STRAPPED

STRAPPED

Why America's 20- and 30-Somethings Can't Get Ahead

TAMARA DRAUT

ANCHOR BOOKS

A Division of Random House, Inc.

New York

FIRST ANCHOR BOOKS EDITION, JANUARY 2007

Copyright © 2005 by Tamara Draut

The Library of Congress has cataloged the Doubleday edition as follows:
Draut, Tamara.
Strapped: why America's 20- and 30-somethings can't
get ahead / Tamara Draut.—1st ed.
p.   cm.
Includes bibliographical references and index.
1. Young adults—United States—Social conditions.   2. Young adults—United
States—Economic conditions.   3. United States—Social conditions—21st
century.   4. United States—Economic conditions—21st century.   I. Title.
HQ799.7.D73 2005
305.242'0973'09045—dc22
2005048497

Anchor ISBN: 978-1-4000-7997-1

Book design by Michael Collica

www.anchorbooks.com

Printed in the United States of America
10   9   8

For Stuart

Contents

STRAPPED

They say music feeds the soul. When you're flat broke, it can also feed your stomach. Several years ago, my husband and I found ourselves sitting in the middle of our living-room floor, our entire CD collection spread out before us. We had not a dollar between us and payday was three long days away. It wasn't the first time we'd been strapped for cash, but we never imagined we'd be peddling our wares for food money at the age of 30.

By the time of our CD purge, becoming adults had left us with $57,000 in student loan debt and $19,000 in credit card debt.

We were so far behind in fulfilling our own expectations, our parents' expectations, and society's expectations, we didn't know whether to laugh or cry. We weren't clothes hounds, we didn't take vacations, and we seldom went out to dinner. Most of our economic woes could be traced back to eight years of start-up costs (pots, sheets, a bed), flights for family visits and friends' weddings, unstable incomes from shoestring salaries, three bouts of unemployment, a gig at graduate school, and one major career change.

And we weren't alone. When we talked to people our age from all walks of life, it became clear that we weren't the only ones who were strapped. While my husband and I were dismantling our CD collection to make some cold hard cash, other young adults were facing tougher decisions and making bigger sacrifices. Across the country, young adults of different cultural, social, and economic backgrounds were confronting brick walls on their path to adulthood.

- Cecilia graduated from a California high school in 1999. It was the height of the tech boom and many of her classmates were dreaming of fast money and early retirement. Cecilia had a different dream: this second-generation Latina wanted to go to college and become a teacher. Despite a good grade-point average and athletic awards in several sports, Cecilia didn't earn the much-needed scholarship money to pay for school. So she did what millions of graduating seniors do each year: she applied for financial aid. But her working-class parents earned too much money to qualify her for aid, yet not enough to afford the state university where Cecilia was accepted. And so with her heart still set on becoming a teacher, she enrolled in the local community college, worked part-time, and lived at home to save money. Three years later, Cecilia has her associate's degree and is working at the mall. She still wants to be a teacher. She still wants to be the first person in her family to graduate from college.

- Rob and Laura, a white couple now in their mid-thirties, are further along in their journey to adulthood. When they first got married, they thought they were on sound financial footing. Though neither finished college, Rob became trained as a heating and air-conditioning technician while Laura got a job working in the accounts-receivable department at the local plastics plant. They made $50,000 between them, which enabled them to live comfortably, but not extravagantly. When Laura became pregnant with their first child, Rob's parents gave them the down payment to buy a house. Their "first child" turned out to be twins—and, overnight, comfortable became very uncomfortable. Without the option of affordable child care, Laura had little choice but to quit her job and take care of the twins. Just then her husband's business took a dive. With their savings dwindling, credit cards went from occasional aids to lifelines. Today, the couple have three young children and $40,000 in credit card debt. They never dreamed that starting a family would plunge them into such deep financial and emotional straits.

• Wanda and Jerome seem like the quintessential middle-class African American couple who have captured the American dream. Both aged thirty-two, they are a dynamic duo with multiple college degrees. Wanda has a master's in human relations and Jerome has an M.B.A. Getting these credentials also got them $30,000 in student loan debt. Thankfully the couple resides in Montgomery, Alabama, where the cost of living is low. But with a five-month-old baby, a six-year-old son, and a twelve-year-old daughter, this family of five is living paycheck to paycheck. They are unable to afford child care, so Wanda's mother has been living with them for five months, and they don't know what they'll do when she leaves. After Jerome was laid off from his account-manager position at a Fortune 100 company, they ran up a couple of thousand dollars in credit card debt. His layoff was an especially bitter pill, since it was this job that brought them to Alabama in the first place. They would like to move out of Montgomery because the educational system is poor, but right now they're biding their time and trying to pay down their debts.

The lives of Cecilia, Rob and Laura, and Wanda and Jerome are at once strikingly different and fundamentally similar. Three different backgrounds. Three different classes. Three different life experiences. They did all the right things, but they're all struggling to make ends meet. And they're not alone. All across the country young adults are sinking economically. The question is, why?

Behind each of these individual stories is a broader tale of economic and political changes that have occurred over the last three decades. For our parents, who grew up during the 1950s and early 1960s, establishing oneself as an adult was a fairly straightforward process. Moving out of your parents' house, getting a job, and starting a family—the three major markers of adulthood—unfolded in a rather swift and orderly fashion. There was little time between graduation, landing a well-paying job, getting married, and having kids. But in the late 1960s, the baby boomers, then in their twenties, began charting a different course to adulthood. Driven by social, economic, and political forces, young adults began delaying definitive "adult" behaviors such as getting married and having kids. As college and career opportunities expanded for women and minorities, more young adults began going to college instead of directly into the labor market after high school. The transition to adulthood was becoming less rigid and more ill defined. A generation later, these trends became more exacerbated. The path to adulthood for today's young adults is a full-blown obstacle course of loop-de-loop turns and jagged-edged hurdles.

When our parents were starting out, three factors helped smooth the transition to adulthood. The first was the fact that there were jobs that provided good wages even for high school graduates. A college degree wasn't necessary to earn a decent living. But even if you wanted to go to college, it wasn't that expensive and grants were widely available. The second was a robust economy that lifted all boats, with productivity gains shared by workers and CEOs alike. The result was a massive growth of the middle class, which provided security and stability for families. Third, a range of public policies helped facilitate this economic mobility and opportunity: a strong minimum wage, grants for low-income students to go to college, a generous unemployment insurance system, major incentives for home ownership, and a solid safety net for those falling on hard times. Simply put, government had your back.

This world no longer exists. The story of what happened is well known. The nation shifted to a service- and knowledge-based economy, dramatically changing the way we lived and worked. Relationships between employers and employees became more tenuous as corporations faced global competitors and quarterly bottom-line pressures from Wall Street. Increasingly, benefits such as health care and pension plans were provided only to well-paid workers. Wages rose quickly for educated workers and declined for those with only high school diplomas, resulting in new demands for college credentials. As most families saw their incomes stagnate or decline, they increasingly needed two full-time incomes just to stay afloat, which created new demands and pressures on working parents. Getting into the middle class now required a four-year college degree, and even that was no guarantee of achieving the American dream.

Although adults of all ages have endured the economic and social changes wrought by the postindustrial era, today's young adults are the first to experience its full weight as they try to start their adult lives. But the challenges facing young adults also reflect the failure of public policy to address the changing realities of building a life in the twenty-first century. Government no longer has our back.

As young adults are working to get into the middle class, they're being hit by a one-two punch: the economy no longer generates widespread opportunity and our public policies haven't picked up any of the slack.

Becoming an adult today takes longer, requires taking more risks, and is rife with more stumbling blocks than it was a generation ago. To get a sense of how much longer the traditional path to adulthood takes, we can compare the percentage of young women and young men meeting a traditional definition of adulthood in the years 1960 and 2000: leaving home, finishing school, becoming financially independent, getting married, and having a child.[1] Four decades ago, 77 percent of women and 65 percent of men aged 30 had completed all of these transitions. In 2000, only 46 percent of women and 31 percent of men had completed all these transitions by age 30.[2]

From the price of a college education to the new cutthroat realities of the economy, young adults are trying to establish themselves in a society that has grown widely unequal and less responsive to the needs of ordinary citizens. At each step in the obstacle course to adulthood—getting an education, finding a job, starting a family, and buying a house—our nation's public policies have failed to keep up. Young adults are left to drift alone, shouldering more of the financial burden and risk than previous generations. Far too often, social critics place the blame squarely on our shoulders, maligning everything from our work ethic to our spending habits. If only it were that simple.

College: A Luxury-Priced Necessity

Every September, local evening news programs across the country inevitably cover the ritual of parents sending their kids off to college. In their best slice-of-life reporting, they capture the twin emotions of excitement and anxiety as long lines of overstuffed minivans inch their way toward student dorms. Stressed-out parents struggle with boxes full of their kids' clothes, CDs, computers, and stereos. Exuberant 18-year-olds stick their heads out of dorm-room windows, waving good-bye to parents and hello to freedom.

What fails to find its way into the news stories is the widespread stress, fear, and anxiety that are now the hallmarks of the college experience. Soaring tuition prices, along with anemic levels of federal student aid, have created a debt-for-diploma system that is stunting many young adults' economic progress as they try to start their lives. It crushes the aspirations of others, who either enroll in two-year institutions instead or just forgo college altogether, knowing all the while that the rest of their lives will be shaped by whether or not they get through college.

College students today are graduating on average with close to $20,000 in debt. Those who take the plunge into graduate school can plan on carrying about $45,000 in combined student loan debt.[3] Those who want to be lawyers or doctors will be lucky to escape with less than $100,000 in debt. Back in the 1970s, before college became essential to securing a middle-class lifestyle, our government did a great job of helping students pay for school. Students from modest economic backgrounds received almost free tuition through Pell grants, and middle-class households could still afford to pay for their kids' college.

That was before tuition began to spiral ever upward and student aid fossilized. Inflation-adjusted tuition at public universities has nearly tripled since 1980, up from $1,758 in 1980 to $5,132 in 2004.[4] To be fair, the federal government is spending more money than ever before on student aid, over $81 billion in the 2003–04 school year. But 70 percent of this aid is in the form of loans, while grant aid only makes up 21 percent and tax credits the remaining 9 percent.[5] Federal grant funding hasn't kept up with rising enrollments, so what little grant aid is available gets spread more thinly across a greater number of students.

As a result of soaring college costs and dwindling financial aid, in 2001 half a million high school graduates who were college-ready either downscaled their dreams by enrolling in community college or skipped college altogether. Congress has responded to this crisis in educational opportunity by merely tinkering with grant and student loan amounts—a bit like the fire department pulling up to a five-alarm fire with a garden hose. Case in point: The maximum Pell Grant award—the nation's premier government program for helping low-income students pay for college—covers about 40 percent of the costs of a four-year college today. It covered nearly three quarters in the 1970s.[6]

Thirty years ago, in 1976–77, the average cost of attending a *private* college was $12,837 annually, in inflation-adjusted dollars. Today, the average cost of attending a *public* college is $11,354— which means the burden of affording a state college today is equivalent to that of paying for a private college in the 1970s.[7] These figures include tuition, fees, and room and board. While tuition at four-year public colleges has soared, tuition at private colleges has entered the stratosphere, costing an average of $27,000 per year. Adding to the financial pressures is the new credential craze that all but mandates a master's degree to get out of the entry-level track in business, marketing, social work, teaching, and many other professions. Already in the hole for a bachelor's degree, many young adults find that the demand to get even more education leaves them up against the ropes. They want the better jobs but can't take the risk of going even deeper into debt.

Young adults have been given the signal loud and clear that getting a degree is now the only way into the middle class. As the burden of paying for college has shifted to the individual, more students are going into debt, dropping out, or not enrolling at all. As we'll see throughout the book, the potential for young adults to create decent lives increasingly depends on whether they clear this first hurdle as college-haves or college-have-nots.

The Real "New" Economy

During the overheated economic boom of the 1990s, two popular stereotypes gained currency. The first was the twenty-something millionaire. The second was the zany new office culture of the so-called "knowledge worker." One of the major software companies ran commercials giving us a glimpse of this e-revolution: employees riding around the office on scooters, shirttails flapping in the wind. As the camera panned over brightly covered walls, we saw young workers with their legs propped up on their desks and keyboards on their laps. Romper room had replaced the boardroom. Public intellectuals started writing about the "creative class," new legions of knowledge workers who challenged traditional structures, forging a creative ethos that would revitalize our nation's urban centers and our culture. An office revolution was under way, and young adults were the major winners.

Of course, the ebullient labor market implied by the commercials was never as ubiquitous as it seemed. This became painfully clear when the high-tech and stock market bubble burst in

2000–2001. So what does the real job market for young adults look like?

In a word, depressing. Compared to older workers, young adults are more likely to be unemployed, hold part-time jobs, or work as temps. Almost half of temp agency workers are in the 18-to-34 age group. That's half a million young adults stuck in the temp system, and another 2.2 million who are independent contractors. These job arrangements rarely offer health care or other benefits, such as pensions.

For college grads who land a job with an actual firm, it's still far from sure that they'll be offered health or retirement benefits. One out of three young adults—a full 17.9 million 18-to-34-year-olds—don't have health insurance, making this the age group with the largest percentage of uninsured. They're not going without health-care coverage out of some sense of invincibility either; in fact, only 3 percent of young workers are uninsured because they declined available coverage.

In addition to often working in a benefit-free zone, moving up the wage or career ladder in the new economy is more difficult than it was a generation ago. The well-paying middle-management jobs that characterized the workforce up to the late 1970s have been eviscerated. Corporate downsizing in the 1980s and 1990s slashed positions in the middle of the wage distribution, and now outsourcing threatens to take thousands more. Instead of becoming more financially secure with each passing year, many young adults in their late twenties and early thirties find themselves struggling ever harder as they start having children and taking on mortgages. What they're experiencing is paycheck paralysis.

Today, America's economy looks like an hourglass. Job growth is concentrated at the top and bottom, while the middle is increasingly whittled away. According to the Bureau of Labor Statistics, jobs requiring a bachelor's degree or higher will account for 29 percent of total job growth from 2000 to 2010. Many of these new jobs are what we think of as "hot jobs"—those clustered in the tech and computer sector. The *largest* job growth, accounting for 58 percent of new jobs, will be those requiring only work-related training. These jobs are primarily in the low-wage retail and food sector, including such jobs as sales associates, food preparation, cashiers, and waitstaff.

Young adults who came of age in the mall culture are still trolling the malls—only this time they're looking for work.

As the job market has changed, so have the paychecks. Young adults across the board are earning less today than they would have twenty or even thirty years ago. In 1974, the typical earnings for males aged 25 to 34 years old with a high school diploma was $42,697 (in 2004 dollars). In 2004, the typical earnings for high school grads had dropped to $30,400. Typical earnings for young males with a bachelor's degree or higher have also declined, from $51,223 in 1974 to $50,700 in 2004.[8]

Living paycheck to paycheck is the new norm for young adults. College grads may have a better shot of slowly digging their way out of the insecurity, but it most likely will not happen until they hit their forties. Today's paycheck paralysis makes it almost impossible for most young adults to get ahead. Dwindling salaries and rising costs mean less leftover money to put into savings, less to contribute to a 401(k), and less to put into their own kids' college funds. And all the while, they're racking up credit card debt to pay for any additional expenses, like going to the dentist or fixing the car, at exorbitant interest rates that rob them of even more money.

Generation Debt

If there is one common experience that young adults share, it is the experience of living in debt. Compared to previous generations, today's young adults have been forced to borrow to get a life. This life of debt serfdom often begins in college. About a quarter of all college students report using credit cards to pay for tuition and books. So what about the other three quarters? Chances are their credit card debt represents what we tend to think of as frivolous debt. Visa and MasterCard have no doubt funded a great many pizzas and spring breaks. Many college grads who have only $1,000 or $2,000 in debt upon graduation feel like the college memories are worth the price.

The problem is that after finishing school, the need for credit often morphs into a whole new category: survival debt. Making the transition from college grad to full-fledged working adult takes more than a good résumé. It takes a credit line. In 2004, 25-to-34-year-olds averaged $4,358 in credit card debt—47 percent higher than it was for the late Baby Boomers in 1989. The rise in credit card debt combined with the massive student loan debt means that 25 cents of every dollar in income goes to paying off debt. Most of that 25 cents is all going to nonmortgage debt: primarily student loans, car loans, and credit cards. Add in a mortgage payment and young adults are likely spending well over half their income on debt service.

The explosion in credit card debt is linked to the earnings crisis hitting young adults. They are earning less than their parents did at the same age, but are facing higher start-up costs for housing, and they're coming out of the gate with bigger student loan debts than ever before. After paying rent, student loan bills, and the car payment . . . the paycheck is gone. Any extra expense—an out-of-town wedding, a busted computer, dry cleaning—gets charged to the credit card. The little charges here and there quickly add up to big trouble. And thanks to a completely deregulated industry, credit card companies are charging interest rates that make the loan sharks of yesteryear look like charity workers.

Home, Elusive Home

Most people now leave their parents' home at the age of 24. That's two years after college graduation, for most young adults, and six years after graduating from high school. But it may not be "for good," because a full 40 percent of young adults who leave their parents' home return at least once. One of the main reasons these "boomerang kids" come back home is that housing costs have risen faster than inflation, and faster than entry-level wages. For college graduates, big cities are still the best place to go for launching a career, but there is a steep price for chasing a good job. Between 1995 and 2002, median rents in nearly all the largest metropolitan areas rose by more than 50 percent: in San Francisco, 76 percent; Boston, 61 percent; San Diego, 54 percent; Denver, 62 percent.[9] Given the high price tag of living in a thriving city, it's not surprising that rent eats up more of a young adult's paycheck than it did a generation ago. In 2002, the median percentage of income young adults spent on rent was just over 22 percent, up from 17 percent in 1970.

Most people in their early twenties choose to rent because they are moving around, are figuring out their lives, and simply aren't ready for the responsibilities of home-ownership. But even when they're ready to go home shopping, they'll find out the hard way that more money buys less house or condo today than it did thirty years ago. Home-ownership rates have fallen among young families since the 1970s, and it's no wonder. Soaring property values, along with record-low interest rates, have been a boon for existing home owners, who have been able to trade up to bigger and better homes. But the starter market has practically disappeared, particularly on the two coasts. Out on Long Island, America's first postwar suburb and development, Levittown, created to make home ownership affordable for returning GIs and their new families, is now off-limits to young middle-class families, as homes there now easily fetch $300,000 and higher on the market. In the New York metropolitan area, median home prices rose 80 percent between 1998 and 2002. California dreamin'? Well, dream on. Even once-affordable alternatives, such as Oakland, now come with near–San Francisco prices. The median home price in Oakland is now $400,000, up from $225,000 in 1997. In Philly, median prices went up 42 percent between 1997 and 2002.[10]

When young adults do manage to escape the rental wasteland, they are taking on much greater risk. Many are financing 100 percent of their home purchase, taking out massive mortgages that eat up as much as half of their income. An unregulated mortgage industry has unleashed a tidal wave of "innovative products" designed to bilk new home owners of their scant resources with extra fees, points, and complex pricing schemes that can spell disaster for the unwary.

The Perils of Parenthood

As the first children-of-divorce generation, GenXers have embraced the notion of family with renewed vigor. Poll after poll shows that young adults today place more importance on family than on their careers, in sharp contrast to the boomer generation at the same age. But this generation's embrace of family bumps up against obstacles on the tough economic road they're traveling.

With student loans to pay back, higher rent payments, and lower starting salaries in general, young adults are increasingly delaying marriage and childbirth for financial reasons. And when they do take the leap into parenthood, they'll experience firsthand a new economic crunch. The United States is alone among industrialized nations in refusing to provide paid parental leave or a system of affordable, high-quality child care. For young adults still reeling from student loan debt, the extra cost of a baby can put them over the edge financially.

Raising a family has become such an economic struggle in the twenty-first century that being able to get by on one income just isn't possible for most young families without a major downgrade in lifestyle. Today, 61 percent of mothers with children under the age of three are in the workforce, up from just 40 percent in the 1960s. But having two incomes to raise a family doesn't provide the security blanket one might think. In fact, two-income families with children are more than twice as likely to declare bankruptcy as those without children. Why? In a nutshell, two-parent families may earn more than their single-earner counterparts of a generation ago, but they have less to spend. The biggest culprits: housing, child care, and the additional car. Child care can cost as much as $10,000 per year for each child under 4, which most parents can't afford. As a result, lower- and middle-class families are often stuck putting their children in mediocre care, which is sadly all too widespread in the child-care market.

Starting a family also exacts a heavy price on young adult women. The pay gap between mothers and nonmothers under 35 is now greater than it is between young men and women.[11] Without paid maternity leave and access to affordable child care, many young adult women will temporarily drop out of the labor force or reduce their working hours when they have a child. In families that can't afford to lose a parent's income, Mom is back at work in less than three months after giving birth. Far too often, well-paid moms are dropping out of lucrative careers because employers won't accommodate part-timers or give flex-time. Still other mothers are choosing part-time work when they'd rather be working full-time. It's a rare young mother who truly gets to decide for herself how to balance her desire for both work and family.

Today's young parents aren't the first to struggle with the economic challenges of adding a new baby to the family. Having a child has always been expensive, but unlike members of previous generations, today's young parents are more likely to be entering into parenthood still saddled with student loan debt and over-extended in a mortgage. Even if the cost of raising a child had remained steady over the last three or four decades, most likely today's new parents would still find it financially more cumbersome than did the previous generation.

Then Versus Now: The Very Different Experiences of Two Generations

Throughout this book I compare the experiences of today's young adults to those who came of age during the 1960s and 1970s. My point is not that these two decades represented an ideal time, either economically or socially. Poverty rates were higher in the 1960s than they are today. Racial discrimination plagued the country and stifled the opportunities and life prospects of entire generations of African American young adults. Blatant gender discrimination along with strict notions about women's role in society constrained the choices of many young women. Racial and gender disparities continue today because of the failures of our nation in the past to promote equality among all its citizens.

But during the 1960s and 1970s, our nation at least strove to address the structural inequalities and lack of opportunity that had beset large swaths of the population. The economy and public policy worked hand in hand to make a middle-class life possible for millions of young families. During the 1960s, the United States increased the minimum wage, ensuring that anyone who worked full-time would not be poor. Today, the value of the minimum wage is 30 percent below its peak in 1968, and 24 percent lower than it was in 1979.[12] To ensure that all high school graduates had an opportunity to pursue college, Congress in 1965 passed the Higher Education Act, which established the federal financial aid system of grants and loans, the framework largely used today. Several years later, Congress redoubled its efforts to ensure that low-income students could afford college by creating the Pell Grant, named after the bill's sponsor, Senator Claiborne Pell. Three decades ago, a Pell Grant covered the majority of tuition, while today it buys students just a sliver.

It's not my intention to pin the blame for the declining opportunity that characterizes American society today solely on government. The world has changed dramatically since the 1970s, with technology and globalization vastly altering the nature of work. Global competition has put downward pressure on American wages, and the new jobs created in the service economy pay less than the manufacturing jobs they replaced. An emphasis on short-term profits has created pressures for businesses to slash costs and trim employee benefits. In each decade since the 1970s, these trends have made getting into the middle class and staying there more difficult for each successive generation. But we should not accept the downgraded quality of life as an inevitable byproduct of these broad structural changes. All along the way, there were steps we could have taken as a nation to temper the harsh edges of the new rough-and-tumble economy. Instead, our nation has experienced widening inequality the likes of which hasn't existed since the Gilded Age in the late nineteenth century. Social mobility—the very embodiment of the American ideal—is on the decline. And, as I'll argue in this book, much of the giant chasm in opportunity that exists today can be traced to a fundamental shift in our nation's priorities and political ideology. We are bequeathing massive and—if we do not act—possibly permanent inequality to the young adults who will inherit responsibility for our society.

Why have we as a society failed to respond? The sclerosis of government in these areas is part of a larger story about the political and cultural forces that shaped American society in the 1980s and 1990s.

Loss of Faith in Politics

One central reason for public policy's failure is that we, the electorate, have lost faith in government's ability to solve these problems. Many scholars have studied the decline of trust in government, tracing the phenomenon back to the government's handling of the Vietnam War and the Watergate scandal. But the fallout from government corruption and mismanagement has been compounded by the concerted efforts of conservative leaders to undermine the roles and responsibilities of government. During the 1980s and 1990s, Americans were bombarded by antigovernment rhetoric. A statement made by President Reagan epitomizes the extent of government bashing by our nation's highest officials: Reagan actually said, "The nine most terrifying words in the English language are, 'I'm from the government and I'm here to help.' "

The distrust of and skepticism about government has profound implications. Young adults do not follow politics, vote regularly, nor even keep up with current affairs. If the whole political system is ineffective, why bother to get in the game? Since 1972, voter turnout among the under-30 population has declined 12 percent. Even in the 2004 presidential election, which shattered records for young-adult turnout, only 52 percent of under-30s showed up, compared to 60 percent of the voting population overall. Our voting record in midterm elections is even worse, with only about one third of citizens under 30 voting in nonpresidential elections. When it comes to political participation, the distrust and skepticism toward government expressed by our nation's highest-level politicians has left young adults turned off and tuned out.

This antigovernment sentiment also affects how young adults view their own struggles. Compared to previous generations, today's young adults learned at an early age to look to themselves for their own security and success. Now, as they struggle to buy homes and start families, they're questioning their own self-reliance and self-worth rather than whether our nation's priorities are in the right place. The last place they'd look for help is the government. And that's exactly what conservatives hoped to achieve.

The New Brand of Capitalism

The last twenty-five years can be characterized as a period of "hypercapitalism," in which the "market" became the arbiter of all that was good and acceptable in society. Public policy moved toward a hands-off approach, putting more risk on individuals by leaving them to rely on the market to provide security and opportunity.

This new economy has increasingly become a winner-take-all system in which most of the spoils go to the top—the CEOs, big shareholders, and top executives. While technology allowed America's productivity to soar, unlike in past eras, since about 1980, less and less of these gains have been shared with workers. Productivity grew 74.2 percent between 1968 and 2000, but hourly wages for average workers fell 3 percent (adjusted for inflation). In fact, according to research in the book *Raise the Floor*, if wages had kept pace with rising productivity between 1968 and 2000, the average hourly wage would have been $24.56 in 2000, rather than $13.74.

This slide in workers' earnings happened as corporate profits were climbing. Domestic corporate profits have risen 64 percent since 1968, adjusting for inflation. The king of the low-wage sector—the retail industry—has done fantastically well. Retail profits have jumped 158 percent since 1968. Wal-Mart, our nation's largest private employer, is a typical employer of low-wage workers. Wal-Mart also typifies the anti-union sentiment that has spread across the country since the early 1980s.

In the old economic order, unions were a big part of why so many blue-collar workers could toil their way into the middle class. The decline in unionization is attributable to the fact that the service economy is harder to unionize, but the loss of union rights has also been deliberate. Emboldened by President Reagan's firing of striking air-traffic controllers, businesses began more aggressively fighting workers' attempts to unionize. Back in 1950, firing workers for trying to organize unions was rare: there was one illegal dismissal of workers for every twenty union elections. By the 1990s, the National Labor Relations Board found illegal dismissal of workers in one out of every three union elections.[13] Orientation for new employees at Wal-Mart includes watching a video that depicts unions as a threat to the company and its workers. The message being sent by employers is crystal clear: organizing a union means putting your job at risk. So far, the strategy has proved remarkably successful: not a single Wal-Mart store has a union. Young adults understand the benefit a union could have on their pocketbooks. Over half of nonunionized workers under 34 say they would join a union tomorrow if given the chance, but the reality is that the chance won't be offered or taking the chance will cost them their job.[14]

There are broader implications to the widespread insecurity created by the new economic order. In an economy characterized by less security, individuals are more likely to worry about their own prospects than about how their neighbors are doing. In this dog-eat-dog economic climate, our national spirit has shifted from "We're all in this together" to "Hey, look out, I'm about to step on you."

Rising Economic Inequality

America's new brand of capitalism has also resulted in widening economic inequality. A few statistics illustrate this: By 2000, the top 1 percent of households had more wealth than *the entire bottom 95 percent*. Focusing on income alone, the top 1 percent of earners, 2.7 million people, receives 50.4 percent of the national income, more than *the poorest 100 million people combined*. And these figures don't take into account the latest income tax cuts or cuts on income from capital gains, both of which will further increase inequality.

The rewards of our economy are no longer being shared by the majority. Only a handful of winners now lays claim to the spoils of what is still the greatest economic engine in the world. Rising inequality hasn't skipped our generation either. While those under 34 may not be fat cats just yet, there are certainly fatter kittens among us. In 1975, the top income quintile (20 percent) of households aged 25 to 34 received about 36 percent of the nation's income for that age group. By 2003 it had grown to 46 percent. Young-adult households in the lower quintiles inescapably saw their share of their age group's income fall over the same time period. Let's put some dollar figures on these numbers. In 2003 the average income for a 25-to-34-year-old household in the top 5 percent of earners was $228,441—more than double the inflation-adjusted $109,589 enjoyed by the fat kittens a generation ago.[15]

Widening economic inequality in the United States brings with it a host of cultural and social implications relevant to my argument about why young adults are stuck on an obstacle course stacked against them. New research shows that inequality results in lower levels of trust and social cohesion. Times of historic progressive change have come about when Americans banded together to protect their common interests. The current inequality has broken that collective spirit apart.

"Young Adults" Defined

Throughout *Strapped,* I'll use the term "young adults" to describe people aged 18 to 34—born between 1971 and 1987. By age 34, most adults have indeed completed all of the transitions to adulthood, including getting married and having children. This age grouping is also commonly used by demographers, social scientists, and economists, and most government data are published using this age category. Although the economic challenges described throughout the book indeed apply to people in their late thirties and even early forties, my analysis focuses on what is happening to those under the age of 35.

Admittedly, the transition from adolescence to adulthood now defies traditional age boundaries, as much as the process can no longer be defined by the markers that once signified someone had reached "adulthood." Most Americans of all ages, including young adults themselves, believe the three most important criteria

for whether or not someone is an "adult" are: accepting responsibility for one's self, making independent decisions, and financial
independence.[16] But the completion of actual events that most
believe critical to reaching adulthood are finishing school, working full-time, being able to support a family, and being financially
independent. That's a tall order, particularly given that most people
still believe that a person should have done all this by the age of
25.[17] Even young adults themselves believe it all should have come
together by this age.

As the transition to adulthood has changed in the United States
and across industrialized nations, social scientists have used various
terms to identify the now-prolonged period of time between adolescence and adulthood. Some refer to this stage of life as "emerging adulthood" whereas others use the term "adultolescence." A
January 2005 cover story in *Time* magazine about people aged 18
to 25 gave them the unfortunate label "Twixter," describing this
age as "betwixt and between." Far too often this stage of life is portrayed as a period of great self-exploration, in which college grads
backpack across Europe. This notion of a responsibility-free stage
of life between adolescence and adulthood is a reality for maybe
just 10 or 15 percent of the young adult population, and yet it has
spawned these terms. Meanwhile, the widespread insecurity of this
generation remains woefully underexamined.

In this book I've avoided trying to attach yet another glib new
generational label and have chosen to refer to those adults between
the ages of 18 and 34 as "young adults." I also describe the experiences of this age group by referring to them in generational terms,
since so much has been written about Generation X and their
younger brothers and sisters, the Millennials.

Throughout the book I write regularly about three different
generations: Baby Boomers, Generation Xers, and Millennials. In

trying to define the age boundaries of these three generations, I looked to generational scholars and demographers, among which there is a surprising amount of debate. For the purposes of this book, the baby boom generation is defined as those born between 1946 and 1964, making them aged 41 to 59 in 2005. Generation X, coming after the boomers, is made up of those born between 1965 and 1981 and aged 24 to 40 in 2005. The Millennials are those born after 1981, aged 18 to 23 in 2005.

As of this writing (2005), the bulk of young adults are Generation Xers and so I sometimes use this term interchangeably with "young adults." Because much of my analysis and arguments is focused on comparing the experiences of today's young adults to those of their parents, most of the book compares the social, economic, and political context of Generation X with that of the Baby Boomers. The generational boundaries also correspond well with the two most common age cohorts in which data are presented: 18 to 24 and 25 to 34. Generation X comprises all of the individuals aged 25 to 34; the Millennials are the 18-to-24-year-old population.

The Why Behind this Book

Why should we care about what's happening to young adults? If you're a nervous flyer like me, you know that the first ten minutes of flight are critical. If something is going to go disastrously wrong, it's likely to happen during those initial minutes. Becoming an established adult is the same way: it is during the first ten to fifteen years after school that the outcome of the rest of adulthood is determined. The first decade of labor-market experience exerts a heavy influence on overall lifetime earnings. These are the years when decisions about college and careers are made. A miscalculation about career choices or the inability to buy a college degree will have a strong effect on where the rest of a young person's life is headed. It is during young adulthood that people marry and start families. The capacity for new parents to provide all the education, nutrition, and nurturing that babies and toddlers need is pivotal to the future of our nation. It is during a child's early years that the capacity to learn, grow, and flourish is formed—and it is young adults under 34 who are tackling the responsibilities of parenthood. As we look at how young adults are faring in the twenty-first century, we can also see how well our country is living up to its promise of opportunity and fairness.

Today, most young adults are holding tight to the armrests, desperately trying and hoping to avoid a major crash during these first ten years.

Over the last year I have interviewed young adults across the country. Some were in their early twenties and just getting started on their paths. Others were in their early thirties, about to welcome their first or second child into the world. I talked to young people of diverse racial, ethnic, and economic backgrounds. Some grew up with parents who were college-educated, others did not. Some of the people in this book have college degrees, some have even attained several. Many others got stuck along the way. The stories in this book are those of real people, though I have changed their names to protect their identity. While some were willing to use their real names, others preferred to remain anonymous. To maintain consistency and avoid asterisking the real names from the fake ones, I have chosen to use pseudonyms for all the people in this book.

This book covers a wide range of experiences, but it does not cover them all. The life stories missing from this book are those of illegal immigrants, high school dropouts, and those who are officially counted as "poor" by the American census. Every person in this book graduated from high school and most went on to take at least one college class—often at a community college. Why leave out the most vulnerable—the "poor"—young adult population? In many ways, that topic requires a wholly different book. My goal in writing this book is to examine why so many young adults who are following the playbook—finishing school, getting jobs, and raising families—are finding it so hard to get ahead, and what could have been done differently to avoid the widespread insecurity plaguing today's young adults.

In the following pages, I'll illustrate how the path to adulthood has become harder, longer, and more risky—and why. Throughout each chapter, I'll connect the experiences in the here and now to broader social and economic changes. After all my research and conversations with young adults, one thing is crystal clear. Without bold thinking and the courage to uphold our nation's most sacred values, a whole generation of young adults will come of age in an America that doesn't reward hard work, family values, or collective responsibilities. I have no doubt that the grim economic reality and choked opportunity facing young adults didn't have to happen. And it doesn't have to continue.

CHAPTER ONE

Higher and Higher Education

Renee, a white 26-year-old, grew up in St. Paul, Minnesota. Her parents wanted nothing more than to send her to a four-year college when she graduated from high school, but unfortunately, it was priced out of reach. Instead, Renee began taking business classes at a nearby community college that specialized in business training and got a full-time job. She worked during the day and took classes at night.

Some time later, Renee accepted a new job at a nearby printing company. A nice increase in pay was the upside; working the midnight shift was the considerable downside. Suddenly, balancing school and work became a lot more difficult. Renee would work until 8 A.M., sleep in the afternoon, and go to school at night. Eventually, racked with exhaustion, financially stressed out, and supporting an unemployed boyfriend, Renee dropped out of school. Money played a big role in her decision. She had already taken out student loans and burned through a small inheritance from her grandfather. Already $4,500 in the hole with student loans, Renee didn't want to sink any further into debt.

It is now four years later and Renee is still making loan payments. She anticipates it will take at least eight or nine more years to clear the debt. Today, Renee works as a legal secretary, earning $28,000 a year, which must support both her and her son. In the hopes of boosting her earnings potential, Renee has re-enrolled in school, taking correspondence classes with the aim of becoming a paralegal. When I asked Renee if she wished she could have done anything differently up to this point in her life, she didn't hesitate with her answer: "Number one, I would have finished college. I would have actually gone to a four-year college and had a real degree."

Renee is not alone. This is the story of downscaled dreams.

Soaring tuition costs combined with cuts to financial aid have forced students into massive debt and priced many smart kids out of four-year colleges altogether. Every year, 410,000 *college-qualified* students—just like Renee—from households with incomes less than $50,000 enroll in community college instead of going to a four-year college.[1] Another 168,000 *college-qualified* students don't enroll in college at all. These students took the SATs, had good grades, and were college-ready. They just didn't have the money. And they weren't willing to play the debt-for-diploma game.

Thirty or forty years ago, skipping college was much less important. While a college degree has always been considered a stepping stone to higher status and greater prosperity, it certainly wasn't expected of everyone. Jobs for high school graduates were plentiful, and many blue-collar workers made good money. Back in the 1970s, an accountant with a B.A. and a steel worker might live on the same block, drive the same cars, eat at the same restaurants, and send their kids to the same public schools. But as the pay difference between high school grads and college grads has widened, so too have the life outcomes. In 1977 there was only a 6 percentage-point difference in home-ownership rates between those with college educations and those without. Today, there is a 20 percentage-point difference. Today the college-haves and the college-have-nots live in different worlds.

College: From Nicety to Necessity

Nowadays, entering the real world with only a high school diploma is like going into battle armed with only a squirt gun. Over the last thirty years, earnings for workers with high school diplomas have taken a beating. By 1994, males 25 to 34 without college degrees were earning roughly the same amount as their similarly educated grandfathers earned in 1949.[2] High school students saw the writing on the wall and more began enrolling in college. In 1975, just over half of all high school graduates continued their education after high school. Today, nearly three quarters of high school graduates enroll in some type of college after high school.[3] But those numbers are deceptive. Although young adults may be swarming into college, most are failing to complete their studies. Less than a third of young adults aged 25 to 29 had a bachelor's degree or higher in 2003—a percentage that hasn't kept pace with enrollments.[4] The kind of family someone comes from and the amount of money they can pony up exert a heavy influence on whether a student ends up at a two-year or four-year college and whether or not they will complete their degree. Which means that today's bachelor's degree holders are still a rather select group.

During the same time that a B.A. has become the new entry pass to the middle class, tuitions have soared and our federal financial aid system has fossilized. Of the $70 billion a year the federal government spends on student aid, the vast majority is loan-based aid, and in any case it is nowhere near generous enough to help many students pay for college. As a result, nearly two thirds of students graduate with student loan debt, and low-income students are most likely to be borrowing.[5] As this Red Sea of debt has risen, policymakers have dithered. Every four years or so, Congress votes on whether to make changes to the maximum amount a student can borrow or receive in grants to pay for college. During the 1980s and 1990s, grants to low-income students were bumped up a tad and student loans were made available to families regardless of their income. And yet, the amount of money a student can borrow is still the same as it was in 1992. The maximum Pell Grant award, the nation's premier program for helping poor kids pay for college, covers about one third of the costs of a four-year college today. It covered nearly three quarters in the 1970s.[6] But only 22 percent of Pell Grant recipients get the *maximum* award[7]—the *average* award in 2003 was $2,421, which covered only a quarter of the costs of a four-year public college.[8] How is it possible that as college has become more important, access to college has become more out of reach?

Perhaps our members of Congress, the majority of whom are Baby Boomers or older, don't remember just how good their generation had it when it came to being able to afford college. For any Baby Boomers reading this book, I'm about to offer you a trip down memory lane. And for young adults, I'm about to show just how badly we've been short-changed.

The Glory Days of Financial Aid

America prides itself on being a nation of unlimited opportunity. Go to school. Go to work. Go to Florida and retire when you're fifty-five. That's the theory, anyway. While European countries rely heavily on taxes to fund social policies that minimize inequality, America has historically looked to education as the great equalizer.

I don't know where we're looking now. As more people want to climb the ladder of educational opportunity, we're simultaneously sawing off the rungs.

The vast system of public universities that exists today was the result of purposeful action by the federal government. In 1862, Congress passed the Morrill Act, named for its sponsor, Congressman Justin Morrill of Vermont, which provided federal land to the states to establish public colleges. The goal of these first land-grant colleges—such as those in Wisconsin, Michigan, Illinois, Indiana, and Minnesota—was to educate the entire population and produce research to support emerging industries. In 1890, a second Morrill Act provided land to establish the country's first black colleges.

The nation continued to promote higher education throughout the twentieth century, expanding access to college as a way to redress inequality, foster democratic ideals, and spur economic development. The pledge to kick open the doors to college began in earnest with the "GI Bill of Rights." Officially known as the Servicemen's Readjustment Act of 1944, the goal behind the GI Bill was to help millions of returning veterans "readjust" to civilian life and provide them with the education, skills, and money to successfully reintegrate into society and the economy. The GI Bill provided grants to help veterans pay for tuition, books, and health insurance. It also provided a monthly stipend to help college students pay for living expenses. Back in 1948, veterans received a grant of $500 a year—enough at the time to pay for all but $25 of tuition at Harvard.[9] On top of that, they received a monthly stipend of $50—that's $400 in today's dollars. As a point of comparison, in 2003 the average federal grant to students was $2,421, which falls $24,000 short of tuition and fees at Harvard.[10]

The GI Bill was key to building the massive middle class that exists today.[11] The hundreds of thousands of accountants, teachers, scientists, and engineers educated under the GI Bill helped fuel the long economic expansion of the postwar era and as a result changed the social and economic landscape of America. About 8 million veterans took advantage of the GI Bill, and 2.3 million of these attended colleges and universities. By 1960, half of the members of Congress had gone to college on the GI Bill. With the additional benefits of no-down-payment policies and low-interest mortgages, the GI Bill fostered the great exodus to the suburbs and the establishment of a wide middle class that came to symbolize our country's prosperity and the achievement of the American dream. Not a bad payback for a mere $91 billion investment (in today's dollars).

The kids who grew up in this new middle-class security are today's Baby Boomers. Like their fathers (it was mostly men who profited from the GI Bill), Baby Boomers benefited from generous financial aid policies and dirt-cheap tuition at colleges all across the country. But this time around, Baby Boomer women joined the college stampede.

A new law was passed to reaffirm the radical American idea that anyone should be able to go to college—and be able to pay for it. The Higher Education Act of 1965 (HEA) established the college grants and student loans on which today's system is largely based. Whereas the GI Bill focused on veterans, the HEA sought to ensure access to college for all individuals. As President Lyndon Johnson said when he signed the bill, "The Higher Education Act of 1965 means that a high school senior anywhere in this great land of ours can apply to any college or any university in any of the fifty states and not be turned away because his family is poor."

As a result of this landmark legislation, the number of low-income students in American colleges and universities nearly doubled between 1965 and 1971.[12] For poor kids, grants were generous enough to cover the cost of going to college. For the middle class, tuition was low enough that most students could foot the bill with Mom and Dad's help and a part-time job.

Back in 1977, the largest high school graduating class in the nation's history, the Baby Boomers born in 1959, was headed for college. Their record numbers, in addition to the slumping economy, made it a particularly bad time to be entering the labor market. The good news, though, was that college was affordable. Average tuition in the late 1970s for a four-year state college was just over $1,900, in 2003 dollars.[13] Add in room and board, and the total cost was just over $6,000. For Boomers of more substantial means and grander expectations, the tuition at a private college was around $8,000, and with room and board the total cost was $12,000, again inflation-adjusted. High school graduates hoping to learn a trade after high school could easily fork over $900 for a year's tuition at a community college.

Borrowing one's way through college just wasn't the norm. In 1977, college students borrowed about $6 billion (2002 dollars) to help pay for college, compared to $28 billion borrowed by students in 1993.[14] By 2003, the amount of borrowing had doubled, to $56 billion. The rise in loan volume cannot be completely explained by increases in college enrollment. The number of students enrolled in college grew by 44 percent between 1977 and 2003, but student loan volume rose by 833 percent. Over the last decade, the average student loan per year rose from $2,713 per student to $4,903, in constant dollars.[15] The older Baby Boomers had it even easier than the younger tail because the 1960s marked the heyday of college affordability and generous financial aid. Both the youngest and oldest of the Baby Boomers (and their parents) made it through college without much financial struggle and certainly without the debt burden Gen Xers have on their shoulders.

The Debt-for-Diploma System

To illustrate how nonexistent student loan debt was for previous generations, I conducted a simple Nexis search. When I typed in the words "student loan debt" for the years 1971 to 1980, the search yielded *no articles*; not a single article on this subject appeared in any newspaper or magazine in the entire country. The next decade brought only a handful of articles, only sixty-seven about student loan debt between 1981 and 1990, to be exact. It's worth noting that the first articles that appeared, in 1982, were exclusively devoted to the high rate of default on student loans by doctors. It wasn't until 1986 that there was a newspaper article voicing concern about rising student loan debt in general. Continuing the Nexis query, I searched "student loan debt" for the decade 1991 to 2000. The search was interrupted because it would yield more than 1,000 articles. The debt-for-diploma system had arrived.

The debt-for-diploma system is a pernicious beast. It stunts young adults' economic progress as they try to start their lives, draining precious dollars out of their paychecks for more than a decade. The evils of the debt-for-diploma system aren't restricted to those who take out student loans. Anytime a bright but lower-income student settles for a two-year institution or forgoes college altogether, the debt-for-diploma system has claimed another victim.

It shouldn't be surprising, then, that many of the gains made during the 1970s in expanding access to college have disappeared. In fact, the gap in college enrollment among whites, blacks, and Hispanic students has actually widened over the last thirty years: in 2000, the enrollment gap between white and black students was 11 percentage points, up from only 5 percentage points in 1972. The enrollment gap between white and Hispanic students was 13 percentage points in 2000, up from a 5-percentage-point gap in 1972.[16] One result of debt-for-diploma is that the highest-performing students from the lowest socioeconomic backgrounds enroll in college at the same rate as the lowest-performing students from the highest socioeconomic households. To put it more bluntly, the smartest poor kids attend college at the same rate as the dumbest rich kids.

And these days, there are more smart poor kids than ever before. The college-enrollment gap by class and race has widened during a period when academic preparation among lower-income students has been improving. More than half of high school seniors in households with incomes below $36,000 have completed college preparatory courses, up from just over one third in 1987.[17] To be sure, many of our high schools are failing students, particularly urban and rural low-income students. But even for those who do well, the options are dwindling.

To fully grasp the financial challenges facing young adults in their quest for academic credentials, we need to look more closely at how "going to college" has changed over the last fifteen years. In far too many ways, what happens at this first marker of adulthood—getting an education—will ripple through the lives of today's young adults. The degree they earn, if they manage to get one at all, and the amount of debt they accumulate in the process will color every aspect of their adulthood. It will determine the size of their paycheck, the safety of their neighborhood, the reliability of their car, and, perhaps most important, the opportunities they will be able to provide for their own children.

Better Than Nothing: Community College

If you've ever spent time on any of the nation's 1,132 community college campuses, one thing you're bound to notice is the diversity of students. And I'm not talking solely about racial diversity. Today, community colleges enroll 44 percent of all undergraduates attending colleges, and the breadth of learning and the diversity of students at our community colleges is quite amazing.[18] You'll find fresh-faced 18-year-olds working on the first two years of their bachelor's degrees, recent immigrants learning English or studying for their citizenship test, and workers of all ages boning up on technical skills or learning new ones. You'll also find students simply trying to get the basic reading, writing, and math skills our public schools failed to provide. This smorgasbord aspect of community college can make it less than ideal for students whose ultimate goal is a bachelor's degree. Unlike universities, community colleges aren't geared solely to the needs of undergraduates. Community colleges are guided by a commitment to serve the needs of the entire community—which means offering a wide array of classes all in one institution. A community college is often the only place for students who want to get more education or learn a job skill, but aren't academically prepared or financially set for a university. The problem today is that community college has become the consolation prize for smart kids who can't afford a "real college," which makes it much more likely they'll never get a "real degree." A 2002 survey of college borrowers found that 40 percent had delayed going to college or had gone to a less expensive college to avoid the burden of large student loans.[19] A 2004 survey of recent high school graduates found that the majority of students would have chosen a different school if money hadn't been an issue.[20]

Though community college is still considered a bargain, it's gotten harder to escape debt-free. Today, the average debt of a former community college student is $8,700.[21]

Natalie, a white 26-year-old, had everything going for her when she graduated from high school. She had earned good grades, done well on her SATs, and gotten accepted by the college of her choice. She had chosen to go to Monmouth University, a small, rather selective private college in New Jersey. Natalie grew up in the suburbs and both of her parents attended college. Her mom has an associate's degree in nursing and her father is an engineer. But like many middle-class families, Natalie's parents couldn't provide much in the way of financial support. Monmouth costs about $27,000 a year, including room and board. Thanks to money she inherited from her grandmother, Natalie was able to pay $13,000 out of her own pocket for the first year. The rest she took out in student loans. Like most students her age, she was excited about living in the dorms and looked forward to the college experience. But after one semester of classes, Natalie's outlook changed dramatically. "I felt the classes were irrelevant. I was going to school with a lot of people who were there because they had the money, not necessarily the brains." Natalie said she "wasn't going to pay an astronomical amount of money for something she didn't feel was worth it." So she packed her stuff and moved back in with her parents.

Because Natalie knew she had to earn some kind of degree, she immediately signed up for classes at the local community college. For $1,000, she was able to take a full load of classes for a semester. After a half year of course work, Natalie decided to enroll in the Art Institute of Philadelphia to study multimedia and video production. The program takes three years and awards an associate's degree. Natalie loved her coursework and thrived in the nontraditional atmosphere. She felt passionate about the work and unlike with her one semester at Monmouth, she felt she was really getting her money's worth.

Since graduating from college in 1999, Natalie has had four different jobs, all administrative in nature. All told, she has $20,000 in student loan debt, plus a car payment. Her current job pays $37,000, but after taxes are taken out and her bills and rent are paid, Natalie is often short of cash. When that happens, she scrolls through a mental list of people she can call to lend her $10 for something to eat. Her landlord recently jacked up her rent by $133 a month, forcing Natalie to move back home. It's the third time she's gone back to the nest since graduating from high school.

Natalie has regrets about her college experience, but feels it's too late for her to start over. As Natalie told me, "I'd love more than anything to have a four-year degree. But it's not economically viable for me. I have a lifestyle I need to maintain now and bills to pay and I wouldn't receive much financial aid because I make too much money. But I don't make enough to pay for college. You're in a catch-22. There's nothing you can do about it. You just do what you can."

Natalie blames part of her situation on a lack of guidance or direction from her parents. But there's a long list of people who could have helped Natalie better navigate her way through college. First, Natalie took a full course load at community college without any interaction with a student counselor. She signed up, took the courses, and left. If someone had explained to her that she could have taken her undergrad courses there and then transferred to a state college or university, Natalie could have made a more informed decision. But because community colleges are open-enrollment institutions, students can just sign up for classes willy-nilly. There's often no academic adviser to help plan a course of study or discuss your goals for enrollment, though some community colleges have begun formalizing their transfer programs to better meet the increasing demand for this type of education.

Even for students whose intention is solely to earn an associate's degree, the dropout rates from community colleges are sky-high.

These students have chosen an educational path that is available only at community colleges, and yet most won't complete their two years. Why? Unlike students at four-year colleges, 18-to-22-year-olds at community colleges are more likely to be working full-time and attending school on a part-time basis. Far too often, the pull of work wins out over school. Five years after entering community college, only about one in five students who enrolled with the intention of getting an associate's degree has accomplished that goal.[22]

What Renee, Natalie, and countless others have learned is that there is no margin for error anymore in young adulthood. Those years that fall between adolescence and adulthood are supposed to be full of exploration and identity building. Young adults who go to college, study full-time, and live on campus have the luxury of structure, support, and guidance to exploit this life stage to its fullest. They can dabble in economics, psychology, sociology, and art history without having to choose between paying the rent and taking classes. No such padding exists for most community college students. Unlike four-year-college students, who attend institutions where the exploratory aspect of college is built in—a person can change majors three or four times and still graduate on time—community college students purchase their education one course at a time.

As the cost of four-year colleges has risen, more students are choosing to start down the bachelor's degree path at a community college. The research is mixed on the success of this strategy. One study finds that about 40 percent of community college students who enrolled with the intention of transferring end up doing so.[23] Other studies find that students seeking bachelor's degrees who enroll in community colleges with the intention of transferring to a four-year college are much less likely to earn their B.A.s.[24]

Among students who start at four-year colleges, 53 percent complete their bachelor's degrees in five years. Among students who first enroll in two-year colleges and then transfer, only 26 percent earn a bachelor's degree after five years.[25]

The class cleavage that has developed in college choice is being driven by dwindling grant aid and soaring tuition costs. Of all college entrants, half of low-income students attend community colleges compared to just one in ten high-income students.[26] Some observers attribute the disparity in college paths between poor and rich students to differences in academic preparation rather than to the ability to pay. Our nation has a long and ignoble history of equating poverty with stupidity or laziness.[27] When the GI Bill was passed, some college presidents feared that the new students, most of whom weren't considered "college material," would lower the pedigree of college campuses. James B. Conant, the president of Harvard University, worried that the bill did not "distinguish between those who can profit most by advanced education and those who cannot."[28] The president of the University of Chicago, Robert M. Hutchins, claimed that the GI Bill "threatens to demoralize education and defraud the veterans."

Opposition to spending money to help lower-income young adults go to college is nothing new. It's a little cognitive trick that allows people to justify their own successes and accept no responsibility to help anyone left behind. It's not uncommon to hear someone argue that most low-income students aren't ready for college. Given the justified negative attention our public schools have garnered over the last two decades, this is not too surprising. But academic preparation can only go so far in explaining why poor students and students of color are disproportionately enrolled in community colleges. A study conducted by the Advisory Committee on Student Financial Assistance, a body that was created by Congress in 1986 to advise on student aid, found that *college-ready* students from households with incomes below $50,000 are much less likely to go to four-year colleges than those from better-off families. The blame for this was placed squarely on the shoulders of our failing financial aid system. According to the committee's 2002 report, *Empty Promises: The Myth of College Access in America,* "The financial barriers to a college education have risen sharply due to shifts in policies and priorities at the federal, state, and institutional levels, resulting in a shortage of student aid, and, particularly, in need-based grant-aid, as well as rising college tuition. As a result, students from low- and moderate-income families who graduate from high school fully prepared to attend a four-year college confront daunting financial barriers with major implications for these students and the nation."

The staggering array of associate's degree options and the number of students who now enroll in community colleges is a relatively new phenomenon. Back in 1965, when the Baby Boomers were first becoming college-aged, only about 1 million students were enrolled in for-credit courses at community colleges. Today, there are about 5.5 million students enrolled for credit. Similarly, there's been dramatic growth in the number of associate's degrees conferred. In 1965, about 111,600 Baby Boomers earned an associate's degree; by 2001, that number was five times as high. Indeed, the rate of growth in associate's degrees has been much greater than that in bachelor's degrees. If the number of bachelor's degrees had grown as fast since 1965 as associate's degrees, an additional 1 million students would be earning their bachelor's degrees each year. I like to think that Natalie and Renee—and the hundreds of thousands of other smart students who tend to come from lower-income households, and as a result are disproportionately African American and Latino—would be among them. As we'll see in the next chapter, the lifetime earnings difference between a worker with an associate's degree and a worker with a bachelor's degree is wide and growing.

The accelerated growth in the number of associate's degrees is troubling because it reflects a widening of inequality in access to higher education. The credential for entry into the middle class is now a bachelor's degree, yet students are piling into two-year colleges and, more often than not, leaving without any degree. It's not because they don't know how important college is. It's because the combination of work, school, and debt becomes unsustainable.

The inequity in college choice that is driven by dwindling grant aid and soaring tuition costs means many young people either won't clear this first hurdle of adulthood, or they will start their adult lives settling for less than their talent or aspirations entitle them to. Kids growing up in households with parents who didn't go to college don't grow up dreaming of getting associate's degrees. They dream of becoming the first in their family to go to a four-year college and graduate. When the doors of college are closed to thousands every year because of price, it undermines our nation's bedrock principles of fairness and equality of opportunity as it saps young adults of their potential and quest for a better life. In my final chapter, I propose a better way to model our federal financial aid system, one that would ensure that all qualified students have the means to pay for college, and that they'd know this as early as the eighth grade.

While the cost of a bachelor's degree sends many bright kids of modest economic means running to the nearest community college, it also straps many young adults into a financial straitjacket of student loans that can feel impossible to wiggle out of.

Costs More, Worth Less: The Bachelor's Degree

The media lavish endless attention on college sports, misbehavior on spring break, and the binge drinking that so often occurs on college campuses. But what goes badly underreported is the high-stakes pressure cooker that college has turned into for many students and their families.

Most college students are working more hours than ever before and are taking longer to complete their degrees. College enrollments are up—way up, in fact—but the percentage of students who actually complete their degrees isn't nearly as high as the surge in enrollments. The average student borrows almost $20,000, and low-income students and students of color take on even higher debt levels. And widening the gap even further, wealthy families are pulling out all the stops to boost their children's chance of success. They hire tutors and essay consultants, and pay for expensive test-prep courses. As a result, the nation's elite schools are overwhelmingly filled with students from the very top of America's income distribution.

Going to college has become an intense, competitive game. Unfortunately, however, a bachelor's degree is fast becoming little more than an entry-level pass. As Nancy Goldschmidt, the associate vice chancellor for performance and planning for the Oregon university system explains, "A bachelor's degree is clearly what a high school degree used to be in terms of basic education for an economy based on knowledge."[29] What remains elusive for so many lower-income students is now considered the bare minimum required to function in the new economy. Now, most professional occupations want their employees to have graduate degrees, and there's no end in sight to this trend. So even after piling up debt for a bachelor's degree, young adults are under more pressure to go further up the credential ladder.

Let's look at each of these trends from the top, starting with how students are dealing with the rising costs of college by working and borrowing, both in excessive amounts.

All Work and No Play

In the fall of 1997, Shaney, who is now 27, enrolled in the University of Arkansas. She chose the state college because it was close to home and the nearby private colleges were financially out of the question. Shaney's excellent grades in school scored her a $10,000 scholarship to help cover the cost of tuition for four years. The scholarship was an enormous relief for Shaney and her family. Neither of her parents had gone to college and they couldn't offer any financial support for her studies. With tuition covered by the scholarship, Shaney was confident she could earn enough for room and board through part-time jobs. She opted out of living in the dorms, choosing instead to get an apartment with a friend from high school.

Shaney worked a lot of hours during school, holding down two or three jobs at all times. During summers, Shaney was unable to capitalize on internship opportunities that would have helped her gain better work experience because the pay was too low and she had to continue to earn. She waited tables instead, trying to save as much money as she could before school started again in the fall. She regrets not being able to accept an internship that would have helped her build more impressive and relevant experience for her résumé.

Shaney's college days were a far cry from the keg parties and dorm room shenanigans that dominate our popular conception of college. Tuition increases made her scholarship money run out sooner than expected. Because Shaney was a French major, she opted to study abroad in France for a year, which she paid for with student loans. She also took out loans to deal with tuition increases. All told, Shaney left school with $25,000 in student loans. After working two or three jobs for the last four years, Shaney was looking forward to being done with school and having a regular nine-to-five job and her nights once again free.

For all of Shaney's hard work, she graduated into one of the worst job markets in recent history and has yet to find a job. Staring down the barrel of $25,000 in loans, Shaney is understandably worried about her financial future. She's begun to question the value of going to college and finds herself wondering whether it wasn't all a waste of time.

Stress-filled college days like Shaney's are much more common than they were twenty or thirty years ago. Full-time on-campus students work more hours at paying jobs while in college than did students in the 1970s or 1980s. According to an analysis of U.S. Department of Education survey data, today three quarters of full-time college students are holding down jobs.[30] Like Shaney, nearly half of them work twenty-five hours or more a week. Working while going to school isn't inherently a bad thing—in fact, some studies show that working on-campus for fifteen hours or less per week can help foster better academic performance. On-campus jobs, which are often work-study slots, provide a chance for students to deepen their connections to the campus through contact with other students, faculty, and staff. The problem is that more and more students are working off-campus at multiple jobs and for longer hours. Students who work twenty-five hours or more a week are much more likely to report that work affected their grades and interfered with their class schedule. Grades suffer as studying time declines and so does the free time to participate in academic clubs and social activities.

Not everyone can handle the added stress of long work hours

on top of college. Too often students give up under the pressure. As anyone who has made it past their first two years of college can attest, the second half is when college becomes really interesting; it's the whole four-year package that provides the analytical, problem-solving, and writing skills that distinguish a bachelor's degree from an associate's degree. But when an 18-year-old is borrowing $8,000 or more a year and working twenty-five hours a week to pay for college, it changes the equation. Under these conditions, a boring class is no longer just a snooze fest—it's an extremely *expensive* snooze fest. It's not surprising that under a debt-for-diploma and work-till-you-drop environment, one third of students drop out after their first year of college. And first-generation college students are almost twice as likely as students with college-educated parents to drop out before their second year.[31]

This is why the percentage of students who actually earn their bachelor's degree hasn't risen nearly as fast as enrollments would suggest.[32] Just over half (53 percent) of all students who enroll in four-year colleges end up getting their bachelor's degrees within five years.[33] Not surprisingly, there are wide disparities by class and race in who completes college. Within five years of entering college, 40 percent of students from the top socioeconomic quartile (25 percent) will earn a four-year degree as compared to only 6 percent of students in the lowest quartile.[34] Over a quarter of white students who enter college will earn a bachelor's degree, whereas only about 15 percent of black and Hispanic college students will complete their degrees.[35]

Upping the Ante

As middle-class and first-generation students have been struggling to afford a decent education from state universities over the last decade, their upper-income counterparts have been engaged in a battle of a different nature. They are competing for slots at the nation's most elite schools, fearing that getting into anything less than a name-brand school will result in a life of mediocrity, or complete failure. Fueling this race is a profound sense that being one of the "winners" is the only sure way to the good life, defined in purely material terms. As the spoils of our economy are increasingly concentrated in a small group of top performers, more and more students are viewing the shrinking winner's circle as the only circle to aim for.

The college application process for high-income students, who already enjoy the advantage of attending the best private and public high schools, is of a completely different nature from that of Middle America. For first-generation students, who tend to be either working or middle-class, going to college usually means going to one of the state universities. Even though I excelled in high school and was in the advanced placement courses, it never occurred to me to explore smaller liberal arts colleges or even an out-of-state public university. A private college was just out of the question. There was no touring of campuses in the hopes of finding the perfect social and academic fit. I made my selection on the basis of brochures and the reputation of each school's journalism program and chose to attend Ohio University in Athens, Ohio. When it came to taking the SAT, I didn't take any prep courses, I just showed up at the school cafeteria at the specified time with my number 2 pencil and tried to do my best. My scores reflected that casual approach. As for many first-generation students, the whole process of getting into college was fairly low-key compared to the new standards set by today's elite.

It wasn't until I moved to New York City that I got a glimpse of this college mania. I've suffered through many Monday mornings listening to my bosses recap their weekend college-hunting excursions and bemoan brilliant young Janie's or Johnny's problems with the SAT. It's an exhausting and tiresome drama, for the parents and the coworkers alike.

But well-educated families, who tend to have higher incomes, are simply responding to the mainstreaming of bachelor's degrees as a bottom-line requirement for a decent job. As more students go to college, it's made attending a selective college even more attractive and necessary for society's upper 10 percent to ensure that the next generation stays in the upper echelon. This new quest to get into the "best" colleges is similar to the "trading up" that's happened with every other major commodity on the market. Now that middle-class families can buy a deluxe range from, say, GE, upper-middle-class families are opting for a top-of-the-line Viking. Similarly, it's no longer good enough to have just any old bachelor's degree. Now, upper-income parents are focused on giving their kids the distinction of a degree from a top college, which in turn will help ensure they can get into the best law schools, medical schools, and graduate programs. And in turn provide *their* children with a top-notch lifestyle and education.

All the private tutors, college consultants, and individual meetings with college recruiters pay off. Nearly three quarters of students at the nation's top 146 colleges come from families in the top quarter of the socioeconomic status (SES) scale, as measured according to a formula that combines family income and the education and occupations of parents.[36] Only 3 percent are from the lowest SES quartile and only 10 percent are culled from the entire bottom half of the SES distribution. These 146 colleges represent the top two tiers in *Barron's Guide to College,* comprising the most selective 10 percent of the 1,400 four-year institutions in the nation. Racial diversity on elite campuses still needs improvement, too, though class homogeny is now more severe. Black and Hispanic students make up only 6 percent of the freshman classes at these selective institutions, while making up 15 percent and 13 percent, respectively, of the 18-year-old population.

It's been over ten years since I was an undergrad, so I did a little online research to find out just how much it costs to pay your way through the admissions process. How much are those SAT prep courses, anyway? I was shocked to learn that a run-of-the-mill prep course from companies such as Kaplan or Princeton Review costs $800. Individual tutoring offered by the same companies can run from $1,900 to $4,199, depending on the number of hours. And that's just the cost of trying to score well on the SAT. Test prep is just the tip of the iceberg. There is now a whole cadre of professionals for hire to help students get into the best schools. Parents can hire their very own admissions consultant, for $150 an hour or for a package rate from $1,500 to $3,000. What exactly do these consultants do? They help students find the right college for their abilities and aspirations, they coach them on interviews with admissions officers, and they help add sparkle and shine to a lackluster college essay. This is to say nothing of the intellectual boot camps that allow students to take college courses and get a feel for the campus environment. Getting a sneak peak at the college experience doesn't come cheap; these trial runs cost about $4,000 to $6,000.[37]

In addition to tutors and consultants, there are special tours that allow students to visit different campuses with other ambitious students. For example, College Campus Tours offers a package to visit all the tony East Coast schools—Georgetown, Dartmouth, Columbia, Barnard, Yale, Harvard, and others—for just over $2,000.[38] That price doesn't include air fare or meals, which would bring the real cost closer to $3,000 or more.

While media stories make it seem as though test prep and consultants have become ubiquitous, these advantages are the province of our nation's elite. According to the trade association for professional education consultants, only 6 percent of high school graduates get help from outside professionals. But that's up from 1 percent in 1990.[39] Now compare that to the amount of free college guidance offered at high schools, a statistic we can round down to zero. Which isn't really that surprising when the average high school guidance counselor has a caseload of nearly 500 students a year.[40]

So what does all this high-priced professional help add up to? The benefits of attending the nation's best colleges are multiple. Students in selective colleges are more likely to graduate and more likely to get into top-notch graduate schools. Studies differ on the wage premium for attending an elite college: One study found no wage differential between similarly qualified students who attended selective compared to less selective institutions.[41] Other studies have found that graduates from selective colleges earn more, but not much more.[42] It does, however, appear that students from families with low socioeconomic status benefit more from attending highly selective colleges.[43]

Of course, there are also intangible benefits to going to the nation's top colleges. Elite schools offer inroads into the nation's power corridor and lifelong connections to a student body that is more likely to become America's next generation of movers and shakers. Given the high-stakes character of our winner-take-all society, the new college mania seems almost rational. As Robert Frank and Philip Cook detail in their book, *The Winner-Take-All Society,* the rewards at the top of professions are so much greater than those enjoyed by the middle that there is enormous pressure to get the best of everything right up-front.

Economically well-off households have actually been helped in this new meritocratic battle. In the early 1990s, state governments and public colleges began shifting their aid dollars to merit-based rather than need-based awards. This shift happened rather quickly and coincided with rising enrollments and rising tuition costs. Between 1991 and 2001, spending by the states on need-based scholarships for undergraduates increased 7.7 percent annually, but spending on merit-based programs increased by 18.3 percent annually. The proportion of state grants awarded based on merit rather than need rose from 11 percent to 24 percent during this period.[44] Why the switch? During the recession of the early 1990s, middle-class families voiced growing concern about their ability to pay for college, as states grappled with budget shortfalls by cutting back on support for higher education. As tuitions shot up at state colleges across the country, middle-income households felt the squeeze. In response to affordability fears, many states began engaging in an all-out scholarship battle aimed at attracting and keeping the best students in their home states by means of attractive aid packages. The first state to engage in this new meritocratic bidding war was Georgia. In 1993, then Governor Zell Miller implemented the HOPE Scholarship—Helping Outstanding Pupils Educationally. Georgia high school students graduating with a B average in core curriculum can receive a HOPE scholarship that covers tuition, fees, and book expenses. A study of Georgia's HOPE scholarship program found that it was successful in raising college attendance among middle- and high-income youth, but that the program also widened the gap in college attendance between blacks and whites, and between those from low- and high-income families.[45]

A few years later, at the federal level, President Bill Clinton would further solidify the shift away from need-based aid. The HOPE Scholarship and Lifetime Learning Tax credits, initiated during the Clinton administration, now account for about 8 percent of federal financial aid. It was claimed that the tax credits would help families pay for college, and perhaps they have, but they've done little to ebb the tide of student borrowing, which has risen steadily. In addition, the benefits of the HOPE tax credit overwhelmingly go to middle- and upper-income individuals.

There is a real problem with state governments choosing to offer grant money on the basis of merit alone, rather than on need and merit combined. When student aid is based on merit, defined solely by grades and test results, rather than need, it tends to go to students from better-off families who could have afforded the college tuition without the aid. The students who score highest on aptitude tests and pen the sharpest essays tend to come from well-educated, high-income families—who can spend thousands of dollars on private tutors, consultants, and essay coaches. These students also tend to come from the best high schools, where guidance counselors are on intimate terms with admissions committees and can help students tailor their extracurricular activities and courses to give them an edge at their school of choice. The scholarship is merely icing on the cake. A merit award is more likely to affect which college a student attends, not whether or not they attend college at all. The same can't be said for need-based aid. The availability of grant aid has a big influence on whether lower-income students will enroll in college.[46] The availability of loans doesn't change this equation for lower-income students anywhere near as much as grants.

Students from middle- and lower-income households don't stand a chance in this game. They can't compete with the thousands of dollars spent on perfecting essays and traveling the country with their parents to find the perfect school. As financial aid has become more focused on loans and less on grants and as both state-level and institutional aid increasingly goes to the best-prepared and brightest, the average smart kids are left to borrow their way through the state university system. The only choice they have is whether they're willing to fork over a good chunk of their future earnings for the "gotta have it" bachelor's degree.

Unfortunately, making it through four years of college will only get you a toehold in the new economy. These days, most professional positions require credentials higher up the food chain.

Hot Shots and Second Thoughts: The Advanced Degree

If the bachelor's degree is the new high school diploma, the master's degree has become the new bachelor's. A bachelor's degree is the bare-minimum requirement for attaining a middle-class lifestyle, but it often no longer suffices to keep you there. As I'll detail in the next chapter, the people who move up the career ladder tend to be the super-educated. The labor market just doesn't reward run-of-the-mill bachelor's degrees the way it used to.

There's a credential craze going on in America's professional class. Occupations that used to require only bachelor's degrees have been steadily upgrading their educational requirements. To get to the management level in any business field now requires an MBA. Even social workers, librarians, and teachers are expected to earn master's degrees.

The demand for advanced degrees began growing in the late 1970s as American society transitioned from an industrial to a knowledge-based economy. Judith Glazer, a scholar who studies trends in higher education, points to several related factors behind the increasing proliferation of advanced degrees: individuals wanting job advancement and mobility, a demand from employers for more highly trained practitioners, and an eagerness in many professions to enhance their status by upgrading the degree requirement for entry to the occupation.[47] Prior to the mid-1970s, the master's degree was mainly the province of academia. Most master's degrees were in nonprofessional fields that stressed theory and pure knowledge over practice. The motivation for getting a master's degree wasn't a better job or better money—it was an intellectual pursuit. Not anymore. Most grad students are in school to help advance their careers, not to experience the life of the mind. Today about 85 percent of all master's degrees are practice-oriented, as opposed to theoretical.[48] Business and education are the major dominators in the master's degree craze, each representing about 25 percent of all advanced degrees.

The result of the new credential craze is that the number of master's degrees being awarded is growing faster than that of bachelor's degrees. The number of students earning graduate degrees rose 58 percent between 1986 and 1999, to just under 500,000 annually. The number of bachelor's degrees rose only by 25 percent, to just over 1.2 million.[49] Just as the rich have gotten richer since the 1980's, the well-educated have gotten supereducated.

However, many of these high-achieving students are paying more of a debt penalty for their ambition than they expected. Wanda and Jerome, both African American, in many ways represent the new face of master's degree holders. Wanda has a master's in human relations and Jerome has an M.B.A. Their combined student loan debt, which is mostly from graduate school, is just over $30,000. Jerome went back to school to get his M.B.A. because he wanted to move up in corporate America, particularly at the Fortune 100 company where he was an account manager. Tired of watching his friends with advanced degrees earn more money, he enrolled in business school and took classes at night. But before he could finish his M.B.A., he got laid off. Today, Jerome is trying to start his own business and is also bartending and teaching aerobics to help make ends meet. When I asked Wanda whether she thought their advanced degrees were worth the sacrifice, she said not really. She didn't need the degree to get the job she currently has as a nonprofit program manager. Jerome managed to complete his M.B.A., but still hasn't found another full-time job. In the meantime, this supereducated couple is struggling to pay the bills.

This couple is not alone in racking up debt in the chase for better credentials. According to a survey conducted by the Nellie Mae Corporation, a leading provider of federal and private student loans, the average graduate student racks up $45,900 in combined student loan debt. That works out to an average monthly payment of $388, or 13.5 percent of their average annual income after graduation.[50] For doctors and lawyers it's more: their average student loan debt is over $90,000, and the cost of their education can easily eat up about 20 percent of their paychecks each month. If we look at graduate student loan debt by major, only one field had annual earnings higher than the amount of student loan debt required for the field. That field was business. In 2002, M.B.A.'s had average yearly earnings of $57,000 and student loan debt just below $40,000. Now compare that to the poor idealists who want to teach for a living. Young adults with a master's in education degree have about $32,000 in debt and mean annual earnings of about the same. A fact unsurprising to this author, who accumulated over $55,000 in grad school loans alone, is that more than half of all graduate borrowers in the Nellie Mae survey felt very burdened by their debt—regardless of what field they studied.

Enough bad news. There is also a bright side to this story. Unlike at the undergraduate level, the faces at our nation's graduate schools have changed greatly in a generation. Today's master's candidates are much more likely to be women and students of color than they were back in the late 1970s. In fact, women now out-number men at graduate school.[51] The number of black students has more than doubled and the number of Hispanic and Asian students has tripled. But there is still a long way to go in terms of proportional representation. White students still make up more than two thirds of enrollees at both graduate and law and medical schools, and black students account for 8.5 percent and Hispanic students for 5.2 percent—both lower than their proportion in the population generally.

Even though enrollments are growing among women and students of color, the hyper-credentialed crowd is still a very select group. Numerous studies have found that among students who *wish* to pursue an advanced degree, those with high levels of undergraduate debt are less likely to actually pursue additional study.[52] Here again the debt-for-diploma system continues to exert a powerful influence on the decisions young adults make about their futures. Shaney, whom we met earlier in the chapter, told me she would like to go to grad school. But she can't imagine going through the madness again of working nearly full-time and going to school full-time. And she can't imagine taking out student loans on top of the $25,000 she can barely pay back as it is. Students with high levels of debt are more likely to have parents without college degrees, come from low-income backgrounds, or be students of color. The surging demand for advanced degrees by employers has put many first-generation bachelor's degree holders at a disadvantage. As we'll see in the next chapter, the earnings of many college graduates are often much more modest than we (and they) might expect. For graduates working in professional fields such as business, education, public policy, and human resources, a master's degree is pivotal to gaining the upper hand in the economy.

New Challenges Around the Corner

Today, in the midst of historic income inequality, our nation's primary engine of social mobility, education, is broken. Gaps in college enrollment by class and race are as wide as or wider than they were thirty years ago. Despite rapidly rising enrollments, whether or not a young person today will finish college is still highly predicted by whether their own parents went to college. African American, Latino, and lower-income students of all races are increasingly funneled into community colleges while wealthier students are engaged in a costly meritocratic battle for a seat at the nation's best colleges. And the increasing demand by employers for graduate degrees has further exacerbated the level of educational inequality in our nation.

Demographic changes already under way have the potential for widening the credential gap even further. Over the next ten years, between 2000 and 2015, the college-age population is predicted to explode and grow by 16 percent.[53] The high school graduating class of 2008 will be the largest in our nation's history.[54] But the composition of the up-and-coming cohorts of high school graduates is different than that of previous cohorts. This generation will be more ethnically diverse, better prepared for college, and more likely to need financial aid for college. By 2015, 43 percent of the college-age population will be nonwhite, and students from low-income families will represent an increasing proportion of high school students.[55]

Without major new efforts to widen access to college by both federal and state government and our nation's colleges, a new social inequality will emerge. We'll have a well-educated minority that is mostly white and a swelling, undereducated majority that is increasingly Hispanic and African American. As the college-age population swells, our nation's financial aid system will leave millions of college-ready students without the means to continue their education and fulfill their dreams. The Advisory Committee on Student Financial Assistance projects that if current enrollment trends persist, over the next decade 4.4 million *college-ready* students from households with incomes below $50,000 will not attend a four-year college and 2 million students will not attend any type of college.[56] And those are conservative estimates. Who knows how many scientists, engineers, teachers, and doctors we will lose as a result.

The loss to both individuals and to society is just too large to allow such social cleavages to develop.

As we'll see more clearly in the next chapter, the potential for young adults to create decent lives increasingly depends on whether they become college-haves or college-have-nots.

CHAPTER TWO

Paycheck Paralysis

Duro the hot boom of the 1990s, Gen Xers were the darlings of the new economy. We were on the covers of national magazines. We were rubbing elbows with celebrities and becoming millionaires overnight. Little did we know, or anybody else know for that matter, that the tech bubble was going to burst and we'd be put back in our rightful place as a generation of ya-hoos—and forgotten as the generation behind Yahoo. But even before the stock market tanked, most young adults weren't feeling like winners in the new economy. Most just wondered when the supposed spoils of the new economy would arrive in *their* lives.

No, the reality of the labor market was, and still is, far different than the version promoted by Madison Avenue and promised by Wall Street. Most young workers were and still are struggling to find a job with health-care benefits, not obsessing about the best time to cash in their stock options. We were on the sidelines of the whole game even though the buzz said otherwise. Looked at today, four years into a weak economy, the whole period seems almost farcical. In fact, the whole argument of this book—that it's become harder and more costly to become an adult—would have seemed heretical a few years ago. But since the tech boom went bust, the blinders have come off.

As the first generation to grow into adulthood in the new economy, in both its boom and bust phases, we've had to readjust our thinking about paychecks and careers. We were promised an era of prosperity, but we inherited an economy where the idea of "making a living" right out of the starting gate seems at its worst a Sisyphean struggle. Most days the economy seems to be taunting our attempts to earn a decent living.

The Real New Economy: Fewer Teamsters, More Tempsters

America's economy began shifting away from manufacturing to services after World War II, but it would take several decades for the "new economy" to mature into what we know and experience it as today. Many excellent books have been written about the new economy and the ways it has altered work arrangements. My intention here is to provide a very brief overview of how the new economy has fundamentally changed the quality and quantity of jobs available today. Then we can examine the particulars of how young adults are faring.

In 1956, William H. Whyte, an editor at *Fortune* magazine, published *The Organization Man,* an influential bestseller that delved into the inner life of the 1950s corporate manager. The eponymous "organization man" went about his work with the quiet security of steady hours, generous benefits, and reliable raises. After thirty or so years with the company, this man could retire with a comfortable pension plan and a gold watch as a token of gratitude for years of loyal service to the organization.

Up until the late 1970s, the "organization man's" economic life wasn't all that different from that of a "factory man." Blue-collar workers enjoyed many of the same perks as the suit-and-tie crowd. Wages were high enough for blue-collar workers to afford a nice house in the suburbs and a vacation once a year. Benefits were generous and included health care and guaranteed pensions. And if the family needed a little extra money, Dad could always work an extra shift or two, earning time and a half for the sacrifice.

The defining characteristic of the U.S. labor market from the 1950s to the mid-1970s was stability. This stability and the upward mobility of workers was in large part due to the presence of a widely unionized workforce. A union card in your pocket meant good wages, good benefits, and the collective bargaining power to prevent those wages and benefits from being capriciously stripped away. Today's labor market, by contrast, is characterized by instability. Job security today isn't defined as knowing that you'll be at the company a year from now. It's knowing you'll be there *a month from now.* Union membership has dropped from 30 percent of all private-sector workers in 1973 to just 8.6 percent in 2003.[1]

Young workers no longer start work at a company with the intention of staying until retirement. In fact, it's a stroke of good fortune if they're still on the company phone list two years later. And then there's the sizable portion of today's young workers who never appear on the company's official phone list. They're brought in on a project-to-project basis and maintain only short-term connections to any firm or organization. Upward mobility is no longer taken for granted. Many young adults are working longer hours for less money than their parents did. The closest they'll get to the high life is opening a cold bottle of Miller.

It is certainly true that all workers, not just young adults, have had to cope with the changing labor market. Many Baby Boomers suffered through the onslaught of corporate downsizing in the 1980s, when CEOs were razing middle management jobs like farmers during high harvest. Those jobs never came back, something labor economists politely refer to as "displacement." Men and women with college degrees who thought they had achieved a comfortable middle-class existence found themselves out of work and out of fashion in the new economy. The 1980s were also when high school grads first dealt with the reality that their dad's factory jobs were no longer available. My intention is not to engage in a debate about who has it rougher, the middle-aged adult struggling to regain his or her foothold or the young adults struggling to find their footing. It's rough and tumble out there, whether you're 45 or 25. What I want to illuminate is how this new labor market is affecting people as they try to establish independent adult lives.

The bulk of today's under-34 crowd entered the labor force during the 1990s, the decade that saw the culmination of America's postindustrial transition. By the beginning of the 1990s, the rules of the game had been totally rewritten. Wall Street investors were pushing short-term profits over long-term stability. Global competition created new pressures for companies to cut costs. The new economy had found its sea legs. Generation Xers became the first group of young adults faced with building their lives in this volatile new economy.

You know the old expression about how people must either "sink or swim"? Today young adults do both. They swim for a while, then sink, then swim again and then sink. And back and forth it goes. Rapid ups and downs make for great roller-coaster rides, but they are not exactly how you want your career trajectory to play out. Especially given that most of the wage growth over a lifetime happens during the first ten years in the labor market.

What happens job-wise in your twenties and early thirties will ripple through the rest of your life. Once you've been bumped off the track, it's hard to regain your position.

Young adults are trying to handle the curve balls of the new economy in three major ways. There are the Bouncers—college graduates who bounce from job to job in search of the elusive salaries and benefits that a college degree supposedly should command. Then there are the Jugglers, who work in relatively low-paying jobs and often juggle school on the side or juggle two jobs. And finally, there are the Tempsters, who don't have "real" jobs. They get their work through a temp agency, or may be part of what I like to call the Pajama Class—people who work for themselves, turning their apartments into offices.

The Bouncers

Today's Bouncers aren't the big beefy guys who determine who gets into the latest trendy nightspot. They're young college-educated adults who bounce from one job to the next in search of a better deal. Or they may be Bouncers who job-hop because they routinely get pink-slipped. Whatever the case, most Bouncers are moving from one dead-end position to another. Their salaries tend to hover between the mid-twenties and low forties, and each job-hop generally gets them just a thousand or so more dollars up the wage ladder.

Susan is a quintessential Bouncer. It's been six years since she graduated from college and she's already on her fifth job. She has been an assistant at a law firm, a manager at two different hotels, a sales rep for a start-up telecommunications company, and a sales associate at a fine jewelry store. She's now enrolled in law school and working for a nonprofit.

Not exactly the résumé one might expect of a Cornell University grad. Susan got her bachelor's degree in hotel and restaurant administration in 1996—which makes those hotel jobs less tangential than at first glance. Her first job out of school was at a law firm. She took the job because she thought she might want to go to law school and her mom suggested she work at a law firm before plunking down serious money on a law degree. After about a year at the job, making $25,000 a year, Susan left the position so she could be closer to her husband, who was still finishing law school at Cornell. To make money, she did research for a professor on hotel law while her husband hit the books. By the time June rolled around, the couple who just six months earlier had said "I do" decided that, actually, they didn't. Broke and demoralized by her divorce, Susan decided to return to Orange County, California, her childhood home. "With my tail between my legs," Susan told me, she moved back in with her mom.

After a few weeks of wallowing around the house, Susan went out to get a job. Thinking she should at least get something related to her major in college, she found a position managing the front desk at a hotel chain in a little seaside town. She got paid $8 an hour. When the owner decided to sell the hotel just six months after she had started the job, Susan was convinced the new owner would clean house. Instead, after learning about her educational background, he promoted her to general manager at a yearly salary of $28,000. After another ten months there, Susan got a job offer from a beautiful historic resort in Santa Barbara to manage the front office—for $6,000 more a year. She moved out of her mom's house and got a small apartment in Santa Barbara. At an annual salary of $34,000, Susan was able to make ends meet despite paying $750 in rent for what she describes as a "rundown one-bedroom apartment with intermittent plumbing." She was in charge of the front desk, reservations, valet parking, and bell staff.

Susan was excited about the opportunity to work at a classy hotel and to have been given so much responsibility. It was exactly what she had envisioned when she decided to major in hotel and restaurant management in the first place. But, alas, dream jobs are sometimes just that: a dream. Susan worked sixteen-hour days and had trouble commanding obedience from staff who were twice her age. After ten months of being miserable, Susan gave her two weeks' notice. Lacking a backup plan, she drove immediately to a temp agency and told them she'd take anything. Following Susan's job history was a little like piecing together a puzzle, so let me recap. At this point, Susan had been out of college for three years, had just left job number three, and was on her way to the temp agency. Susan got placed right away, at a telecommunications company. It was 1999 and the economy was on fire. About a month into the temp job, the company offered Susan a full-time job for $35,000 a year—which she was very excited about. For Susan, this salary was enough money for her to start getting ahead. She started saving half of every paycheck, prudent advice gleaned from her parents.

After a year and a half at the telecom job—her lengthiest employment yet—two of the directors decided to start their own company in Las Vegas. They offered Susan what seemed like the deal of a lifetime: a base salary of $60,000, plus incentives equal to 40 percent of her salary. And the cherry on top: a 20 percent bonus if the directors met the company's goals and another 20 percent if Susan met her goals. Viva Las Vegas! Susan, like anyone with a gold carrot dangled before her, bolted for the desert. It was the year 2000, the first year of the new millennium, and the tech market was still booming. As you probably guessed a few sentences back, the timing turned out to be not so good. The tech sector began to tank and the gamble in Vegas became a bust. Just a year and a half after the company opened its doors, it collapsed.

But Susan is a survivor and a planner. She had stashed a good deal of that hot tech money away in savings and retirement plans. She had about seven grand in cash and much more in a 401(k) plan and an IRA. Some sort of nihilistic pride kept Susan from signing up for unemployment until six months after the company had folded—during which, despite pounding the pavement, she couldn't get work. She applied for jobs at the mall and at hotels, but nobody would hire her for fear that she was overqualified and would quit when something better came along. Almost eight months had passed when, through a friend of a friend, she landed a job selling high-end jewelry at a posh Vegas resort, making $10 an hour. Susan still talks about the big perk that came with the job: a free meal every day from room service. To save money, that was the only meal she'd eat all day.

By the age of 30, Susan had held five jobs since graduating from college. Other than the job with the start-up—which turned out to be a fluke—this Cornell grad has not surpassed the $35,000 mark. Her eight-month unemployment zapped her savings and landed her $12,000 in credit-card debt. Susan, who manages humor in spite of the ups and downs that come with being a Bouncer, blames Murphy's Law: "When times are down that's when your car needs tires."

Bouncing from job to job is sometimes chalked up as a generational character flaw, rather than a by-product of a flawed economy. But it's not as if Gen X rode into town and rewrote the rules of the economy. The rules were being rewritten when we were young tykes in the late 1970s and high school students with bad hair in the 1980s. Today's young adults aren't that different from previous generations in their basic values about work and life. They want jobs with good wages and good benefits. They're shooting for a comfortable, decent middle-class life. But whereas jobs that offered that kind of security were relatively plentiful thirty years ago, they've come closer to extinction every day. And so they bounce.

The Jugglers

Jugglers—young adults who work full-time and juggle college—are not a new phenomenon, but the practice has become much more common among young adults than ever before. Most Jugglers are the half of all high school seniors who don't enroll in a four-year college. For them, the real world starts immediately upon high school graduation. The Jugglers I've met are super-motivated people. They work in low-wage jobs like retail or fast food, or they do grunt work at an office, and manage to squeeze courses in at a community college, study every minute that they're not on the job. These young adults, who are typically in their early- to mid-twenties, often seem tireless. I felt exhausted just listening to their accounts of chaotic, time-crunched lives.

When Anna, now 28, graduated from her Colorado high school in 1996, she traded in her job at the mall for a receptionist position, where she made $7 an hour. Her working-class parents couldn't afford to pay for college, so Anna was on her own. A difficult relationship with her mom prompted Anna to move out right after high school. She immediately enrolled in community college and for the next three years worked as a receptionist and took classes at night. Despite relatively low tuition, Anna had to work at a clothing store on the nights she wasn't in class to scrape together enough money for tuition and books. During the holiday season, she'd often add another retail job. Despite juggling several jobs,

Anna often couldn't enroll every semester because money was always stretched to the breaking point.

In March 2000, Anna was laid off from her receptionist job. Panicked, she quickly signed up for placement with three temp agencies. But work was hard to find and Anna often found herself applying for three jobs a day. One day she placed twelve different applications. After three months, she finally got a two-month assignment doing administrative work at a government agency. Just a short time later, the agency hired Anna as a full-time assistant to one of the directors. The hourly pay was $9.02. Now that she was earning two dollars more per hour than on her last job, Anna was finally able to stop juggling a second job. Her new government job offered health insurance—but it was too expensive and the benefits weren't that great. Having gone three years already without a health plan, Anna just continued going to urgent-care clinics when she got sick.

Anna worked at the agency for nearly three and half years, right up until she left for art school in San Francisco. At that time, Anna was making just under $20,000. Her college education had added a debt of $12,000 in student loans—the bulk from one semester at a "real" college. I talked with Anna after she had moved to San Francisco and started art school. She is living with four roommates, which makes her rent much cheaper—just $600 a month. Anna didn't waste any time in getting a job. Her first day in the new city, she got a job working twenty hours a week at a card shop. Not one to stop juggling, she had just taken a second part-time job at a clothing store. Most of her tuition and fees, which are about $7,500 each semester, is paid for by student loans. Everything else is paid from her paychecks. When all is said and done, Anna thinks she'll leave school with about $76,000 in student loan debt.

Anna was candid about just how much of struggle the past eight years had been, but she still managed to laugh it off. When I asked what her financial dream was for the future, she quickly answered: "My dream is to be financially stable. I'd be content making forty thousand a year." Anna would like to work in an art gallery and hopefully one day as a museum curator. But her "big" financial dream is to be able to send her children to college. She wants to have enough money set aside to pay for their college so they won't have to work so hard just to pay off debt. And she'd like to be able to show her children the world and broaden their horizons. The daughter of working-class parents, Anna just wants to live a modest middle-class life. If she stays on track—and I have to believe that she will—she'll be 30 years old when she graduates from college. Her student loan debt will be like paying a second rent, making it difficult for her to come out ahead for at least another decade. Her earnings potential isn't huge, but for Anna it's worth the $76,000 investment if it gets her beyond her working-class roots and into the middle class. Anna's determination and drive make her exceptional. Most Jugglers can't endure the long financial and emotional haul it takes to work full-time and try to earn a degree.

Like Anna, the majority of Jugglers come from modest economic backgrounds. Their parents didn't go to college themselves and often are unable to offer their children much guidance or financial support. As we learned in the last chapter, whether or not someone's parents went to college is the single biggest predictor of where their adult children will fall in the socioeconomic pecking order. Unfortunately, most Jugglers give up on the one thing that could help them get ahead financially over the long run: a college degree. I discussed the high prevalence of "some college" on the résumés of today's young adults in the last chapter, but the point is worth making again. In 2001, just under one third of all 25-to-29-year-olds had earned a bachelor's degree. Another third had gained "some college." The difference in earnings for all three levels of education—bachelor's degree, some college, and no college—has steadily widened over the last thirty years. Today's young adults are sloshing through an economy that increasingly saves its best rewards for well-educated individuals.

Here's the difference between going the extra two years and getting a bachelor's degree, or dropping out after a stint at community college. Over the course of their lifetimes, today's young workers who have "some college, but no degree" can expect lifetime earnings of about $1.5 million. Associate's degree holders will earn slightly more: $1.6 million. On the other hand, young adults who have a bachelor's degree can expect to earn on average $2.1 million. That's about a third more than workers who don't finish college, and nearly twice as much as workers with only a high school diploma. And of course the wage inequality keeps on getting wider as we creep up the credential ladder. A master's degree holder will earn about $2.5 million over a lifetime, and professional degree holders—largely lawyers and doctors—will average out at $4.4 million.[2] The credentials craze has its roots in money. Diplomas yield dollars. The more diplomas you rack up, the better your chances are in today's economy.

Welcome to the Benefit-Free Zone

The disturbing inequality among today's young adults goes beyond earnings. Not only do jobs for college grads offer better salaries, they also offer more fringe benefits such as health care, retirement plans, and paid vacation time. And increasingly, even well-paying jobs may not provide such benefits, with health benefits becoming more and more scarce. Today, young adults make up the single largest group of the uninsured in America—18 million and counting.[3] Roughly 33 percent, or one in three, of those aged 18 to 34 are without health insurance, the highest percentage of any age group.[4] Many people assume young adults decline coverage when offered, out of some sense of invulnerability to illness. But in reality only 3 percent of young adults are uninsured because they turned down coverage; the rest either aren't offered it by their jobs or they can't afford it.

Not surprisingly, it's Jugglers who are more likely to be uninsured. The majority of young adult workers who are uninsured earn under $10 an hour.[5] Even if their employers offer coverage, it's often financially out of reach. Here again is a bitter pill for Jugglers and the rest of the sheepskin-less crowd: low-wage employers tend to require workers to make larger dollar contributions to health insurance plans than do higher-wage employers. The lower your earnings, the more you're expected to pay for your health-care benefits. In 1987, 68 percent of 25-to-34-year-olds had employer-based health care coverage; in 2003 this figure was down to 61 percent.[6]

Going without health insurance is not only bad for young adults' health, it often lands them in the financial hurt box. Ed, whom we'll meet again later, didn't have health insurance even though he worked full-time as a cook at a local restaurant. When he got sick and ended up in the hospital, he was stuck with a $5,000 medical bill. It took Ed about three years to pay off the debt. Ed's not alone. About half of young adults aged 19 to 29 without health insurance reported having problems paying medical bills.[7]

If health-care benefits are on the endangered list, guaranteed pension plans are on the verge of extinction. A guaranteed pension plan, usually called a defined-benefit plan or traditional pension, used to be the means, along with Social Security, by which workers managed to retire in some comfort. The company did the investing and guaranteed each worker a monthly retirement payment that was based on their salary and years at the company. In these plans, the amount of money earned for your retirement wasn't based on how much you could scrape together in savings. In 1974, 44 percent of workers in the private sector were in a defined-benefit plan. Today only 17 percent are in such plans.[8] The days of guaranteed income for retirement are long gone and show no signs of returning. In their place are defined-contribution plans, commonly known as 401(k) plans. In these types of accounts, employees contribute a share of their income to an individual account and the employer contributes either directly or through a match. The investment decisions are generally left to the employee. In employer surveys, most young adults say they prefer 401(k)s to the traditional plans anyway—in large part, no doubt, because we grew up with the Wall Street–dominated corporate culture.

But there is a huge trade-off to managing your own account: you are rolling the dice on the chance of achieving good investment returns—and, unlike traditional pension plans, 401(k) plans are not insured by the federal government. As the Enron, World-Com, and Global Crossing scandals made sickeningly clear, it's not just about putting your money into a 401(k), it's about putting your trust in the market and your faith in the integrity of the system. Saving for retirement means deftly navigating the world of stocks, mutual funds, and bonds.

Of course, not all young adults get the chance to save for retirement. In 2000, just under 50 percent of all private-sector workers were covered by any sort of pension, including 401(k) plans.[9] And like health-care benefits, pension benefits are primarily the province of the well-paid. About 73 percent of those in the top quintile of earners had a pension plan, as compared to only 18 percent of those in the bottom quintile.

Faced with meager paychecks and unequal access to retirement benefits, it's not surprising that only 35 percent of young workers are saving for retirement. In a later chapter, I'll look more closely at how young adults are doing in terms of their wealth accumulation and savings. But for now, let's get back to how the under-34ers are trying to make a buck in the new economy.

The Tempsters

So far, I've talked about Bouncers, who tend to have college degrees and are constantly job-hopping in the hopes of boosting their earnings or building their career, and Jugglers, who tend to have lower incomes and combine full-time work with school. That brings us finally to the Tempsters.

Temporary work—or contingent work, as it's often called—has spread through the economy like a nasty virus. Until the late 1980s, temporary work tended to be seasonal, in industries such as construction, farming, and tourism. It was such a below-the-radar phenomenon that the Bureau of Labor Statistics didn't start collecting information on contingent workers until 1995. Today contingent workers make up 16 percent of the workforce.[10] If part-time workers are included, contingent workers make up 33 percent of the nation's workforce.

How did temping become mainstream? The rise in temp jobs is part of a much larger story about changes in the economy. Global competition, technological changes, and increasing pressure to deliver short-term economic gains to Wall Street all played a role in driving employers to shift their corporate focus from stability to flexibility. These pressures ushered in the infamous "downsizing" of the 1980s, when corporations slashed jobs and closed factories in the quest to become "lean and mean" at the behest of Wall Street.

Companies began contracting out many services, from building maintenance to receptionists, as a way to cut their labor costs. Many of the parents of today's under-34ers got slaughtered during the 1980s downsizing and never made it back to their previous earnings.

"Temping" became the way for employers to get the job done without giving anyone a real job. Temp agencies started springing up all over the country to satiate the new corporate thirst for "flexibility." During the 1990s, the number of jobs handled by temp agencies more than doubled, growing from just under 1 million jobs to over 2 million by the end of the century.[11]

Before we go any further, it would be good to be clear about what contingent work really is. The Bureau of Labor Statistics defines contingent work as "any job in which an individual does not have an explicit or implicit contract for long-term employment." Essentially, contingent work is temporary work. And it runs the gamut from independent contractors or freelancers to day laborers to temporary help–agency workers. Young contingent workers are a motley bunch. They're culled from both the highest and lowest educational backgrounds and they work in positions up and down the scale, from librarians and receptionists to scientists. The jobs with the highest percentage of contingent workers are professional specialty occupations such as college instructors and scientists, administrative support occupations such as receptionists and data entry clerks, and farming.[12]

Across the board, Tempsters earn less than they would if they were doing the same job on a permanent basis.[13] They're also much less likely to have health-care or pension benefits.[14] Contingent workers are more likely to be young, female, and nonwhite—particularly Tempsters who work for a temporary agency.[15]

But the biggest drawback of being a Tempster is the instability and financial insecurity that comes with the territory. Paychecks may be sporadic, and unemployment is always one project away. Which helps explain why nearly half of all Tempsters would prefer a permanent full-time job.[16]

Life as a Tempster can be rough. Tempsters have higher rates of unemployment and are more likely to hold multiple jobs than their permanently employed counterparts.[17] But it isn't easy to lump Tempsters into one big class. They are as likely to be high school graduates as they are to have bachelor's or advanced degrees, so the earnings and quality of their jobs vary greatly. For example, computer programmers who work on contract make $400 an hour in Silicon Valley, while temps doing filing or receptionist duties make $15 an hour. It's hard to plan a financial future on sporadic, unpredictable employment (unless you're the rare Tempster making $400 an hour).

Contingent work can be a blessing when it allows young adults to quickly get a paycheck after college or after losing a job. Being a Tempster is better than nothing. For the youngest Tempsters, temp work allows them the flexibility of combining school and work. Indeed, the highest percentage of Tempsters are between the ages of 16 and 24, the majority of them working while enrolled in school.[18]

Temp work has helped many young adults manage the roller-coaster ride of the new economy. But for many, the Tempster stage can feel like a houseguest that stays too long.

Dylan is a 32-year-old editor and writer living in New York City, where she grew up and went to college. She's multiracial, with black, Irish, and Native American roots. She studied screenwriting at New York University while living at home but nonetheless needed $15,000 in student loans to help pay for tuition. When Dylan graduated from NYU in 1994, the job market was sluggish, so she took a job as a receptionist at a production studio, making $17,000 a year. As it happened, a coworker told her about a job at a new magazine. Dylan hit it off with the editor and went to work as the magazine's office manager. She stayed there for two years, helping out with editorial assignments because the staff was so small. They moved her to the editorial division, which required her to give up her benefits and work as a freelancer. Her next job was with another magazine—again as a freelancer, though they dangled the carrot of a full-time position in front of her. The full-time job never materialized, so Dylan continued to freelance, working for several different magazines over the next couple of years. The lack of a stable income took its toll on her finances. Dylan had managed to get through four years of college without any credit card debt, but she racked up a lot of it as a Tempster. By the time she finally landed her first full-time salaried position, five years after graduating from college, she was carrying almost $10,000 in credit card debt. The job paid $35,000, which was quickly eaten up by rent, groceries, and bills. (Remember, she lives in New York City.) The financial struggle was an emotional drain on Dylan. No matter how many meals she skipped or how many one-dollar slices of pizza she ate for dinner, she still couldn't get ahead. Every dollar of her finally stable paycheck went to bills. She finally decided her best bet was to file for bankruptcy, which she did in late 1999.

Today, Dylan is feeling better about her financial situation. She still works for the same magazine and now earns roughly $45,000 a year. She can pay her rent and afford groceries. She gets health-care benefits through work, allowing her for the first time to go to a dentist and doctor on a regular basis. Plus, Dylan managed to secure one of the last great steals in Manhattan—a studio apartment for just $650 a month. It all sounds pretty good until you remember those student loans, which can't be erased by bankruptcy. Dylan owes $15,000, so her net worth remains in the minuses. Her dream of someday joining the ownership class looks to remain a dream for some time to come.

The Pajama Class

In cities with a high proportion of creative industries, freelancing has become the typical way of life for many writers, designers, editors, and photographers. You'd be hard-pressed today to find any magazine, advertising agency, book publisher, or newspaper that didn't rely on freelance talent for some or all of its creative tasks. Businesses utilize these independent contractors in large part because they cannot afford to pay payroll taxes and provide health-care benefits and 401(k) benefits to a full workforce. Often these freelancers work from the comfort of their homes, so I've taken to calling this class of workers the Pajama Class.

The Pajama Class tends to be white and well educated. They also are more likely to prefer their work arrangement over a full-time, permanent job. And why not, when their commute takes only five seconds? One in five in the Pajama Class is between the ages of 20 and 34.[19] Many having turned to freelancing when they were laid off from their previous full-time jobs. My husband, for instance, works in advertising and over the years has earned money as a freelance writer, both by choice and by necessity. Granted, some members of the Pajama Class, 83 percent, according to data collected by the Bureau of Labor Statistics, prefer the flexibility and freedom that comes from living life as a hired gun.[20] The rest, however, like Dylan, are de facto Pajamas who'd much rather have the security of a full-time job.

Both run-of-the-mill Tempsters and Pajamas often go without health insurance for very long periods of time. And it's no wonder: buying health insurance on the open market is prohibitively expensive. Depending on the state, health insurance can cost anywhere from $300 to $500 a month for basic individual coverage. In New York City, which probably has more Pajamas per capita than any other major city, the monthly premium for a standard HMO plan is at least $513.[21] Freelancers tend to fall in that fragile terrain known as the middle class. They don't make enough money to buy things like health care, vacations, or retirement plans, but they make too much to qualify for any subsidies for health care. A survey conducted of independent workers in New York City found that their average income was $45,000.[22] In the same survey, 84 percent reported it was difficult to afford health insurance. Like Dylan, nearly half went without insurance coverage sometime during the year.

The Bouncers, Jugglers, Tempsters, and Pajamas that make up today's young workers face a bleak economic future. No matter how young adults try to cope with the new insecurity of today's labor market—juggling school and work or temping through the rough patches—they can't escape a simple reality. They will be the first generation who won't match the prosperity of their parents. Not only do entry-level jobs pay less than they did thirty years ago, but wage growth has slowed to a trickle. So instead of becoming more financially secure with each passing year, many young adults in their late twenties and early thirties find themselves struggling even more as they start having children and taking on mortgages. What they're experiencing is paycheck paralysis.

The Incredible Shrinking Paycheck

Many of the young adults I spoke with told me that their parents just don't understand why they can't get by on what seems to them a decent salary. What parents often fail to understand is that basically, their money went further than ours does. Much of the earnings made by today's college graduates is earmarked for paying back student loans, exorbitant rents, and expensive health-care coverage—expenses that were kept in check until the 1980s, and have grown faster than inflation, particularly in the 1990s. Young adults without college degrees have it even tougher, as the well-paying manufacturing jobs have been replaced with lower-paying occupations in the service sector.

Put in this context, it shouldn't be too surprising that young adults are barely keeping their heads above water. Even during the boom years of the late 1990s, many twenty-somethings and early thirty-somethings lost ground because their paychecks didn't grow nearly as fast as their costs. Those who did make gains quickly lost them when the market soured and the economy slumped. The 2001 recession was particularly brutal to young adults. Between 2000 and 2002 alone, household income for those under 35 dropped by 14 percent—the biggest decline of any age group.[23]

For young adults in their early thirties, this recession was, in fact, their second lashing at the hands of the new economy. They started work in the early nineties, at the tail end of a recession, and then, ten years later, were forced again to live through another round of pink slips and dwindling salaries. As I'll detail in the next chapter, the vicissitudes of the economy have left many young adults burdened with credit card debt and possessing no savings to speak of.

In order to truly appreciate how bad things have gotten, it's important to look back thirty years and see how the previous generation was faring at this age. Table 1 (p. 80) shows that median earnings for 25-to-34-year-olds have dropped considerably for those with only a high school diploma. Back in 1974, the typical male high school graduate in this age group earned nearly $43,000, in inflation-adjusted dollars. Three decades later, male high school graduates in this age group are earning just over $30,000. That's $13,000 less each year than their counterparts in the early seventies. Even in the recession of the early 1980s, workers with only a high school diploma still made more money in real terms than they do today.

What about college graduates? Young college-educated women have seen their incomes grow impressively in three decades—a trend I'll discuss more in this chapter. But their male counterparts have experienced slight declines. In 1974, typical earnings for a young-adult male with a bachelor's degree or higher were $51,223, in inflation-adjusted 2004 dollars. In 2004, young male college grads earned $50,700. You read right—today's college grads are making less than the college grads of thirty years ago.

Table 1. Median Annual Earnings of All Wage and Salary Workers Aged 25 to 34 (in 2004 dollars)						
	Males			Females		
	High School Diploma	Some College	Bachelor's Degree or Higher	High School Diploma	Some College	Bachelor's Degree or Higher
1974	$42,697	$44,257	$51,223	$25,913	$29,556	$35,674
1984	$36,773	$39,806	$46,775	$24,449	$28,263	$35,030
1994	$29,996	$33,650	$45,629	$22,604	$26,938	$37,363
2004	$30,400	$36,400	$50,700	$24,400	$28,800	$40,300

Source: From the National Center for Education Statistics, based on data from U.S. Department of Commerce, Bureau of the Census, Current Population Survey, March Supplement, 1972–2004.

The obvious question is: If young adult college grads are making less than they did thirty years ago, why is college more important today? There's a lot of confusion about the so-called "college premium." It's more advantageous today to have a college degree not because college grads earn much more than they used to—it's because high school grads earn much, much less than they used to. Unlike in the 1970s, most workers with high school diplomas simply can't make it to the middle class.

Victor, a 35-year-old African American, has the labor market experience typical of someone without a college education in today's economy. He's worked in manufacturing, fast food, hotels and restaurants, and, most recently, for a bank. He even worked two jobs for a couple of years. After graduating from high school in 1988, Victor worked for a year and a half stocking shelves at a grocery store for minimum wage. When it became clear there was no potential for a raise, Victor took a new job at a factory that made car parts. He earned $3.50 an hour, but was laid off when the owner closed down the plant and moved it to Mexico. His next job was at Domino's pizza, where he started as a driver making $5 an hour plus tips. During his three years on the job, he was promoted to a shift leader and eventually to assistant manager, making $8 an hour. While at Domino's, Victor also worked part-time at a delivery service, altogether putting in about sixty hours per week. He and his wife had just had their first child and so Victor was trying to bring in more money to support his family. He finally quit the job at Domino's and went full-time at the delivery service. He worked there for two years and then got a job at a new Embassy Suites Hotel in room service, making $2.33 an hour plus tips. He was part of the staff that helped get the hotel ready for its grand opening and he took pride in his work.

The hotel promoted him to restaurant manager and paid him $25,000 a year plus benefits. With only two or three days' training, Victor felt he had been thrown into the position unprepared. Working sixty to seventy hours a week and still unable to get all the work done, he asked his manager for an assistant. His boss responded by asking him to step down to assistant manager and train someone new to become the manager. When Victor agreed to take the demotion but said that it was against his will, his boss fired him. At the time, Victor's wife was working at Taco Bell and the couple was relying on both their incomes to get by.

Unlike with his other jobs, Victor was devastated when he was let go from the hotel. "I had given my heart, my time, and my wit and everything to the job. I was there from the beginning when the hotel opened. It was really, really, really hard and heavy on me when I lost the job." Three months later, in January 1999, Victor got a job as an assistant manager at McDonalds. He was making slightly less money, $22,000 a year. It was hard for him because he felt as though the position was a step down from his previous hotel job, but he stuck it out for six months and then got a job in customer service with a mortgage company making $11 an hour, or roughly $23,000 a year. After working at the mortgage company for five years he was laid off when the company merged with another bank. It took him a couple of months to find a new position with another mortgage company. Victor is still working there, as a loan officer, and now earns $30,000 a year. After fifteen years of solid experience in the labor market, Victor's income is still well below the $42,630 median earnings for someone of his age and education in 1972. And, as we'll see in the next chapter, the slow growth in his earnings has created another problem: a steady accumulation of debt to deal with car and home repairs.

It's bad enough that young adults are dealing with bigger bills on smaller paychecks. But as many in their early thirties can attest, this generation can't rely on aging into better earnings. The labor market of our parents' time was like an escalator: productivity went up and so did wages, so young workers back then experienced a steady and swift progression in earnings. Today's labor market is like an automated airport walkway: the economy grows faster, but wages remain flat. That's the paycheck paralysis in a nutshell.

As we've seen, about two thirds of a worker's lifetime wage growth occurs during their first ten years of labor market experience.[24] So it's important to compare the experiences of different generations at the beginning of their working lives. By now, it should come as no surprise that Gen Xers such as Victor are coming up short compared to Baby Boomers. Several studies have confirmed the lackluster wage growth experienced by most young adults; they indicate that all demographic groups of young workers are having more difficulty attaining middle-class earnings.[25] Wage growth is slower, and even though today's young adults are known for their job-hopping, it doesn't pay off the way it used to. Each new job adds less dollars than it did a generation ago.[26]

The summary of our generation's income trajectory is this: we earn less from the start and our earnings aren't growing as fast as they did a generation ago. This is especially true for certain subgroups of young workers. Young African American men and young non-college-educated men are severely disadvantaged in the new economy. Young black and Hispanic men have higher unemployment rates and lower wages than any other group. In 2002, about 9 percent of white adults under the age of 30 were living in poverty, compared to 25 percent of African American young adults and 15 percent of Hispanic young adults.[27]

In an article in *Monthly Labor Review,* two economists from the Bureau of Labor Statistics summed up perfectly how the economic well-being of today's young adults compares to that experienced by young adult Baby Boomers: "With the possible exception of having a larger array of entertainment and other goods to purchase, members of Generation X appear to be worse off by every measure."[28]

Which brings us to the next part of the story: The earnings of Generation X are marked by widening inequality. In chapter 1 I pointed out that young adults with only a high school diploma can no longer come close to matching the lifestyle of those with college degrees. But there's another type of inequality that's important to examine. Even among college degree holders, there is much more polarization in incomes than there was a generation ago. Some college grads end up earning modest middle-class incomes (if just) while others garner spectacularly high salaries. The winners are winning more than ever before. In 1975, the average income of young adults in the top 5 percent of earners was about two and a half times as great as the average income of young adults in the middle fifth; in 2003 it was nearly five times greater.[29]

It wasn't supposed to be like this. Up until the 1990s, many forecasters had projected that Gen Xers would benefit across the board from their small numbers, compared to the baby boom that preceded them, as they entered the workforce. With fewer of us than the Baby Boomers, it was predicted that jobs would be more plentiful and our raises would be fast and large. Sadly, the predictions were off, way off. Not only did overall median wages decline, but they did so across all major occupational groups.[30] Another way to look at how young adults' earning power has changed is to compare their earnings to that of the rest of the adult population.

In 1979, young adults earned about 95 percent of what all adults earned.[31] That means that young workers just starting out were earning about the same amount as their parents at the time. But by 1996, young adults were earning only 89 percent of what all adults earned. Between President Reagan and President Clinton, our generation lost more ground than other workers.

Why are young adults earning so much less than they used to? One reason is that the types of jobs available have changed dramatically. As the economy has transitioned away from manufacturing industries and toward service industries, the pay and quality of jobs have changed as well. This transition began after World War II, but it wasn't until the mid-1980s that it really accelerated. Feeling pressure from foreign competition, many companies slashed manufacturing jobs permanently. As a result, many of the high-paying blue-collar jobs were no longer around for Generation X. On top of that, unions began to disappear and the minimum wage lost ground against inflation, leaving young workers without college degrees in a serious pinch.

Much of the research on wage growth examines the trends for male workers only. Why? One reason is that up until the 1980s and 1990s, researchers didn't collect much data on female workers. But what we do know is that women have made impressive gains in the labor market since the 1970s. Women's earnings have steadily risen for both high school— and college-educated women. Unlike their male counterparts, young women today earn considerably more than their mothers did in the 1970s. Of course, some of the steep growth in their earnings is due to the fact that women work more hours and more continuously than they did in the 1970s, particularly women with children. But the gains also come from a decline in sexism that for all intents and purposes kept women from pursuing careers in anything other than nursing or teaching. And finally, women didn't suffer nearly the unemployment losses that men did as manufacturing jobs moved overseas. The deindustrialization of the U.S. economy has created new employment opportunities for women. However, many of the new service jobs where women predominate are low-paying, such as retail sales associates (75 percent of workers at Wal-Mart are women), child-care workers (99 percent women), and home health-care aides. These are the positions where you will find many young Jugglers punching out from one lousy-paying job just to punch in at the next.

Hard Work, Hardly Worth It

One of the things that separates the United States from other countries around the world is our promise of upward mobility. Though rags-to-riches stories have always been the exception rather than the rule in reality, we as a people take great comfort in their very possibility. The belief that hard work guarantees just rewards is part of our country's longstanding social contract between citizen and government.

That social contract is in tatters.

Nancy and Ed are a typical white couple living paycheck to paycheck in a suburb outside of Cleveland, Ohio. Last year, Ed earned $21,000 as manager of a local restaurant. His wife is a medical assistant and over the same period of time earned $12 an hour, roughly $24,000 a year. When Nancy started at this job, four years ago, she was making $9 an hour. Over the last four years, however, her health-care costs have increased and gas prices have soared, both growing faster than her pay increases. Nancy would really like to go back to school and earn her nursing degree, but she and her husband can't afford the loss of her income. Sadly, the financial obstacles she and Ed face have meant that they cannot get ahead—even though their combined income of $45,000 puts them squarely in the middle class. But as Nancy keenly observed, "today's middle class is very different from the middle class of my parents."

The truth of the matter is that Nancy and Ed are the lucky ones. Ed, as a manager of a local restaurant, works in one of the largest growing occupations in the country. Nancy, on the other hand, works in one of the *fastest* and *largest* growing occupations in the country. That being said, medical assistants are not considered one of the "hot jobs" for college grads, probably because the pay tends to top out at $18 an hour, or $37,000 a year. In discussing the current and future job market, it's important to understand the distinction between *fast*-growing and *large*-growing jobs. The fastest growing jobs are those that are growing quickly but not necessarily adding the most number of new jobs. They are growing faster than other jobs, but probably will never achieve the numbers of those jobs that do not require a college education.

The fastest growing occupations—the ones that get all the attention, especially from college counselors—are jobs in technology, such as computer systems analysts and computer software engineers. According to the Bureau of Labor Statistics, the fastest growing jobs will be those requiring at least some college education. And that includes medical assistants, who must attend a six-month program and a 250-hour externship.

The other half of the story about job growth has to do with the *largest* growing occupations—those adding the most number of jobs—which include food service and preparation, like Ed's restaurant job. Most of the largest growing occupations will be in jobs that pay low wages and don't require any education beyond high school (nursing and teaching are two exceptions; see below). Grasping the distinction between occupations with the *fastest* growth versus those with the *largest* growth becomes clear when you look at the raw number of jobs. The *fastest* growing occupation between 2000 and 2010 will be for computer software engineers. The number of job openings is expected to double, to 760,000. The average salary of a computer software engineer in 2003 was over $75,000.[32] So, now let's look at one of the occupations that's the *largest* growing, that is, the occupations that will add the most jobs in the economy. Topping the list is food service and preparation, with 2.9 million jobs predicted in 2010, representing a measly 30 percent growth in jobs. These jobs paid on average from $15,000 at the low end to $26,000 at the (not very) high end in 2003.[33]

Between 2000 and 2010, nearly seven out of ten new jobs will be in occupations that require only work-related training. Only 20 percent of new jobs will require a bachelor's degree or higher. About 10 percent of new jobs will require an associate's degree or a vocational certificate.[34]

But there is one glimmer of opportunity in these rather depressing job-growth figures. Two fields—teaching and nursing—will continue to add lots of jobs to the economy over the next decade. Job openings are expected to swell at both the low and high ends of these occupations. At the low end are teaching assistant jobs, medical assistants, and home health-care aides. At the higher end are registered nurses and elementary and secondary school teachers. These are good-paying, solid middle-class jobs that right now are currently going unfilled because there are too few opportunities provided for workers like Nancy to get more training and education to move up the career ladder. In the last chapter of this book, I'll address the need for structured apprenticeships to help ensure that young adults who want to teach or become nurses and can do the work can access the training and education necessary to climb the ladder.

Spoiled Slackers?

In the early 1990s, when Gen Xers first started entering the labor market, they were greeted by a tidal wave of criticism. Gen Xers were portrayed as lazy and unambitious. Maybe the grunge style got lost in translation. Compared to the baby boom's yuppies in their starched khakis and button-down shirts, Gen Xers were indeed more casual with their wardrobe. But a little slack in their slacks doesn't make them lazy or apathetic. So, do Gen Xers really shun hard work? Maybe we should ask the millions holding down two or three jobs. Young adults are more likely than any other age group to hold more than one job. In fact, young adult men aged 25 to 34 have the highest rate of multiple-job holding of all male workers. The highest rate of multiple-job holding overall, however, goes to young, single women.[35] Gen X employees are also working longer hours than their Baby Boomer counterparts did at the same age. In 2002, Gen Xers worked on average 45.6 hours a week, nearly three hours more than young Baby Boomers worked in 1977.[36]

Living paycheck to paycheck is the new norm for young adults. College grads may have a better shot at slowly digging their way out of the insecurity, but it most likely will not happen until they hit their forties. Today's paycheck paralysis makes it almost impossible for most young adults to get ahead. Dwindling salaries and rising costs mean less left-over money to put into savings, less to contribute to a 401(k), and less to put into their own kids' college funds. All the while, they're racking up credit card debt to pay for any additional expenses, like going to the dentist or fixing the car, at exorbitant interest rates that rob them of even more money. And the holes just keep getting deeper.

CHAPTER THREE

Generation Debt

First job. First house. First child. These "firsts," when strung together, traditionally signal the arrival of adulthood. Today, we can add dodging debt-collection calls and filing bankruptcy to the list. Between college debt and the spillover effects of paycheck paralysis, piling up debt has become a new rite of passage into adulthood. It's not exactly the kind of generation-defining characteristic we wished for, but debt is perhaps the one shared experience of our diverse generation. If our generation had its own branding campaign, it would be "Debt—you can't leave home without it."

While young people have more debt than previous generations had at the same age, the explosion in credit card debt is a pan-generational phenomenon. Over the last decade, seniors have racked up credit card debt in record amounts. Middle-class families are also sinking into credit card debt. Those little pieces of plastic have become the monkey on the back of our moms and dads, aunts and uncles, and even our grandmas and grandpas.

People struggling to pay back credit card bills get very little sympathy for their plight. This is especially true for young adults, who, conventional wisdom holds, are wildly decadent about their spending. When people think of a young woman in debt, they probably envision a closet full of shoes, Manolo Blahniks, no doubt, and a wardrobe rich with designer brands, splurges courtesy of a generous credit line. And, of course, empty kitchen cupboards because she's out with friends most nights. If it's a young man sinking in credit card debt, the stereotype that springs to mind is a hall closet full of the latest sports equipment, like Calloway Big Bertha golf clubs. The guy's living room is furnished with a flat-screen television, replete with theater-surround sound. Bose speakers, naturally. His refrigerator is stocked with premium beers and not much else because he, too, always eats out.

These "kids" just need to learn some self-control.

Older adults, particularly parents, tend to be censorious about the endemic credit card debt facing this generation. Seventy percent of young adults with credit cards regularly carry balances on their cards that they don't pay off each month, compared to just over half of all households.[1] Journalists love to churn out articles about how young people are profligate spenders and have poor budgeting skills. According to Margaret Webb Pressler of the *Washington Post,* "The growth in credit card debt is about instant gratification and the inability to live within one's means."[2] She has lots of company. In fact, when it comes to credit card debt, America is full of finger-waggers. A survey that asked card holders about credit card usage found that most individuals think that other people don't know how to use credit wisely—but that they themselves do.[3] Typical finger-wagging logic.

In reality, there is very little extravagance behind the under-34ers' credit card debt. Most young adults have several grand in credit card debt with nothing to show for it. So, what exactly then are young adults charging? In interview after interview with young people all over the country, a few explanations emerged. The most common reason was the debt trap parked out front: car repairs.

If the car is going to the shop, you might as well kiss a couple of hundred dollars good-bye, which most young adults don't have in their bank accounts.

Another big budget buster for young adults is travel, particularly for college-educated young professionals, who often live far from family and have friends sprinkled throughout the country. These friends inevitably get married. An out-of-town wedding is a huge expense for young adults, one that contributes to the steady ac- cumulation of credit card debt among twenty-somethings. To beg off is to lose a friend.

Aside from using credit cards to keep the car running, and maintain good relationships with friends and family, many young adults get into debt from charging up the requisite goods that come with leaving the nest. For young people who can't or won't turn to parents for help, credit cards become their high-interest version of a trust fund. It's the money pot that allows them to put a down payment on an apartment and buy a bed, sheets, towels, and a toilet brush. This plastic trust fund also helps them buy the basics of a professional wardrobe: two suits, one good pair of shoes, and a couple of nice shirts—all carefully chosen so the pieces can be mixed and matched, giving the illusion of a much bigger wardrobe. Before a year of postcollege life has passed, most grads are easily in for two to three thousand to the plastic behemoths. Then, if they get their first pink slip, they sink even deeper into debt.

In fact, in her most recent book, *The Money Book for the Young, Fabulous and Broke,* the best-selling financial guru Suze Orman changes her usual antidebt stance when it comes to young adults. Recognizing the weight of student loans and the abysmal condi- tion of the economy, she says it's okay for young adults to rely on credit cards to help meet monthly expenses, offering advice on how to best use credit cards during this fragile start-up period in a young person's life.[4] When one of America's leading personal finance experts acknowledges that establishing an adult life now requires going into credit card debt, we're seriously in trouble.

Her acknowledgment that young people often must and should rely on credit to get through the rough-and-tumble twenties reflects the upside-down reality of our lives. The need to rely on credit cards after college stems in large part from the enormous student loan shackles that define young adults' entry into the real world. With the average college grad having to commit $200 or more every month to student loan payments, there's a lot less wiggle room in the budget. If we took away some of that burden, it's very likely credit card debt among young people would decline.

Choked by Student Loans

One of the perks of living near New York University is that every May, I get to witness the ritual of college graduation. The sidewalks of my neighborhood become dotted with purple commencement gowns and flooded with proud parents. One by one these students will go to receive their diplomas, shake someone's hand, and pause for a photo that will grace their parents' mantel for years to come. It's nice that this exuberant moment is captured for posterity, because just six months later, the joy will quickly vanish when the first student loan bill shows up in the mailbox.

During the 1990s the percentage of students who borrowed money for college rose dramatically. In the 1992–93 school year (the year I graduated from college), just over 49 percent of graduates from four-year state universities had taken out federal student loans. By the end of the decade, nearly 65 percent of college grads had taken out such loans.[5] The growth in student loan debt occurred after 1992, when Congress established a new unsubsidized

federal loan program open to all students, regardless of their income. This legislation was triggered by the growing squeeze on
the middle class, whose incomes had stagnated and weren't keeping up with rising college costs. The new loan program allowed
middle- and upper-income students to relieve some of their parents'
financial burden by taking on some of their own. In the decade
since the legislative change, inflation-adjusted student loan volume
has risen by 137 percent.[6] Of course, students from low-income
households are still more likely to borrow than their wealthier
counterparts.

Statistics from the Department of Education confirm that rising tuition and the relaxation of loan eligibility mean that more
students are borrowing, and are doing so at higher amounts. Since
1992–93, the average college grad's student loan debt has grown
from $12,100 to $19,300 in 2003 (inflation-adjusted dollars). What's
more, over a quarter of graduates had debt higher than $25,000, up
from 7 percent in 1992–93.[7] Even students who attend two-year
colleges can't escape the noose of student loans: their average debt
is now $8,700.[8]

In the first chapter I examined how the debt-for-diploma system affects young adults' choices about college, including where
they enroll and whether or not they complete their degrees. But
the debt-for-diploma system continues to exert a powerful influence on young adults even after they leave college. It influences
decisions about where to live, what job to take, and even when to
get married.

According to a survey, conducted by the Nellie Mae Corporation, of young adults who are currently paying back student loans,
student loan debt is stifling their aspirations. The surveys, conducted in 1997 and 2002, provide snapshots of postcollege debt
in the early and late 1990s. The average college grad pays $180 a

month to repay student loans, eating up nearly 10 percent of their current earnings.[9] The first couple of years after college are particularly rough on young people's budgets, when loan repayments slough off 16 percent of their earnings. You would think that as young college grads' salaries rise and student debt takes up less of the monthly paycheck, young adults would feel less of a burden. But that's not the case. In fact, young adults who have been paying back their loans for at least three years feel *more* burdened than those who are in their first years of repayment. After paying back loans for three years, some young adults are less likely to agree that the benefits of a college degree make the debt worthwhile.

Borrowing for college is a lot like buying a new car. By the time that great "new car smell" wears off, so does the joy of owning the car.

The three-year itch notwithstanding, most young adults do believe that the personal growth and career opportunities of a college degree make the debt worthwhile. They wish they could have borrowed less, but wouldn't trade their college degree for a debt-free existence. Which isn't too surprising. If given a choice, most people would rather be $20,000 in debt and working in a decent office job than not have student debt and be working at Wal-Mart.

Still, paying off undergrad loans well into your thirties is a major drag.

Lori, a 33-year-old African American living in Manhattan, can't believe she's still on the hook for $40,000 in student loans. When Lori first moved to New York in 1997, she got a job as a social worker and community organizer, making $16,000 a year. Her salary kept inching upward as she changed jobs, but not enough for her to pay rent, bills, and student loans. So she deferred payments on her student loans until just three years ago. That means that for six years, while Lori wasn't making payments, the interest on her

$40,000 loan just kept building. As a result, she is now paying $250 every month just to chip away at the interest. Lori feels like she hasn't made a dent in her student loans and doesn't see how she'll ever pay them off. "I'm going to die with these student loans," she jokes. Nine years after graduating from college, Lori is still beholden to the debt-for-diploma system.

Natalie, whom we met in Chapter 1, has $20,000 in debt from student loans. She's actually one of the few young people in this book without credit card debt. At the age of 26, she's making $37,000 as an office manager, a job that doesn't utilize her degree in multimedia production. Making ends meet every month is tough, says Natalie. In the five years since finishing school, she has had to ask her parents for money more often than she'd like. As it is for many families, this is a source of tension between Natalie and her mother.

Natalie knows her mother is frustrated. Natalie is frustrated, too. She feels as though she is doing everything right but can't get ahead. "I don't spend frivolously. I live responsibly. I don't think my mom understands how hard it is for me to ask her for money. It's degrading. I shouldn't have to be doing this. I'm twenty-six years old, I live on my own, I have a full-time job. I shouldn't have to ask my mom to feed me."

Natalie stays motivated and focused by using a spreadsheet to track her progress at paying off debt. She doesn't use credit cards and doesn't shop. The only things she spends her money on are gas, tolls, and food. The rest goes to pay off her student loans and car loan. "I get so frustrated sometimes. It's not fair that I have to struggle so hard when there are people out there who have it so easy. All I want to do is go out and eat a cheeseburger, but I have to eat this bag of bread." Natalie told me that she actually has dreams about shopping for clothes because she hasn't done it in years.

Although debt-for-diploma is preferable to no diploma at all, heavy doses of student loans are causing more grads to report serious side effects. In 2002, 14 percent of young adults reported that student loans caused them to delay marriage, up from 7 percent in 1991.[10] One in five said their debt has caused them to delay having children, up from 12 percent in 1991. Forty percent reported they delayed buying a home because of their loans, compared to just one quarter in 1991. And 17 percent, significantly, changed careers as a result of their student debt, about the same as in 1991. Young adults from low-income families are much more likely to report these side effects.

But student loan debt is only part of the Generation Debt story. Over the last ten years, young adults have racked up record levels of credit card debt. When they lose a job or the car breaks down, that credit line quickly becomes a lifeline. And the reliance on credit cards starts early, just the way the credit card companies intended.

Prior to the early 1980s, credit card debt was virtually nonexistent. Credit cards weren't yet widely available, and they certainly weren't marketed to college students. According to data from the Federal Reserve, in 1983, the median consumer debt for 25-to-34-year-olds was $3,989 (in 2001 dollars).[11] By 2001, the median consumer debt for households under 35 had tripled to $12,000.[12] Consumer debt lumps together all debt other than mortgages, so it includes things like student loans, car loans, and credit card debt.

By the end of the 1980s, credit cards had sprung up like weeds and could be found in the wallets of most Americans. The story of how we became so indebted is in part a tale about deregulation, and in part a tale of economic change. As wages dropped or stagnated during the 1980s and 1990s, more and more people turned to credit cards to stay afloat. The new demand for credit cards was easily met by a hungry credit card industry, newly unbound from the chains of regulation. Since the early 1990s, the credit card companies have unleashed a tidal wave of direct-mail solicitations, television ads, and campus marketing. I should know: my first job out of college was writing those pesky direct-mail credit card offers. We would alter the wording or terms of the offer and then wait to see which "pitch" would lure the most responses. For cardholders who had failed to charge anything to their card for a while, I'd have to write a pithy letter trying to convince the slacking cardholder to use the enclosed free "convenience checks" to pay other bills or transfer balances. In 1993—the first year of my job—the credit card industry mailed out 1.5 billion credit card solicitations. By 2001 it was sending out over 5 billion offers—none of which, thankfully, were written by me.

In addition to ramping up their marketing efforts during the 1990s, the credit card industry has also gotten much more aggressive about raising interest rates and levying high fees for quite minor infractions. Cloaked by deregulation and protected by a powerful Washington lobby, credit card companies are making record profits. And fleecing young adults.

The Dirty Deregulated Business of Credit

During the 1980s, entire industries, including banking, were deregulated under the rationale that intense competitive pressures would compel corporations to police themselves. The paladins of laissez-faire ideology also propagated the myth that deregulated markets would empower individual citizens with more choices and cheaper products. In addition, freeing corporations from pesky regulations would enhance our democracy, as consumers took more control of their lives.[13] But like other sectors that were deregulated (energy being a good example of bad deregulation), the deregulation of the banking industry has proved especially bad for individual investors and borrowers—and fantastically good for CEOs and shareholders.

The story of deregulation of the credit card industry begins back in 1978 with a Supreme Court decision. In *Marquette National Bank of Minneapolis v. First Omaha Service Corp.* the Court interpreted a dusty old statute, section 85 of the National Banking Act of 1864, as allowing a national bank to charge its credit card customers the highest interest rate permitted in the bank's home state—as opposed to the rate in the state where the customer resides.[14] As a result, regional and national banks moved their operations to more lender-friendly states, such as South Dakota and Delaware, where there were no laws limiting the amount of interest that banks could charge for credit card loans. In domino-like fashion, states began loosening their own usury laws, limiting the chances for consumers to get a lower rate from a local or state bank.[15] Today, twenty-nine states have no limit on credit card interest rates.[16]

Look at the next bill or credit card solicitation that comes in your mailbox. Chances are it came from South Dakota or Delaware. Why? These states have no usury laws limiting the amount of interest on credit cards, so the credit card companies can charge any interest they want. Thanks to another decision by the Supreme Court in 1996, the same rules that apply to interest rates apply to fees as well. Prior to both of these cases, states set the maximum amount of interest and fees that lenders could charge. Most states outlawed interest rates above 20 percent and limited fees to $10 or $15. High rates and fees that were once considered usurious are now just considered profit for the credit card companies. The average late fee is now $32, which in 2004 provided a cool $10 billion in revenue for the card companies.[17]

The *Marquette* ruling had tremendous impact on the growth of the credit card industry and its profitability. Before *Marquette,* complying with fifty different state laws represented a high cost burden for the credit card companies. Also, during the high-inflation years in the 1970s, interest rates bumped up against state usury laws. The *Marquette* decision allowed banks to nationalize credit card lending and take full advantage of the ease of centralized processing provided by the Visa and MasterCard system. Better technology combined with the removal of interest caps also allowed credit card companies to expand their business to less creditworthy households by offering higher rates and fees for customers deemed a higher credit risk. As a result, credit cards, which were once the province of the wealthy and elite business class, quickly became part of mainstream American culture.

The rise in credit card debt during the eighties and nineties reveals how quickly credit cards swept the nation: in the two decades between 1980 and 2000, credit card debt grew from $111 billion to nearly $600 billion (both in 1999 dollars).[18] Today, Americans have $800 billion in credit card debt. And this debt doesn't come cheap, to say the least.

Although our mailboxes get stuffed with offers for low rates like 5.9 percent for one year, the credit card companies have gotten very creative in finding ways to raise that "teaser" rate once you've gotten the card. Thanks to new "gotcha" tactics such as tripling the interest rate for a late payment, credit card companies are routinely charging interest rates of 29 to 34 percent—a rate of return that the old neighborhood loan sharks wouldn't dare charge. And "late" means being merely one minute past 1 P.M. or 2 P.M. on the specified due date. If a payment arrives a minute late, the credit card company will also charge a late fee.

But it's not just late payments that can land you in the penalty zone. Credit card companies now routinely scan their cardholders' credit scores and if they see a credit problem elsewhere will raise the interest rate on your card—even if you've never been late or missed a payment. The industry rationalizes this preemptive strike by saying they are adjusting to a change in risk. But the logic doesn't hold. If the credit card companies were really concerned about risk, they would lower the customer's credit line to stop further indebtedness—not jack up their rates to 29 percent or more.

Shaney, the University of Arkansas grad we met in the first chapter, is so scared and stressed out by her credit card debt that she just looks at the amount due and stuffs it back in the envelope. She owes $6,000, a big chunk of which was for the security deposit for her apartment. Shaney is having a tough time paying down her debt because all of her cards have high interest rates and she can afford to pay only the minimum amount. "I feel like I'm getting eaten alive by the percentage rates on my credit cards. A lot of them are at twenty-five percent, and right now I only have enough to pay the minimum amount due, which just covers the interest . . . It's not like I'm using my credit cards to buy clothes or things I don't need. I use them for gas and groceries, things I would buy each month anyway. I'm very good at living within my means." When I talked to Shaney, she had just made an appointment with a credit counselor.

The credit card industry gets away with something most other lenders can't do. Next time you get a credit card solicitation, look at the fine print below the boxes that state how much the interest rate is on the card. On a BankOne solicitation I got in the mail recently, it said, "We reserve the right to change the terms (including APRs) at any time for any reason, in addition to APR increases which may occur for failure to comply with the terms of your account." There are plenty of rules for cardholders to follow, including getting their payment in by the minute, but absolutely none for the credit card companies. They can do what they want, when they want, for whatever reason.

But there's more to the capriciousness of these credit card contracts. When a credit card company increases the rate on the card, the new APR is applied retroactively to the entire balance. Now, it'd be one thing for the company to raise your rate on any future purchases, but to apply the new rate to everything you've purchased with the card is essentially raising the price of everything ever bought on the card that hasn't been paid for. Let's say you buy a new computer on your Citibank card at the normal interest rate of 12.99 percent. One month your payment arrives a day late. As a result of this tardy payment, Citibank raises your rate to 27.99 percent. That computer just got a lot more expensive.

The sheer audacity of these practices led me to wonder just how in the world an industry can get away with such tactics. It wasn't too hard to find the answer.

After all, behind every deregulation story (energy, pharmaceuticals) is a tale of political contributions and powerful lobbies. And the banking industry is no slouch when it comes to fighting for its way in the nation's capital. Table 2 (p. 104) shows the political contributions made to Congress since 1990 by the lending industry. Republicans appear to be favored over the Democrats, which makes sense, given their penchant for big-business interests and their idolatry of the free market. Although the Republicans' portion of the pot has been climbing steadily, Democrats do receive a substantial amount of money from the industry. Which might explain why majorities in both parties supported the bankruptcy "reform" legislation of April 2005, which the credit card industry had fought for since the mid-1990s.[19] The bankruptcy legislation

President Bush signed into law will make it harder for people to erase their credit card debts and force any disposable income to be paid to the card companies.

Table 2. Political Contributions by Finance and Credit Companies, 1990–2004

Election Cycle	Total Contributions	Percentage to Dems	Percentage to Repubs
2004	$7,978,034	36%	63%
2002	$7,377,468	37%	63%
2000	$9,688,276	31%	69%
1998	$4,613,403	29%	71%
1996	$4,676,693	33%	67%
1994	$3,395,037	47%	53%
1992	$1,887,883	51%	50%
1990	$704,990	59%	42%
Total	$40,321,784	36%	64%

Source: Center for Responsive Politics (http://www.opensecrets.org/ industries/indus.asp?Ind=F06)

The main argument for deregulating any industry is to provide a more competitive market, which in turn should lead to lower prices and more choices for consumers. Like so much of economics, what is supposed to happen in theory is often the opposite of what happens in practice. Since deregulation of the credit card industry in the early 1980s, debtors now actually have less choice and are paying more in interest and fees. The wave of major mergers among national banks facilitated by deregulation means that today fewer companies control the credit card market than ever before. In the year before *Marquette,* the top fifty issuers of cards controlled about half of the market. By 1990, the top ten issuers controlled 56.6 percent of the market. The latest bank mergers, between J. P.

Morgan and Bank One, and Bank of America and Fleet, mean that now the top ten card issuers control nearly 90 percent of the market.[20]

So what has been the effect of all this on prices? Credit card interest rates began to soar in the high-inflation post-*Marquette* environment, reaching averages of 18 percent, and have remained relatively high in comparison to drops in the federal funds rate, the amount of interest banks pay to borrow money overnight from the Federal Reserve.[21] Several economists have remarked on the reasons why consumers continue to pay, and card companies continue to charge, exceptionally high interest rates. Some point to the high consumer transaction costs involved in switching accounts, and others point to a lack of competition in the credit card marketplace.[22] Whatever the reason, credit card companies did not lower their rates when inflation slowed and national interest rates came down. As a result, the card companies' "spread," the amount charged above what it costs them to lend funds, has remained consistently high—at or above 10 percentage points over the last fifteen years.

This trend persisted in the past decade, even as the federal funds rate and the prime rate (the rate banks offer their best customers) dropped to historic lows. For example, in 2001 the Federal Reserve lowered rates eleven times, from 6.24 percent to 3.88 percent.[23] But these savings didn't get passed on to cardholders: during the same period, credit card rates declined only slightly, from 15.71 percent to 14.89 percent—and penalty rates shot through the roof.[24] Deregulation has been very bad for consumers and very good for the industry. The credit card industry rakes in $2.5 billion in profits each month.[25] No one would argue that the credit card industry shouldn't be profitable, but those profits should be made fairly and through good and transparent business practices. Neither of these characterizes the modern-day American credit card market.

Both political parties have looked the other way when it comes to regulating or at least reining in an industry that flagrantly engages in abusive and deceptive practices. It's the Wild West in the credit card industry and there's no Wyatt Earp coming to our rescue. According to the Center for Responsive Politics, MBNA Corp., the second largest issuer of credit cards, was the largest campaign contributor in the lending industry, and was George W. Bush's biggest campaign contributor in the 2000 election. How did both the presidential candidates fare in the 2004 campaign coffers race? George W. Bush received $592,575 from the lending industry; John Kerry, $105,916. It's clear whom the industry favors, both in Congress and the White House.

For now, young adults are stuck paying high rates, getting slapped with exorbitant fees, and having their welcome wagon at college sport MBNA, BankOne, and Citibank logos. Young adults are borrowing their way into adulthood, and it's costing them greatly. Each payment to a credit card or student loan company is one less opportunity to save for the future. The average 25-to-34-year-old now spends about one out of every five dollars on debt payments. That's less money for the piggy bank or a house down payment or a 401(k) account.

It Starts with a Free T-Shirt

If you've strolled through a state college campus lately, chances are you've witnessed a huge phenomenon known as tabling. It used to be tabling was the province solely of student campus groups, with table after table offering pamphlets and sign-up sheets for everything from the ultimate Frisbee team to the Young Democrats or Young Republicans. But in the last ten years, tabling has been co-opted by capitalism, particularly by the industry one young adult referred to as those "credit card pushers."

At colleges across America, especially at state universities, credit card companies have taken a page out of the student organizations' playbook and table alongside the best of them. But the card companies have a leg up on the student groups: swag, and lots of it. In exchange for filling out a credit card application, students can get free stuff ranging from T-shirts to mugs to pizzas. The tables are staffed not by marketing representatives from the company but by college students trying to earn an extra buck themselves. On college campuses, credit card companies not only find profitable customers, but cash-strapped minions to do their shilling for them.

But what about the colleges themselves? Where are they in this picture? Far too often, they're in on the profit mongering. This is especially true of big state universities. The University of Tennessee, for example, accepted $16 million from First USA (now BankOne) in exchange for exclusive marketing rights on campus, and hundreds of other schools receive money for every new application filled out by students. According to Robert Manning, author of *Credit Card Nation,* these types of deals yield the 300 largest universities about $1 billion a year.

The marketing onslaught has paid off: in 2002, the average college senior had six credit cards and an average balance of just over $3,200.[26] Many college students are in deeper trouble. One in five students has credit card debt of $3,000 to $7,000. Not surprisingly, student credit card debt increases with each successive year and more than doubles from freshman to senior year.

Recently, some states have closed their open-door policies regarding on-campus credit card marketers. In 2003, West Virginia passed legislation requiring all the public colleges in the state to regulate credit card marketing on campus.[27] Some schools in the state banned the practice outright, whereas West Virginia University simply put an end to swag—at least swag without permission granted from the university. According to a General Accounting Office report in 2001, at least twenty-four states had introduced legislation to restrict credit card marketing on campus, but so far only Arkansas, Louisiana, New York, and West Virginia have actually passed such legislation.[28] Where state legislatures have failed to ban the practice, many individual schools have taken the initiative. In 1998 the University of Minnesota banned credit card companies from campus. Smaller, private liberal arts colleges have been most effective at patrolling card marketing on campus. Enforcement is easier on small campuses and there's less incentive for these elite schools to raise money through deals with the card companies because they tend to have fat endowments and a steady stream of very high tuition monies filling their coffers every year.

But the card companies are nothing if not persistent. Even if they're forbidden to table on campus, they have other crafty methods to reach students. Some colleges make it really easy by selling the card companies their students' information. A report by the Maryland Public Interest Group found that Towson University sells its student list to MBNA—although after the publication of the report it told the authors they would stop this practice in mid-2004.[29] If a college bans a company outright, the friendly campus bookstore will usually help out the card mongers by agreeing to stuff its bags with credit card offers.

Elaine, now 27, told me she still has her free Discover Card T-shirt from her campus days. Unfortunately, the logo has faded much faster than her balance. It's been five years since she graduated from the University of Wisconsin and she is still paying off credit card debt from college. Elaine, who is white, comes from a modest home—her parents don't use credit cards and her mom was instantly worried when Elaine called from college to tell her she just got her first credit card. Her mother is a teacher's aide and her dad is a farmer. It was important to both her parents that all five of their kids go to college. They provided lots of emotional support but weren't able to help pay for college. During her college years, Elaine lived on credit cards and her financial aid check. She never asked her parents for money. "I made do with what I had or just used credit cards." Elaine was a master of the credit card shuffle. She'd transfer balances to low introductory rates every six months, which allowed her to manage much higher debt than she could have if she had been paying the normal rate on a card. At one point, she had ten cards, but always kept the shuffle in order. But the major issuers have since caught on to these tricks and now typically charge a transfer fee equal to 2 percent of the balance.

After college, Elaine moved to Seattle with her fiancé, and that's when she started putting even more on her credit cards—her balance now tops $40,000, half of it racked up after college. She bought a computer and new furniture. Like many college grads, she wanted her apartment to look like "an adult's apartment," not an annex of her dorm room. Elaine also paid for a lot of her wedding on credit cards and relied on credit to fly back to Wisconsin for family visits.

Elaine entered a debt management program last year. She pays $950 dollars a month to chip away at her balance. On a $35,000 salary, it's not always easy. But Elaine has no regrets. She thinks about the things she did—studying abroad in Scotland, flying to Paris, having the perfect wedding—and knows it would never have been possible without credit. Now she only uses one credit card—for the miles—and pays her balance every month. She now visits her family just twice a year, using her credit card miles to pay for the airfare.

Elaine got snared by the card companies early and for the most part tried to use her credit cards on campus to relieve financial pressures on her parents. About a quarter of students report using credit cards to pay for tuition and books. So what about the other three quarters? Certainly their credit card debt represents in part what we tend to think of as frivolous debt. Visa and Master-Card have no doubt funded a great many pizzas, kegs, and spring breaks.

The problem is that after graduation, the need for credit often morphs into a whole new category: survival debt. Making the transition from college grad to full-fledged working adult takes more than a good résumé. For young twenty-somethings who can't turn to Mom and Dad for start-up money, launching their adult lives often entails going further into credit card debt. And with substantial debt already built up from college, young adults can get caught off-guard and tangled in a debt spiral they most likely never saw coming.

Borrowing to Get a Life

Of course, it's not only college grads who are using credit cards as a private safety net. In fact, the ubiquity of credit card debt among under-34ers makes it hard to categorize young debtors. They're college-educated, non-college-educated, male, female, black, Hispanic, and white. They're receptionists, project managers, teachers, and health-care workers. During the 1990s, credit card debt among those under age 34 grew by 47 percent. But that doesn't mean that young adults don't take debt seriously or that it isn't a major stress in their lives. This generation regards credit card debt as a necessary evil.

Victor and Eloise, whom we met in the last chapter, know from experience the pain of debt at high interest rates. After a series of fast-food management jobs, Victor now works as a mortgage loan officer, making $30,000 per year. Eloise, who also worked in fast food for many years, now works for the state department of motor vehicles and makes $16,000 a year. She also sells Avon on the side, which brings in another $4,000 to $6,000 annually. Even with full-time jobs and two children, aged 4 and 14, the couple finds time to attend church regularly, be actively involved in their children's school, and volunteer in various ways for the community. In fact, they've recently been approved to be foster parents. For all their hard work and goodwill, this family is struggling with $13,000 of very expensive debt from a combination of credit cards, car title loans, and three personal installment loans worth about $8,000, money borrowed from a finance company that offered the couple quick cash at awful terms. Those loans carry interest rates of 28 percent and 30 percent. The rates on the credit cards are 24 percent.

Where did the debt come from? Let's start with the credit cards. Their biggest debt is on their Sears card, about $3,000 at an interest rate of 25 percent per year, or $750 per year just for interest. Those charges were for new tires and alignment work on the car and a new stove. The couple also has three personal installment loans. In 2000, after Eloise had their second child, they needed the money to help cover bills while she was on maternity leave. Victor took out a loan for $4,000 at 25 percent interest from Citi Financial, putting up his 1986 van as collateral. The baby is now 5 years old and they are still paying off their loan-funded maternity leave. Their second installment loan was taken out three years ago, when Victor opened the mail and was offered a $4,000 loan, with a 30 percent APR. The loan was used to buy a car, and he is still chipping away at the balance, which is difficult given that it is growing by a third, or $1,320, every year. After three years, he still owes $2,500. The couple's third installment loan is for $1,100, again at 30 percent, which was used to repair the central air-conditioning on the house.

Victor and Eloise earn about $50,000 a year, but with two kids, an old house, and old cars, they never seem to get ahead. Their economic insecurity has put them smack in the center of the bustling new subprime lending industry. Both Victor and Eloise have always held full-time jobs—in fact, Victor sometimes works two jobs to help make ends meet. So why are they paying extra-high interest rates for their loans? According to Victor, he got a solicitation in the mail from a finance company saying he was preapproved for a loan. The couple, however, has a decent credit rating, as evidenced by their ability to refinance their home from 8.5 percent to a lower mortgage rate of 6.5 percent. They always pay their bills on time and have never missed a credit card payment. But their zip code makes them easy targets for those selling quick, expensive cash.

Every three years, the Federal Reserve collects information specifically on household credit card debt as part of its Survey of Consumer Finances, with 2004 being the latest data available. To compare credit card debt between Gen Xers and the late Baby Boomers we can use survey findings from 1989, when the 25-to-34-year-old population was made up of Baby Boomers, and 2004, when it was made up of Gen Xers. My analysis of the Survey of Consumer Finances indeed confirms that Gen Xers are more indebted than Baby Boomers were at the same age. In 2004, 25-to-34-year-olds averaged $4,358 in credit card debt—47 percent higher than it was for Baby Boomers in 1989. Keep in mind that these numbers are based on self-reported amounts, not actual credit card statements. For many reasons, people tend to underreport their credit card debt. For example, in 2004 the average household credit card debt reported in the survey was just over $5,219. But aggregate data on outstanding credit card debt reported by the credit card industry puts the average household debt at $12,000.[30] New survey research conducted by Dēmos of low- to middle-class households found that the average indebted under-34er had just over $8,000 in credit card debt in 2005. According to these households, the most common reasons cited for their credit card debt were car repairs, loss of a job, and home repairs. Forty-five percent of under-34ers reported using credit cards in the last year to pay for basic living expenses, such as rent, mortgage payments, groceries, and utilities. Not exactly the stuff of the young debtor stereotype.

The rise in credit card debt, coupled with the surge in student loan debt, is the main reason why today's young adults are spending much more on debt payments than the previous generation. On average those aged 25 to 34 years old spent nearly 25 cents out of every dollar of income on debt payments in 2001, according to the Federal Reserve's data. That's more than double what Baby Boomers of the same age spent on debt payments in 1989. The fact that young adults are already spending a quarter of their income on debt is particularly worrisome because most in the 25-to-34 age group aren't homeowners. So that 25 cents is going to nonmortgage debt: primarily student loans, car loans, and credit cards.

The soaring debt among young adults is landing more of this generation in the throes of bankruptcy. By 2001 nearly 12 out of every 1,000 young adults aged 25 to 34 were filing for bankruptcy, a 19 percent increase since 1991.[31] Young adults now have the second highest rate of bankruptcy, just after those aged 35 to 44.

As being young and single has become practically synonymous with being in debt, it's no surprise that when young people find love, they also find more debt. While the economic benefits of living together or getting married are still pretty good—especially in expensive cities—today's young couples aren't getting quite the economic benefit that previous generations enjoyed when they combined incomes. Why? Because in addition to joining together in holy matrimony, young couples today are joining together in debt servitude.

Until Debt Do Us Part

Despite all the stereotypes and reality TV shows about women searching for rich men, most men and women marry people of similar financial background. It's what sociologists refer to as "assortative mating." Most individuals marry someone with the same educational and class background as themselves. Which means that today most young couples aren't combining fortunes. They're combining debts.

On the surface, David and Lisa seem like the quintessential middle-class professional couple. Both of them sport Ivy League degrees, and Lisa has a master's. They live in suburban Cincinnati, where David is an architect and Lisa is an educator specializing in early childhood development. Together they earn about $86,000 a year. Both 31 years old, they bought their home three years ago in anticipation of starting a family. Today, they have two children, aged 4 and 2.

They also have $40,000 in credit card debt, and they have refinanced their home twice to pay off car debts and some credit card debt. As a result, their monthly mortgage payment is now $850, compared to $600 when they first bought the house. Even though David and Lisa have built much of their credit card debt as a couple, they each brought plenty of financial baggage to the relationship.

When they got married in 1998, David had $14,000 in student loans and $10,000 in credit card debt and Lisa had $20,000 in credit card debt. And the credit card debt has continued to mount during their marriage. David calls it "unavoidable debt," much of it from the cost of traveling around the country for friends' weddings, holiday trips to visit their families, and the cost of clothing and feeding two growing boys. David admits that they spend more than they make, which he is somewhat puzzled by because they aren't extravagant spenders. They rarely eat out and don't spend money on clothes, except for the kids. They have only one car, a hand-me-down from David's mom. The big budget buster for this family is travel. David's family lives in Cincinnati, but Lisa's lives in New York, and they both have friends and siblings in places all over the country. David acknowledges that going to weddings and visiting family is a major source of their debt problem, but he and Lisa believe that staying in touch with family or friends takes priority over financial concerns. Of course, the price of traveling is more expensive now with two young children. Many of their family and friends are on the West Coast, so driving is not a possibility. They've refinanced about $20,000 in credit card debt, but still have $40,000 outstanding in credit card balances. It's a way of life that makes them extremely vulnerable should anything go wrong. "We're one catastrophe from everything breaking down." But they have a strong family and social network, which gives them some comfort that if the worst did happen, they'd have help.

Despite their enormous debt, they are adamant about saving money for the future. They have over $30,000 in their 401(k)s, and always keep $1,000 in their checking account and another $1,000 in their savings account. And if times ever got rough, they have another $1,000 put away in an education fund for the kids.

They are now trying to move to a larger house, with a real backyard and enough bedrooms so that each of the boys can have his own room. The house they live in now is in an urban area, so they don't have a garage or a backyard. With the oldest boy approaching kindergarten age, they're trying to move to a suburb with good schools. Making this move has proved slightly more difficult than they first anticipated. They can't buy a new home unless they sell the one they are in now, and so far, they've had no luck.

Seven years after getting married, this couple is basically treading water. Although both now make more money than they did eight years ago, most of the extra money goes to debt payments. Even after turning their house into a wallet by cashing out their equity, their credit card balance is only back to where it was when they first got married.

Scrimpers and Savers

Despite being broke and in credit card debt, many of the young adults I spoke with actually managed to put some money into a savings account. I was somewhat surprised by this because I didn't have a savings account or money to put into one until about two years ago.

Most young adults want to build up an emergency fund and save for retirement. Unfortunately, it often isn't until they hit their thirties that they're able to do both. Ian and Rebecca, aged 30 and 27, respectively, have $3,000 in a savings account. They've recently gotten out of credit card debt and are trying to beef up their emergency fund by putting $600 away each month. But neither one of them is saving for retirement. They recognize the need to put money into a 401(k), but explain that up until now they needed all their extra income to pay down their credit card debt. Ian had a 401(k) account from a previous job, which they emptied for a down payment on the house they purchased two years ago. They are careful about spending and each has a wish list of things they'd like to buy. To beef up their savings account, Rebecca no longer buys new clothes or gets her hair highlighted at the salon. Ian would like to replace his seven-year-old computer, which is "limping on one leg." They're committed to building up their savings to cushion themselves against a job loss and to help with the added expenses of a new baby, something they'd like to have happen in the next year or so.

Young adults aren't alone in struggling to save money. Over the last twenty years, our nation's personal saving rate has plummeted from about 8 percent through the 1980s and early 1990s to zero in 2005—its lowest point since the Great Depression.[32] There is growing concern that Americans now live by the rule "If you have it, spend it." Most social critics hold up the Greatest Generation, those who came of age during the Great Depression, as the moral pinnacle of scrimping and saving. The Baby Boomers took a lot of flack during the 1980s for their spending habits. Remember yuppies? The Baby Boomers seemed to have invented conspicuous consumption. And now that the Baby Boomers have reached the age where they control the commentary on all things social, political, and economic—they've taken to criticizing the younger generation for its spending habits.

Clayton is a 31-year-old African American, living in a small town about an hour away from Milwaukee, Wisconsin. And he is a very good saver. He has a 9-year-old son, Clayton III, and a 5-year-old daughter, Tameka. Clayton is a high school guidance counselor making $42,000 a year. A portion of his yearly income comes from working a second job on weekends at a drug rehabilitation center. All told, Clayton works sixty-four hours a week, every week. He works two jobs so that he has extra money to put away for his children's education. So far, he's saved $7,000 total, or $3,500 for each of them. But all his extra money goes to saving for their future, not for his own. Clayton doesn't have a retirement account, and admits that without that second job, he'd be living paycheck to paycheck. He still has $20,000 in student loans to pay off and spends about $500 a month on child care for Tameka. Child-care costs are more than his rent, which is only $425 a month for a two-bedroom apartment. Clayton lives a very modest life. He has never been on an airplane; a vacation for him is a trip to Milwaukee to see his grandma and family. Clayton is well grounded and his long-term goals are simply to keep improving every year—financially, socially, and emotionally. After ten more years of counseling, he'd like to become an assistant principal. Or try something altogether different.

Since the majority of young adults struggle just to pay back their loans and monthly bills, it's not too surprising that most of them aren't saving for retirement. But, contrary to popular opinion, Gen Xers actually are more likely to be saving for retirement—and at higher levels—than were their baby boom counterparts. According to the Survey of Consumer Finances, in 2004 about 40 percent of workers under 35 were saving for retirement.[33] Compared to young adult Baby Boomers, Gen X is doing a better job planning for retirement: only 27 percent of under-35s had retirement savings in 1989. The typical Gen Xer has also saved more for retirement by this age than had their predecessors: the median value of Gen

Xers' retirement accounts was $11,000 in 2004, up from $5,900 in 1989 (2004 dollars).

Overall, how are young adults' balance sheets? What is their net worth, and is it higher or lower than it was for Baby Boomers of the same age? The answer is they're doing slightly better than were Baby Boomers at the same age, thanks in large part to the rise in home values and low interest during the early 00s. Net worth, which is the amount of a person's total assets minus debts, increased between 1989 and 2004 for under-35ers—from $11,900 to $14,200 in 2004.[34]

Borrowing away the Future

If today's young adults can be accused of wanting it all too soon, the "it" isn't riches, gadgets, or luxury cars. The elusive "it" that today's twenty-somethings are after is financial independence, and then, hopefully, financial security. All the buzz about young bucks making millions in stock options and entrepreneurial start-ups simply distracted attention from a bigger story. The 1990s ushered in the Era of Debt. While the popular media made it look as though riches had landed at our feet, the real new economy meant that obtaining a middle-class lifestyle now required a large credit line and five-figure student debt. And getting the ultimate piece of the American dream—our own home—meant being mortgaged to the max.

CHAPTER FOUR

The High Cost of Putting a Roof over Your Head

A t the age of 33, Lori worries about never owning a home. Her salary, $97,000 a year, puts her in the top class of earners, but for her, becoming part of the ownership class is as elusive as if she earned $35,000. Why? Because Lori is one of the millions of young adults who are becoming permanent renters—"permarenters"—in our nation's largest cities. Buying a place in the city is simply out of reach in such urban centers as Boston, San Francisco, Los Angeles, New York, and Washington, D.C. Young professionals who live in these places face tough choices: be a permarenter or take on a supersize mortgage in the nearby suburbs. Once an affordable haven for young families, starter homes in the nearby suburbs surrounding major cities now routinely top $300,000, leaving many young adults wondering if they'll ever achieve the American dream of home ownership.

Where Lori's housing options seem bleak, the home-owning prospects of Ricardo and Salina are downright hopeless. Ricardo, aged 36, who immigrated to the United States from Mexico eighteen years ago, has worked as a salad maker at an upscale restaurant for the last thirteen years. His monthly paycheck is $1,260. Salina, aged 34, who used to work at a clothing factory for $300 a week, is now at home with the couple's 18-month-old daughter. The young family currently lives in a small one-bedroom apartment in the Bronx. Their rent is $750 a month, plus utilities. They used to share a two-bedroom apartment with another couple, but were lucky to find a new place when the baby was born. Ricardo has consistently been saving for a down payment over the last decade, but still has only $3,000 in the bank. He wants to buy a house or condo so he can pass it on to his daughter when he dies. After living in the city his entire adult life, he isn't willing to move upstate in order to find an affordable place to buy. He loves the people in the city and the fast pace. When I asked him if the government could do anything to improve his economic situation, he said they could raise the minimum wage, "because you can't live like that with the rents going up and the salaries not. Why does the government want people to live with many people in one room? I think they don't know."

Like generations before them, young adults still dream of owning the proverbial house with a white picket fence. But in today's economy, about all they can afford is the picket fence. With dwindling starting salaries and starter homes priced out of reach, becoming a home owner remains an elusive dream for many young adults. And the rental market in major metropolitan areas—where professional jobs are typically found—is brutally expensive, too.

In the struggle to find an affordable place to live, many young adults are turning to a familiar landlord: their parents.

Home Again

Every year, millions of adults under the age of 34 find themselves waking up in their childhood bedrooms. It's not only recent college grads who are returning to the nest. Young adults are moving back in with their parents after going through a divorce or los-ing a job. They may be 22 years old or 32 years old—but the high price of housing has sent them "home again" in record numbers.

The percentage of young adults who are still living with their parents started rising in the 1980s and continued to increase steadily until 1998, when 15 percent of men and 8 percent of women aged 25 to 34 were living with their parents.[1] In 2003, 13.5 percent of men and 7 percent of women aged 25 to 34 were living with their parents, slightly higher for men than in 1970 and about the same for women. According to the Census Bureau, most young adults do not leave home now until age 24.[2] However, this data only captures the percentage of young adults who are *currently* living with their parents. The percentage who move back home at least once after being on their own is much higher: four out of ten young adults detour back to the nest at least once.[3]

Irene never thought she'd be living at home at the age of 33. But a surprising and nasty divorce sent her seeking a temporary haven from rent and the world. Until eighteen months ago, Irene and her husband, Adam, who are both white, lived in a studio apart-ment in Manhattan. By the time they got engaged they had been together for nearly eight years, except for a one-year break. It was the late 1990s when they got engaged, and the red-hot economy had greatly inflated Manhattan rents. Adam's small studio rented for $1,900 a month. Irene was just finishing graduate school and working at an academic center at the university. Her salary started at $40,000 and was raised to $54,000 after a year. Adam worked in corporate law, so his salary was enough to pay the rent and start paying down their debts. Irene had $9,000 in credit card debt and $65,000 in grad school loans. Adam had $12,000 in credit card debt. They lived paycheck to paycheck, and wedding expenses had them in even tighter financial straits. Once the wedding was behind them, they vowed that they would look for a cheaper apartment and Irene would look for a higher-paying job.

But over the next six months, their plans began to slowly unravel as their relationship began falling to pieces. They began fighting regularly; Irene blames much of this on post-traumatic stress that Adam was suffering after September 11. After a major argument, he kicked Irene out of the apartment and told her that he never wanted to see her again. Irene couldn't afford an apartment of her own on her salary, but she couldn't just pick up and leave her job, either. So she stayed in the city, living with a friend who fortunately had a pull-out couch available. For the next three months, she was entangled in a messy and abusive separation with Adam. The whole process left her mentally exhausted. She had arranged to end her employment, so that she could take some "time off" from the real world to recover and regroup. She sought this solitude by moving back to her parents' house in Pennsylvania.

Irene's plan was to give herself four to six months to figure out her life and get through what had become a very messy divorce. That was in August 2003. Two years later, she was still living in her childhood home. She recently got a new job, after an excruciating nine-month search. Her new salary is $50,000. After not working for nearly a year, Irene plans to stay at her parents' a little while longer so she can save up enough to buy a car and rent an apartment. And of course, she'll have to start chipping away at the $65,000 in grad school loans. At age 33, Irene is tired of struggling, tired of being broke, and desperate to be back on her own.

Irene's story indicates just how difficult it is for young adults to get by in the big city. Even if she didn't need a mental break after her divorce, Irene couldn't have afforded to live on her own in New York City. She'd have to get a roommate, which is bearable in your twenties, but not so fabulous when you're in your thirties.

In major cities all across the country, rents have risen spectacularly over the last several years. But these same cities still offer the best career and job potential, particularly for college grads, which is why young professionals continue to favor places like New York, Boston, and Los Angeles. These vibrant cities offer the best chance to launch a career, but as rents climb to Everest-like heights, it's become harder than ever to get ahead in them.

Budget-Busting Cities

The 1990s tested young adults' mettle in so many ways, it's hard to believe we haven't taken to the streets to protest the economic injustice. We entered a new economy that rewarded so very few of us, but made it pricier for most of us to put a roof over our heads. We left college weighed down by debt, only to find we needed a couple of thousand dollars just to get into an apartment. Welcome to the real world, kid: the joke's on you. Young adults leave college with, on average, close to $20,000 in debt. Then, when they start looking for jobs and apartments, they realize that starting salaries and rent prices are rarely in alignment. But they can't live at home forever, so they pay the piper. And the piper is a landlord who wants a month and half rent for security, plus the first month's rent upfront. When half your paycheck goes to rent, it takes the wind right out of your sails.

Why are so many college grads choosing expensive big cities for their launching pads? Because that's where the jobs are, or where the prospects for well-paying jobs are still highest. Many of the most vibrant and attractive industries are still centered in the nation's top twenty metropolitan areas. New York City is still the financial, publishing, and advertising center of the nation. Chicago is tops for sales and management consultant work. San Francisco and San Jose are still meccas for technology jobs. These big cities also tend to offer higher pay for entry-level jobs, though it's not enough to make up for the higher cost of living. And of course, these cities offer the culture, the nightlife, and a plentiful singles population that make them burst with vitality and energy that one can't find in, say, Cincinnati—a top metropolitan area that came in last place for singles to live according to *Forbes* magazine.

But there is a steep price tag for career ambition and cultural stimulation. Between 1995 and 2002, rents in nearly all of the largest metropolitan areas rose astronomically. Median rents in San Francisco ballooned 76 percent; Boston, 62 percent; San Diego, 54 percent; even median rent prices in less costly Denver shot up by 49 percent.[4] Rents in these cities are off the charts. The Department of Housing and Urban Development's Fair Market Rent data show that the average studio apartment in Boston was just over $1,000. In the San Francisco–Oakland area, the average rent for a studio apartment in 2004 was $943. Oakland, once a cheap outpost for aspiring San Fran dwellers, is now sporting average studio rents of $936. It's no wonder so many under-34ers are flocking to the Denver area—a studio apartment there costs "only" about $607 a month.

According to the Census Bureau, between 1995 and 2000, more young, single, college-educated people, defined as those aged 25 to 39, moved into major cities than moved out. In fact, of the twenty largest metropolitan areas in 2000, only three cities lost more young, single and college-educated people than they gained: Philadelphia, Detroit, and Cleveland.[5] While major cities like New York, Chicago, Los Angeles, and the Washington-Baltimore area suffered losses in the overall population, these cities have remained popular destinations for young professionals. But the high cost of living in the top metro areas has sent non-college-educated young adults packing. Many of the same cities that attract young college grads—such as Los Angeles, Boston, and New York—are losing non-college-educated young adults, who are migrating to lower-cost alternatives such as Atlanta, Dallas, Phoenix, Denver, and Las Vegas.[6] Our nation's largest and most diverse cities are becoming virtually unaffordable for young people without college degrees. They're being priced out of the places where they grew up and are flocking to less expensive states. The top destinations for young adults are now Texas, Colorado, and Georgia.[7] In fact, between 1995 and 2000, more Gen Xers moved to Atlanta than to any other location in the country.[8]

For the young professionals who stick it out in the top metro areas, making the rent every month isn't possible without room-mates. Typically, a two-bedroom apartment split two ways in all of these cities costs less than a studio. To make the paycheck stretch even further, recent college grads often double up in the bedrooms. A couple of years after graduating from college, Natalie moved to Boston. After growing up in a small town in New Jersey, Natalie wanted to experience the big-city life. So when a friend called to say she had a cheap place for her to live, she took a leap of faith. "Cheap" was made possible by sharing a four-bedroom apartment with seven people. Natalie shared a bedroom with her friend, each of them paying $250 a month in rent. The roommates were a mot-ley bunch: two flight attendants, a history teacher, a law student, and "someone who made a ton of money." They had turned a stor-age room into a bedroom, which they had to hide from the land-lord. Most of the people in the house weren't on the lease. Natalie described it as a "revolving-door" apartment. Natalie worked as a waitress when she first got to Boston—the most horrible job she ever had. She was miserable and about to throw in the towel on her Boston experience when a friend called to tell her about a much better job opening. She got it: an office manager position paying $38,000 a year, plus benefits and two weeks' paid vacation.

Two years later, the same four-bedroom apartment was being shared by only five people. Natalie finally had her own bedroom, which brought her rent to $490—a major rental coup in a city such as Boston. Nevertheless, Natalie found living in Boston to be a struggle. The winters were harsh and everything was expensive. She ended up leaving most weekends, driving to DC to visit her family and friends. As she racked up miles on her car, she was paying too much in gas and car repairs, so she decided to move to DC. She moved in with her mom, who lived in a high-rise apartment in Alexandria, Virginia, a suburb outside of DC. She got a new job, making $35,000 per year as an office manager. Her mom was going to be remarrying in four months, so it was a temporary arrangement. Natalie took over the lease for $550 a month in rent, including utilities. After living there for a year, she was notified by the landlord that the rent would be raised to $683 a month. That was Natalie's breaking point; she could afford $600 a month, but $683 was out of the question. She was given thirty days' notice about the increase. Unable to find a cheaper apartment, Natalie moved back in with her mother and her mother's new husband. After spending two months on their couch, Natalie moved in with a friend who had just bought a house and needed the rental income. She pays $500 for her own room, plus her share of rent and utilities. Natalie's happy with the deal and relieved to find shelter. At the age of 26, Natalie feels as though owning her own home is something she'll never be able to accomplish. She can barely find a place she can afford to rent and pay her student loan bills, car payment, and all the other fixed monthly expenses.

The Rental Blues

Because young adults are spending more of their paychecks on rent and paying back student loans, renting often becomes a hamster-wheel experience. Once you're on the wheel, you can't get off. Staying on top of the rent and other bills has made it increasingly difficult for young adults to save up for a down payment. Since the 1970s, the amount of time it takes for young first-time homebuyers to scrape together a down payment has steadily increased.[9] What took our parents two years now takes us nearly four years. But even though we are saving longer, rising home prices mean our down payments are smaller as a percentage of the purchase price. In a nutshell, it is taking this generation longer to save less. And now it takes two incomes to do it.

Just how much are young adults spending on rent? In 1970, the median rent paid by 25-to-34-year-olds was $497 in inflation-adjusted dollars. By 2000, those in the 25-to-34-year-old age group were spending 25 percent more on rent—$627.[10] The higher rent paid by today's young adults also eats up a higher percentage of their income. This is somewhat counterintuitive, given that young adults have higher percentages of cohabitation than previous generations and higher education levels. Nonetheless, young adults are spending more of their paychecks on rent: in 2002 they paid a median of just over 22 percent of pretax income on rent; in 1970 the median figure was 17 percent. Rising rents, particularly in central cities, have resulted in a higher percentage of young adults who spend more than 30 percent of their income on housing—the standard threshold of "affordability." In 2000, one third of young adults between 25 and 34 spent more than 30 percent of their income on rent—up from less than 20 percent in 1970.[11] The rise in the percentage of household income spent on rent by young adults could be driven by two factors: increases in rent prices or decreases in income, or a combination of both. One study showed that the decline in affordability during the 1990s is attributable to higher rents, not lower incomes.[12] The excessive rents, combined with lower starting salaries, has made getting out of the rental zone harder for many in this generation.

According to data collected by the Chicago Title and Trust, the average first-time home buyer today is 32 years old, about four years older than in 1976.[13] The Chicago Title and Trust surveys home buyers in the nation's top twenty metropolitan areas, which account for one third of all home sales nationally. The National Association of Realtors has different figures, which show the age of a first-time home buyer has held steady at 31 or 32 years of age for the past twenty years.[14] Whether the age has risen or held steady over the last two decades, the perception among both parents and young adults is that buying a home is more difficult today.

Tony, whom we met briefly in the last chapter, is a 30-year-old middle-school teacher. Tony began his teaching career in San Francisco. After growing up in the Bronx and nearby Rockland County, New York, Tony wanted to explore a different part of the country. He was planning to move to California immediately after college graduation, but when his plans fell through he took a three-year detour working on a cruise ship. Besides seeing the world, Tony was able to save quite a bit of money while at sea. He came back with over $10,000 in savings. By this time, his older brother had moved to Berkeley, providing a base from which Tony could start his real career as a teacher in California. After living on his brother's couch for a couple of months, he and some friends moved into an apartment in San Francisco. His share of the rent was $1,050 a month.

Tony got off to a rocky start financially, because he moved in the middle of the school year and was able to get only a long-term substitute teacher position. Because he wasn't on permanent staff, he didn't get paid for holidays—including three weeks over Christmas break—and he didn't have health insurance. Between the moving expenses, the high cost of living in San Francisco, and the lulls in his paychecks, Tony was quickly draining his savings account. The next year Tony got a full-time position teaching history to seventh- and eighth-graders. His pay was quite good, about $41,000 a year. But that salary doesn't pack much punch in a city like San Francisco. Tony lived paycheck to paycheck. As the tech boom deflated out and his dot-com friends were adjusting to their declining salaries, Tony decided it was time to find a cheaper place to live.

After a weekend trip to San Diego, he fell in love with the city. He used the rest of his savings to pay for moving there. He lived on a couch for a month in a friend's apartment and then got an apartment with a college friend. Tony makes less in San Diego as a teacher, just $36,000, but the cost of living is lower. His rent is now $700. He says living in San Diego is more manageable but he still can't get ahead. Any unexpected expense throws a wrench in his budget. He's had to borrow money from his parents about five times in the last two years, usually for weddings or car repairs. "I don't live an extravagant life. I eat out maybe once a month and go out to a bar maybe two or three times a month. I just make enough to get by." When I asked Tony if his financial situation makes it hard for him to think about getting married or having a family, he tells me how his old roommate just bought a condo with his girlfriend—something his roommate couldn't have done by himself. He admits that having a girlfriend to help contribute financially to a home would make his life less stressful.

As a teacher, Tony's earning potential isn't great. To boost his salary, he is going to start taking classes to get his master's degree in education, which will translate into a $5,000-a-year increase in salary. But even then, he'll need a partner to move out of the rental morass and into home ownership. As for many of today's under-34ers, finding love is not only emotionally beneficial, it's often the only path to upward mobility.

The trifecta of smaller starting salaries, higher rents, and the red-hot housing market has taken a toll on young adults' home owner-ship rates. The dream is slipping through our fingers.

Dreams Deferred

Six decades ago, two enterprising individuals set out to build a new type of suburban community. Alfred and William Levitt en-visioned mass-produced housing that would offer young families an affordable home complete with a backyard, washing machine, and a one-car garage. The first Levittown development was built on a former potato field in Long Island, about 30 miles from New York City near the town of Hempstead, and comprised 17,000 Cape Cod–style houses featuring two bedrooms, a kitchen, living room, and amenities such as built-in bookshelves and fireplaces. The Levitts even sold land at cost for schools and donated land for fire stations and churches.[15] Young couples and families quickly bought up the properties, jump-starting the rapid exodus to the suburbs and launching the widespread lifestyle that would come to define the modern American suburban dream. By 1960, almost 60 percent of Americans owned a home, compared to just under 50 percent in 1945.[16] But it wasn't just private developers like the Levitts who made home ownership a possibility for millions of young former renters.

Postwar suburban prosperity was given a shot in the arm by Congress, which enacted legislation to offer low-cost, zero–down payment mortgages through the Federal Housing Administration

(FHA) and the Veterans Administration (VA). Prior to this time, most private banks required a 50 percent down payment and a mortgage repayment term of only ten years. The FHA and VA offered mortgages up to 90 percent of the value of a home with repayment periods of thirty years. The new loans ushered in a rapid expansion of home ownership and fueled the white exodus from the cities to the suburbs. Between 1950 and 1970 the population in the suburbs doubled, from 36 million to 72 million.[17]

The avalanche of suburban developments sparked a range of criticisms. Some bemoaned the cookie-cutter conformity of the dwellings and streets; others lamented that the extended family was suffering because the one-family houses typical of the suburbs offered no place for older Americans. More serious criticism was directed toward the racial discrimination that barred black Americans from purchasing homes in the Levittowns, including explicit rules prohibiting African American families from buying homes in certain suburban neighborhoods as well as restrictive zoning that indirectly ensured that black families remained behind in the central cities. In his book chronicling the postwar era of American history stretching from 1945 to 1974, *Grand Expectations*, James T. Patterson explains how those policies set in motion a legacy of racial segregation that still exists today. Sixty years after the birth of Levittown, the 1990 census showed that there were only 127 African Americans living in Levittown, Long Island, out of a population of 400,000.[18]

Today the original vision of Levittown as a place for young families to raise children is a distant memory. At the start of the new century, homes in Levittown are sporting price tags way out of reach of the typical young family. A house purchased in Levittown back in 1952 for $6,700 ($44,647 in today's dollars) sold for $300,000 in 2003.[19] Online listings of homes for sale in Levittown in April 2005 were priced from \$315,000 to \$529,000, hardly a starter-home neighborhood any longer.[20] In the late 1940s, most Levittown homes cost only slightly more than two and one-half times the median family income of young adults at the time.[21] In 2001, today those homes are more than six times the median family income.[22] Levittown is just one example of once-affordable areas now sporting very upscale prices. The fast rise in home values has burst young adults' hopes of fulfilling the American dream.

Home ownership rates for young households aged 25 to 34 began declining in the 1980s, falling from 48 percent in 1982 to 43 percent in 1992.[23] But the market rebounded and the 1990s witnessed the largest national gain in the home ownership rate since the 1950s. By the end of the decade, young home ownership rates had rebounded to 47 percent. At the turn of the new century, as home values soared and interest rates declined, more young adults became home owners. By 2005, 49 percent of those aged 25 to 34 owned a piece of the dream. But as we'll examine later in this chapter, many young adults managed the leap into home ownership by taking on massive mortages often with risky terms.[24]

There is some evidence that the gains in home ownership enjoyed by the young population were uneven. While the home ownership rate for young singles was climbing during the 1990s, the home ownership for young households with children declined. In 1977, 63 percent of households without children owned their own homes; in 1997, 66 percent did.[25] Not so for households with children. In the same period the rates for households with one child fell 3 percentage points; the rates for households with two children fell 4 percentage points, and those with three children fell 7 percentage points. Home ownership among households with four or more children dropped 10 percentage points.

The other important trend in young adults' home ownership is the big gap that still exists between whites, blacks, and Hispanics. Just as the legacy of discrimination is still evident in the makeup of Levittown's population today, the differences in home ownership rates are still significant by race. In 2000, as we've seen, 47 percent of all those in the 25-to-34-year-old age group owned their own homes. Those rates are heavily skewed not only by income but also by race. While half of white households aged 25 to 34 were home owners in 2000, only a quarter of black households of the same age group were homeowners. Hispanic and Asian home ownership rates also trailed that of white households, with just over a third laying claim to the American dream. Since 2000, home ownership rates among both lower-income people and minorities rose quite substantially, yet wide gaps remain. For example, between 1960 and 2000, home ownership among African American young adults rose from 22 percent to 27 percent, but is still 23 percentage points lower than the home ownership rate among young white households.

The racial gap in home ownership reflects the legacy of discrimination in lending practices that persisted well into the early 1980s. Now that the first generation to truly enjoy a more fair lending environment has started to purchase houses, we have seen a rise in home ownership among young African American households, offering hope that the gap will continue to close. But in the wake of the recession of 2001, African Americans suffered greater income and wealth losses than both white and Hispanic Americans. And a "housing bubble" in the West and the Northeast continues to plague young households of all races hoping to emerge from the rental blues into the dream.

According to the National Association of Realtors, between 1998 and 2003 median home prices in the New York metropolitan area rose by 76 percent, adjusted for inflation.[26] In dollars, that's a $140,000 increase in the sticker price. The increase in median home prices across the country was 26 percent over the same time period. The New York area is becoming a place where only the rich can afford to raise their families. Renters in the city hoping to escape the closed-in walls of their apartments and provide a nice backyard for their growing baby now find they can't afford to buy anywhere in the area. That's when they become permarenters.

Of course, the ups and downs in home prices are very local in nature. What's happening in the New York City area is very different than what's happening in Cincinnati, where median home prices rose by only 22 percent, or $24,000, between 1997 and 2002.[27] A median-priced home in Cincinnati was $135,000 in 2002, compared to $330,000 in the New York metropolitan area—proof, if any was needed, of the old adage that location is indeed everything. It's probably not surprising to most readers that New York is much more expensive than Cincinnati. But, sadly, New York isn't alone in being too expensive for most young families. California's housing market is mostly out of reach for young families, too; median housing prices even in places like Sacramento have doubled, to $258,000 between 1997 and 2002.[28] How about funky Seattle? The median home price in 2002 was $260,000, an increase of 42 percent in five years. Boston is just as bad. The median home price there is now $413,500. The Northeast and West, along with other major metro areas like Chicago, are fast becoming middle-class-free zones. Today, the typical household lacks the income to buy a median-priced house in thirty-four metropolitan areas, up from fourteen metro areas in 1999. And that spells particular trouble for aspiring young home owners.

Consequently, young Northeasterners are moving away from their hometowns, often migrating south, where the cost of living is still relatively low. The exodus has spawned a phrase that is quickly becoming part of our lexicon: "brain drain." Not surprisingly, it's hit Long Island. From 1990 to 2000, the population in the 18-to-34 group on the Island dropped by 20 percent, five times the nation's average.[29] Last year alone, 18,000 young Long Islanders moved away, and many more are thinking about it: according to a 2003 poll, half of the Island's young adults are considering leaving the area because of the lack of affordable housing, high taxes, and the high cost of living.[30] Boston, too, saw sharp declines in its young-adult population between 1990 and 2000, when the population in the 20-to-34 group declined by 16 percent, compared to 5.4 percent nationally.[31]

There's a popular perception about today's young adults, that they are anything but hometown proud. But the reality is that the majority of young adults in this generation, like those of most earlier generations, want to raise their families in the very same hometowns where they grew up, or no farther away than a couple of towns over. Census Bureau reports affirm the pull "home" has on young adults. When young adults move, the majority move within the same county.[32] In fact, it's older Americans who are the most likely to move across state lines. In 2002, more than a quarter of 55-to-64-year-old movers crossed state lines, whereas only one fifth of 25-to-29-year-olds moved to a different state. For the last thirty years, young adults in their twenties and early thirties have always moved around more than middle-aged or older Americans, but most aren't moving great distances. Single college-educated young adults are twice as likely to move across state lines than the age group as a whole, though the percentage moving out of state is still relatively low, at 22 percent.

Unfortunately, as home prices were rising at record-setting rates in the late 1990s, many young adults found themselves facing a bitter paradox: they couldn't afford a home in the towns where they

grew up, even if they had college degrees and two full-time professional workers in the family. From Boston to California, newspaper
articles describing the emotional pain of not being able to buy
homes in the "old neighborhood" are now all too common. A 2002
Boston Globe article described how families who have lived for generations in towns sprinkled around the city face rising home prices
that threaten to break the family tradition.[33] A similar story appeared
in the *Oakland Review.*[34] It described the dilemma facing a young
couple who tried for several years to buy a home in the county
where they grew up. That county wasn't near any of the big coastal
cities. It was San Lorenzo County, California—a town with strong
blue-collar roots. In 2001, the average home price in San Lorenzo
was $317,000. A household would need to earn more than $90,000
a year to buy such a home. The couple's parents had bought their
home in San Lorenzo thirty-eight years ago, a three-bedroom house,
for $19,500 ($109,000 in today's dollars) with the help of a GI Bill
loan and a $100 down payment. They couldn't afford to buy that
house, which they still live in, today, and neither can their children.

It's a familiar tale to Nancy and Ed, whom we met in chapter
2. When Nancy, age 25, and Ed, age 28, got married they moved
in with Nancy's parents so they could pay off their debts and start
saving money to buy a home. They accomplished the first goal,
but have found buying a home where they both grew up to be
more difficult than they anticipated on a yearly income of $46,000
(which is right at the median). They recently moved out of her
parents' house and into an apartment, where their rent is $730 a
month. The only other monthly bills are utilities and their car payments, which drain their monthly coffers by $700 each month—
and that's not including gas. They don't drive luxury cars. Nancy
drives a 2003 Cavalier and Ed drives a 2004 Sebring. Both Nancy
and Ed grew up in a suburb about thirty miles from downtown

Cleveland. They now live just one town over from their childhood homes. They've managed to put $1,000 away in savings, which is a long way from their goal of having $15,000 or $20,000 to put down on a house. Nancy and Ed share similar life goals—to have a home and children. Nancy almost apologizes for their simple goals, telling me that they're not big on traveling or anything like that. Nancy can't understand why she and Ed, who make the same salary as her parents, aren't able to afford their own home. She sees her older sisters and brothers, who have homes and families, and is disappointed that she and her husband don't. "I'd love to have that, you know, not even a big house, just a house with a yard where the kids could run around with a dog. The thought that that probably won't happen, or if it does, it's not going to be for a long time, that's a big disappointment."

For now, Nancy and Ed will continue paying rent and try to save for a down payment in the hopes that they'll be in position to buy in a few years. Even though Ed and Nancy spend their money wisely and rarely go out, they often have nothing left over. Nancy explained what is an all-too-common reality for young adults: "Every time we try to put money in the bank to save, there's no extra to put away. By the time we get done paying the bills, there's always something else requiring an expenditure—a birthday, anniversary, or wedding—and so there's nothing left."

At the other end of the spectrum, many well-educated and better-paid young adult couples and even singles are able to become home owners only by taking on major mortgage payments that leave them with very little financial cushion. On top of that, many young adults are putting very little down on their homes, which means it will take them longer to build equity. The 1990s gave birth to a new trend for young first-time homebuyers: the über-mortgage.

Mortgaged to the Max

There's a common, and condescending, phrase used for people who own nice homes but are living paycheck to paycheck: "house-rich, cash-poor." And it's a situation all too common among young adult homeowners. Today it is not uncommon to find a couple in their early thirties spending almost half their income to support a house payment. In fact, Gen Xers' housing debt is 62 percent higher than it was for Baby Boomers at the same life stage.[35] What used to be doable for a middle-class family with one earner is today barely doable for a middle-class family with two earners. In their best-selling book, *The Two-Income Trap,* Elizabeth Warren and Amelia Warren Tyagi document this counterintuitive notion. How can a two-parent family with two full-time workers be less secure than a two-parent family with one earner?

Warren and Tyagi crunch the numbers and find that today's two-parent, two-earner households have less disposable income than did a two-parent, one-earner family in the 1970s. Why? The authors point to a number of factors: for example, more of the family budget now goes to fixed expenses such as child care and car payments than in earlier decades. But the biggest culprit is the mortgage, which is bigger in both absolute and relative terms: today's young families have higher mortgages and they eat up a larger percentage of the monthly household budget. This is quite a paradox, when you think about it. Given that households with children now usually have two parents earning paychecks, one would think the percentage of household income devoted to the mortgage would be smaller. But that's not the case.

Census data show that the median monthly mortgage payment for those in the 25-to-34-year-old group grew by almost one third between 1980 and 2000.[36] The percentage of income spent on the mortgage also grew, though by a smaller amount. In 1980, 25-

to-34-year-old households spent 15.7 percent of their household income on the mortgage; by 2000, this percentage had grown to 17.3 percent. But remember, these are medians, so half of households are spending less than 17 percent and half are spending more. The standard rule used by the federal Department of Housing and Urban Development for affordability is that no more than one third of household income should be spent on mortgage or rent. Here's the bad news. The percentage of 25-to-34-year-olds spending more than 30 percent on their mortgage each month rose quite sharply between 1980 and 2000, from 10.5 to 14.5 percent. That's the über-mortgage effect showing up, as well as the slide in earnings for young adults over the last twenty years.

So why are home mortgages so much bigger than they used to be? Warren and Tyagi point to a suburban bidding war rooted in the scarcity of homes in good school districts. As more families have the power of two incomes to leverage, they consistently bid up prices in neighborhoods with good schools, essentially killing off the starter-home market in many communities. They also point a finger at the newly deregulated mortgage industry, which created a range of new mortgage products marketed to lower-income and younger households, who typically struggle to amass enough cash for a down payment. These new mortgages come at a price, though: extra fees, points, and mortgage insurance, none of which help pay down the principal on the loan. So in essence, when young adults buy a home with a zero or low down payment, they'll end up paying a mortgage plus the equivalent of a mini-rent in fees and insurance charges.

Robin and Jack, a white couple (both are 29) from the Northeast, in 2003 bought a new house in Norwalk, Connecticut, a few months after their first child, David, was born. In looking for a home, they wanted to be close to their families and to Robin's job in Stamford. Jack's parents live right outside New York City and Robin's live in Greenwich. Norwalk is about twenty minutes from Robin's parents and about a forty-five-minute drive from Jack's family. As in many areas in the Northeast, home prices in Connecticut are steep, and Jack and Robin's home is no exception: $487,000. They were able to put 10 percent down, because Robin's parents gave them a bridge loan for 5 percent, which they'll repay once they close on their previous condo. Even though Robin and Jack do very well financially, earning over $160,000 a year, they have never been able to build up their savings.

When they first got married, in 2000, they lived in New York City. Paying the rent, about $2,500 for a 450-square-foot apartment, and paying off student loan bills totaling $20,000 and credit card debt of $25,000 tapped them out each month. As for so many other New Yorkers, having a five-figure salary still meant living paycheck to paycheck. So how were they able to buy a home? Luckily, Robin and Jack have one of the most important assets: parents with money in their pockets. Both come from upper-middle-class families who have been central to their escape from the rental wasteland. In 2002, they bought a condo in Scarsdale, a nice community in Westchester County, north of the city, for $150,000. Jack's mother lent them $22,000 for the down payment. Buying the condo lowered their monthly housing costs to just under $1,300. With some much welcome breathing room—both physically and financially—they started chipping away at their debt. After two years, they now have cut their credit card debt in half, to $12,000, and shaved about $5,000 off the student loans.

After the birth of their first child, they were running out of space and wanted to have a real house. They decided to buy the home in Norwalk. They chose to move to Connecticut because it had lower income tax, lower property taxes, and lower sales tax than New York's Westchester County. Despite the half-million-dollar price tag, Robin says the house is a "bargain" because it's on a busy street—if it had been on a quieter street it would have been out of their price range. The monthly mortgage payment runs about $2,500—the same rent they struggled to pay in New York City. Of course, they now make about $30,000 more per year and will enjoy the tax advantages of home ownership, but nevertheless, owning the house is going to be tight for them, when one considers that there are day-care costs and the costs of two cars, not to mention utilities and real estate taxes.

Robin recently ended her maternity leave and went back to work. She wants to work in theory, but ideally would have liked more time off to be with David during the first year. But the couple can't meet their house payment without her full-time salary.

In order to be near family and in a decent school district, this couple mortgaged themselves to the max, and settled for a house on a busy street, which as little David begins to walk may be more of a sacrifice than the couple first realized. From the outside, Jack and Robin are living the American dream. Compared to the lives led by many of the other young adults in this book, this couple seems to have it very, very good. They work in professional jobs and earn high salaries. They have 401(k) accounts and health insurance coverage. And a big, new house.

But Jack and Robin are still living paycheck to paycheck, albeit in more comfort than their non–college-educated peers. They also enjoy the security of parents who can help them out financially. Without the intergenerational transfer of wealth, chances are this couple wouldn't be living in Norwalk in a half-million-dollar home. Perhaps they would have had to move to a less costly area of the country and give up the fifteen-minute drive to family. Robin admits that they could have made different choices and recognizes that without help from their parents, they'd probably still be renting. "Maybe we didn't make the most frugal choices. Maybe we should have stayed in the condo longer, but we were on top of each other and if David made a peep we were miserable. It depends on how much you're willing to sacrifice. I don't make much, but it's great that I work because we were able to afford the house." Despite having a household income more than three times the median, Jack and Robin are living modest lives, except for their house. They can't afford vacations and they can't afford to go out. If we peel away the house and their careers, their day-to-day financial situation is just as precarious as it is for Nancy and Joe in Cleveland, making $46,000 a year. The experiences of both these couples, at quite different points in the income spectrum, illustrate how difficult it is to maintain the standard of living that their parents had at their age and in which they themselves were raised. At the end of the day, if you're lucky enough to own your own house, chances are you'll still be cash-poor, and one job loss away from financial disaster.

As the baby boom generation nears retirement, it may become even harder for young adults to buy a home in the suburbs. Already, communities across the country are making decisions about construction and land use that favor older Americans at the expense of young families. The sheer size of the baby boom generation means there will be fewer vacancies in existing housing stock and enormous pressures for communities to build sprawling retirement villages in lieu of single-family homes.

Zoned Out of the Burbs?

As mentioned earlier in the chapter, young people have launched an exodus out of the Northeast, California, and even metro areas

in the Midwest. In the quest for less congested and more affordable places to raise their families, non-college-educated Gen Xers
have been moving to states like Georgia, Nevada, and Texas. The
short-term implications of this massive migration haven't been too
dramatic, but as the generational giant, the Baby Boomers, begins
aging into retirement, the geographic shift could greatly alter the
economic and cultural environment, as entire communities and
even states become overwhelmingly older. Already, seven of the
ten states with the oldest population are in the Northeast, where
the majority of the population is now over 40.[37] Besides altering
the economic and cultural landscape of these regions, the graying
of the population also means changes in housing opportunities
for the young families that don't make tracks out of their home
states. Towns are becoming far less friendly to young families, even
hostile. In suburbs around Boston, for example, tensions between
the needs of older residents and families with children are already
surfacing.

In May 2004, I was part of a panel convened to discuss the
housing challenges facing young Bostonians. The room was packed
with young professionals under 40 who were frustrated at the
high cost of housing in the Boston area. Joining me on the panel
was a woman named Helen Lemoine. Helen is a past chair of the
Framingham Planning Board, and her insights about the way gray-
panther politics are already impacting young adults' opportunities for home ownership were eye-opening. She spoke about the
politics of town planning boards, which are largely controlled by
people over 65, who have a very high stake in keeping the community focused on their needs. "They are interested in keeping
everything the same," she said. "Communities are becoming older
and we are not allowing young professionals to come in. I am worried about it. I didn't move to Framingham to be in a community

of old people. My children were raised there and want to come back but can't afford to. Young people are the social conscience of any community and we are losing that. If I wanted an old community I would move to Florida. I am getting that in Framingham without the sunshine."

What's happening in Framingham is a harbinger of the battles to come. Already town planning boards across the country are making decisions about priorities for new housing developments. Considering that the bulk of the population is soon going to be over age 55, the pressure to build new retirement communities is likely to win out over the need to build new homes for young families. Why? Because housing a family with children costs the local community more money than it brings in, largely owing to school costs. For example, according to a study by the Massachusetts Administration and Finance Office, each new single-family home brings with it, on average, $800 in education expenses, even after factoring in property tax revenue generated by the dwelling and additional per-pupil state education aid.[38] In a May 2004 *USA Today* article, city officials from Naperville, Illinois, a Chicago suburb, said that developing new housing for those 55 and older is the town's priority partly because the elderly will bring in property taxes, but few schoolchildren.[39] Because federal housing laws prohibit discrimination against families with children, town planning boards use stealth tactics. One such anti-family zoning ploy is to entice developers to build homes with no more than two bedrooms. In Rowley, Massachusetts, for example, developers who wanted to build twenty single-family houses were offered the option of instead building twenty-four new units—but they had to be two-bedroom townhouses.

Young families with children are also being zoned out by a preference for building large, expensive homes. Officials in the town of Plymouth, Massachusetts, on Boston's expensive South Shore, commissioned a report to undertake a cost–benefit analysis of certain types of housing.[40] Here's what they learned: A single–family house occupied by a family with school–aged children would cost the town $8,641 in services. Only houses with a value greater than $464,000 would bring the town more in property-tax revenue than it would spend in services. A third tidbit in the report was that an empty–nester household costs the town only $2,215 in services. The town of Plymouth wasted no time in using the report's findings to inform their development decisions. The planning board approved a plan to build 3,000 new houses ranging in price from $330,000 to $1.5 million—obviously out of reach for most young families. But there's more: one third of the houses must have at least one resident who is 55 or older.

The use of zoning to indirectly price or move families out of the suburbs is likely to become more common in the coming decade. Currently, these practices seem limited to areas with scarce new land for developing. But as the population ages, it's almost inevitable that more towns will face similar pressures. The near tribal trek of young adults from the Northeast and Midwest to the Sun Belt states will hasten a gray-haired monopoly on these regions' housing stock, leaving the young families left behind with fewer options for achieving the American dream. In addition, as suburbs in these regions become increasingly older, these regions may very well face declining economic development and slow economic growth in the future.

Getting a place of one's own is a defining experience of adulthood. Today's young adults are hitting the marker of home ownership later in life and paying more in real terms than their parents did. It now takes two full-time earners to pay the mortgage for a modest house in a good school district—which increasingly is located farther from jobs and families than in the past. Young adults are coping with the affordability crisis by moving in with parents, migrating far away from social and family networks, or getting in over their heads with massive mortgages. In trying to find a home, young adults are taking whatever they can get. And right now, that's not very much.

CHAPTER FIVE

And Baby Makes Broke

Four years ago, when my old college roommate called to tell me she was pregnant, I realized that my friend and I had reached an unspoken, yet pivotal point of adulthood: when news of a pregnancy gets greeted with hearty congratulations, rather than with something like, "Oh, no, what are you going to do?" Like many college-educated women, my friend was 30 when she leaped excitedly across the most epochal marker of adulthood: starting a family.

It's a transition that is coming later and later for young adults, particularly professional, college-educated women. Consider that in 1970, 19 percent of first births were to women aged 25 or older; by 2000 this percentage had increased to over 50 percent.[1] Today the average age a woman has her first child is 25, up from 21 in 1970. The trend toward waiting longer to have children is generally attributed to the rising educational levels of women and a fuller range of career choices. But there is something else at work, too: many young adults are postponing family life because it is taking them longer to get their financial footing.

As we've seen, those five-figure student loan debts don't go away overnight, and credit card debt tends to snowball rather than dwindle after college, thanks to all the start-up costs of getting established as an adult. So today, when a couple marries, the financial debt burdens are often magnified rather than reduced. In my interviews with twenty- and thirty-somethings who were thinking about starting a family, the issue of money always came up. While many of the couples were ready to take the plunge psychologically and emotionally, financially was a different matter entirely. The couples who were already expecting a baby were in a nine-month sprint to save up as much money as possible. As any parent will tell you, there is no ideal time to have a child. Despite the best intentions to erase or reduce debt and sock away some savings, having a child is a major financial commitment and sometimes a crippling one.

The New Baby Math

Kids are expensive. There is simply no way around that fact. But the transition to parenthood has become a much steeper financial challenge for young people today because they're often still living on the financial edge when they start a family. There's a popular perception that the college debt and credit card debt that accrue during the rough-and-tumble twenties will somehow be erased by the time parenthood comes along. Yet college loans typically take a decade or longer to pay off, and young adults who went the extra mile to get a graduate degree will be paying off an average of $45,900 in combined debt well into their thirties and even forties. Adding the extra expense of a baby to the budget can put them further in the hole financially.

One new father, aged 33, told me that he and his wife had never been in credit card debt until they had a baby. Because they were living paycheck to paycheck to begin with, they turned to credit cards to help deal with the extra expenses of a new child. They were charging diapers, baby food, and everything else the baby needed on their credit cards. When most couples today decide to start a family, they are used to having two full-time incomes to help pay the bills. After giving birth, however, there will be a reduction in income as one parent—usually the mother—cuts back on work to stay home with the child during at least the first three months. For most young families, during this leave from work one parent will receive only partial pay, or no pay at all, leaving the family with fewer resources at a time when they need more money. Those first few months of a baby's life are full of new expenses. First there's the cost of the birth itself. A standard vaginal delivery without complications runs about $8,000. Cesarean births without complications are about $14,000. Depending on the type of health coverage, the cost of birth may be zero or as much as 30 percent of this cost.[2] Once the little one comes home, new parents can plan on spending $80 to $130 on diapers each month and about $120 a month on infant formula or baby food.

While it may seem coldly rational to discuss having children in terms of the financial costs, the reality is that having a baby often pushes couples to the brink of economic collapse. Just how much does an infant cost? According to the USDA, which has collected data on expenditures for children since the 1960s, having a child under age 2 today costs a middle-income couple about $800 a month, or just under $10,000 annually. For the average American family, that's a whopping 18 percent of their pretax income. For two kids under age 5, a family will spend nearly double that amount.[3] Given the sobering amount of money needed to care for a young child, it's little wonder that finances are one of the most common concerns facing expectant parents today.

If the websites on parenting are any indication, financial fears are abundant among new parents. They are the subject of countless columns and message boards, edging out other topics like breastfeeding and potty training. In my many conversations with new parents, the discussion about the financial difficulties or emotional stress of raising a child was always followed by some type of declaration about how it is all worth the struggle. We can take the emotional rewards as a given. What's less acknowledged is how big the financial bite is for young families today.

While most couples don't scan the USDA report before getting pregnant, they are fully aware that having a baby is an expensive endeavor. In fact, by the time they're choosing baby names, they've probably already delayed the decision a year or more to get as much of an economic head start as possible. No matter how much love and purpose raising a child provides, there is a sad underbelly to the self-sacrifice that defines parenthood. Today, in the United States, having a child is the biggest predictor of whether someone will end up filing for bankruptcy. Married couples with children are twice as likely as childless couples to file for bankruptcy. They're also more likely to be late paying bills and to lose their homes to foreclosure.[4] A contemporary middle-class lifestyle requires two incomes. Add a baby into the mix and you can also add a second car, a second bedroom, and child care to that list of requirements. These factors account for why the typical two-parent, two-child middle-class family in America is more susceptible to bankruptcy.

Of course today's young parents aren't the first to struggle with the economic challenges of adding a new baby to the family. Nurturing a child has always been expensive, but unlike previous generations, today's young parents are more likely to be saddled with debt and overextended in a mortgage before they even start a family. Even if the cost of raising a child had remained steady over the last three or four decades, today's new parents would still be likely to find it more financially difficult than previous generations.

But just like housing, health care, and college, the cost of raising

a child has also risen. For middle-income families, the cost of raising a child born in 1960 to age 18 was $155,141 (in 2003 dollars).
The cost of raising a child born in 2003 to age 18 rose to $178,590,
a 15 percent increase.[5] Why does it cost more today to raise a child
than it did back then? One might look around at all the techno
toys and frivolous clothing in parents' magazines and think they
know the answer, but they'd be wrong. There's little evidence to
support the notion that families are struggling because of $45 baby
Nikes, $60 LeapFrog Learning Games, or Baby Einstein DVDs. The
real culprit is much more banal: health-care and child-care costs.
Figure 1 shows that since 1960, expenditures on both clothing and
miscellaneous items such as toys have fallen both as a percentage
of the family's budget and in real dollars—so young families today
are actually spending less on clothing and extra goodies than the
previous generation.

Figure 1. Expenditures on a Child up to Age 18, 1960 and 2003

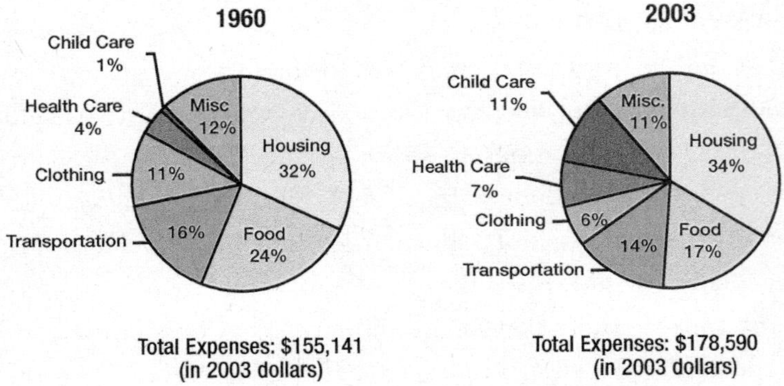

1960

Child Care 1%
Health Care 4%
Clothing 11%
Transportation 16%
Misc 12%
Housing 32%
Food 24%

Total Expenses: $155,141
(in 2003 dollars)

2003

Child Care 11%
Health Care 7%
Clothing 6%
Transportation
Misc. 11%
Housing 34%
Food 17%
14%

Total Expenses: $178,590
(in 2003 dollars)

Source: United States Department of Agriculture, "Expenditures on Children
by Families: 2000 and 2003 Annual Report." Graphs show expenditures
for two-parent middle-income families.

Today the average two-parent family with two children under age 5 spends 11 percent of their budget on child care, up from only 1 percent in 1960. Paying for a child's medical care eats up significantly more of the budget, too. What used to absorb 4 percent of the monthly budget now absorbs 7 percent.

Not So Family-Friendly After All

Young parents in the United States face a much tougher and less generous society than do young parents in most other industrialized nations. Our society does very little to help defray the costs of child rearing, particularly during the first five years. Our tax system provides richer rewards for someone buying a second home than for parents raising a second child. Practically every nation except the United States offers some form of paid parental leave, providing an economic safety net that allows parents to bond with their child without fear of missing a house payment or sliding deeper into debt. As the child gets older, again, most countries help to ensure parents can place their children in high-quality care while they work. And finally, most countries mandate that companies provide paid sick days, so parents don't have to choose between caring for their child and paying the bills.

The United States has always tended to take a more hands-off approach to family policy than other countries. But where Germany, France, England, Turkey, Japan, and every other country in the Organization for Economic Cooperation and Development (OECD) have expanded their supports for families, the United States has remained stubbornly unmoved. When it comes to navigating the many obstacles of new parenthood, in this country you're on your own.

The lack of social supports available to parents helps explain why today's young families end up frazzled by the battle to be good parents and workers. It's hard to underestimate the financial and emotional tug of war facing parents when a child is sick and can't go to school. For nearly half of all workers, taking a day off to be with a sick child means losing a day's pay. And in the worst-case scenario, it could mean losing a job altogether.

The capitalism that has made the United States the richest nation on earth has created a culture that penalizes employees for having any obligation other than work. Despite evidence that employees who have access to work-life supports are better workers, most major corporations don't do much to foster good parental behavior. And despite numerous studies showing that providing access to quality early learning and care would save the government money in the long run through reduced crime and welfare expenditures, our country has no official family policy or child-care policy. For all the political debate about family values, as a society we do little to deliver on the rhetoric. Our nation's hands-off approach to the tremendously important and challenging responsibilities of parenthood has resulted in few desirable outcomes for individual families or for the economy.

After Renee, whom we met in the first chapter, gave birth to her son, Ben, her husband split. Renee was living with her parents and working the second shift, from 2:30 P.M. to 10:30 P.M., at a printing company. Under federal law, Renee was entitled to take three months' leave from her job, without pay, after giving birth. With no husband, no savings, and no benefits from her job, Renee got through her maternity leave by going on welfare. Although her ex-husband is under a court order to pay child support, he often doesn't. Her father and mother, a custodian and a nursing home aide, respectively, weren't in a position to help Renee out financially, other than by giving her a free place to stay. For three months, Renee got help from the state through food stamps and a special program called Women, Infants and Children that ensures babies and new mothers can afford nutritious food. Renee went off welfare as soon as she returned to work, twelve weeks after giving birth. After making it through the first challenge of an unpaid maternity leave, she was now about to encounter the mess that is known as child care in the United States. In order to go to work, Renee needed to find a place to take her child for eight hours a day, five days a week.

Before we rejoin Renee in her quest to find a safe and affordable child-care provider for Ben, let's look at her options up to this point. Suppose that her husband had stuck around to raise his child. The family still would have lost Renee's income for three months, and they would not have qualified for welfare assistance. The first months of a baby's life are critical. Not only is one-on-one time important for the child's development, but it's also important for the mother to get fully recovered from the rigors of pregnancy and delivery. For already financially stretched couples, getting through the first three months with a new baby not only means losing precious sleep and moments together, but struggling to keep the lights on and the food on the table. If ever there was a time when families need a safety net, it is in those first few months after having a child. Instead, our nonexistent public policies leave them unprotected and vulnerable.

Because each week taken off from work after childbirth results in lost pay for most workers, it's not too surprising that most parents don't take parental leave. Taking three months off to be with a new baby is still a luxury in the United States available only to those who work for magnanimous employers or whose incomes are high enough to allow them to get by for three months without a paycheck. This explains why the take-up rates for parental leave are so low in the United States: only 36 percent of women and 33 percent of men take parental leave after having a baby.[6]

So what exactly *does* our society do to help parents bond with their babies without the gnawing fear of losing their jobs?

Up until 1993, the answer was "nothing." Today, the answer is "next to nothing." In 1993, Congress finally passed the Family and Medical Leave Act (FMLA). FMLA requires employers with fifty or more employees to provide up to twelve weeks of *unpaid* leave to care for a newborn or adopted child, or to care for a seriously ill family member. It was viewed as a social policy watershed. Feminist leaders celebrated its passage on behalf of women. Religious conservatives celebrated its passage on behalf of families. Corporate leaders celebrated nothing. They vigorously opposed the legislation, viewing it as an undue infringement on their rights to run their businesses as they saw fit. "It's Congress as personnel director. They want to tell you who to hire, what benefits to provide and even the racial composition of your work force," asserted Fred Krebs of the U.S. Chamber of Commerce.[7] Some Republicans opposed the bill on the grounds that it would squelch free enterprise. Representative John Boehner, Republican of Ohio, who opposed the bill, said, "We don't need the federal government further strangling the free enterprise system in our country."[8]

After nearly a decade of debate and two presidential vetoes by George H. W. Bush, the bill was finally signed into law by President Bill Clinton in 1993, one of the first pieces of legislation he signed. The debate over FMLA demonstrates our nation's reticence to engage in family policy or regulate any aspect of the employee-employer relationship. It's not just Sweden or France, the favorite "socialist" whipping countries, that make the United States look, well, heartless in its stance toward new parents. In the most advanced countries in the world—the twenty-nine countries that make up the OECD—the average childbirth leave for women is ten months, with four months of *paid* leave on average.[9] The countries offering up such "radical" policies include Turkey, Japan, England, Germany, and Hungary. What these countries have realized and the United States has failed to grasp is that providing paid time off to care for a newborn is good for society and the economy. In countries that offer paid leaves, women are more likely to return to their employers and more likely to work in general, and infants get the intensive care that moms, dads, and most everyone else think they deserve. Nor does the cost of offering paid leave break the bank in these countries: in all but two of the twenty-nine OECD countries, providing paid leave costs less than 1 percent of the GDP (gross domestic product).[10] To put that percentage into perspective, the three rounds of tax cuts implemented under the Bush administration in 2001, 2002, and 2003 cost 2.6 percent of the U.S. GDP in 2004.[11] The primary obstacle to providing widespread quality child care in the United States isn't about money, it's about priorities.

In fact, the actual cost may be lower than that 1 percent of GDP, because paid maternity leave policies in fact lead to higher rates of female labor participation, resulting in more government revenues. Savings also come from the positive impact of leave policies on childhood health, with some studies finding paid leave associated with better pediatric health.[12] What we have instead in this country is a flimsy policy that doesn't even cover most workers: 45 percent of U.S. workers don't even qualify for the Family and Medical Leave Act because they work for small businesses with less than fifty employees. And among those who do qualify, many can't afford to take unpaid time off.

Under the law, employers are allowed to require employees

to take any unused sick or vacation days to cover some or all of the twelve-week leave, so many new parents use up all their sick and vacation days in order to take the leave. Then the law does something even more ridiculous—it penalizes the most successful workers at a company. FMLA allows employers to deny leave to an employee within the highest-paid 10 percent of its workforce if the leave would have adverse consequences for the company. In other words, to best take advantage of the Family and Medical Leave Act, it helps if you're sick often enough to have used up your allotted sick days and are not in line for the corner office.

After the birth and the first few months of a baby's life, another problem looms: child care. Two-thirds of parents with children under age 5 are under 34,[13] making raising young children a defining issue for young adults. Having a young child has become one of the trickiest obstacles in adulthood thanks to a largely unregulated, private child-care industry that is overwhelmingly defined by high costs, waiting lists, and mediocre care. Figuring out how to keep the paychecks coming in *and* taking good care of their children is one of the most frustrating and financially challenging tasks for young adults in the twenty-first century.

A Hollow Helping Hand

Over the last three decades, child care has become a necessity for young parents, because today in the "normal" family with young children, both parents work full-time. Back in 1975, only two out of five mothers with a child younger than 6 held a paid job. Today, nearly two thirds of mothers with young children have jobs.[14] Nationwide, about 60 percent of working families with children under 5 pay for child care, at a cost of $325 a month on average.[15] According to the latest Census Bureau figures, about 18 percent of children under 5 were in family or home-based day care and 22 percent were in a formal child-care center. In family day care, children are watched at someone's home, as opposed to in a child-care center. The most common situation was relative care, with over a quarter of young children in the care of a relative, usually a grandparent, and another 20 percent in the care of a parent.[16]

As I've argued throughout this book, our nation's public policies have failed to address changing realities in the workplace, in the economy, and in the home. Child-care problems are a major area where the ball has been dropped. Limited subsidies are available to help lower-income parents, mostly single women transitioning off welfare, pay for child care. The generosity of these benefits is determined by each state, but in general, waiting lists for a subsidized spot can be long and eligibility levels are too low for moderate- or middle-income families to qualify. As a result, child care remains one of the biggest expenses in a young family's household budget, often second only to the mortgage or rental payment. The American brand of capitalism, in combination with our tendency to eschew social spending, has spawned a patchwork system of child care that is overwhelmingly of poor quality.

Panic is the word that best describes what parents go through in trying to find child care. Arrangements fall through, the child-care center turns out to be a dump, or the sweet woman who watches kids in her home is completely booked. It is rare for parents to get their first choice when it comes to child care, and even rarer for them to be completely satisfied with whatever arrangement is finally reached. Far too many parents feel lucky just to find something they can afford. For a bird's-eye view of what is both a financial and stressful situation, it's helpful to compare the experiences of three different families, at the low, middle, and top of the income spectrum: Renee, the divorced mother, and her son, who is now

5; Carolyn and Ryan, a teacher and police officer with two kids under age 4; and Robin and Jack, a computer analyst and program manager with an infant son.

When we left Renee, she had just taken maternity leave and was living with her parents. Ben, Renee's son, is now 5 years old and has had six different child-care providers since he was 3 months old. When Ben was just a toddler, Renee, who was working nights at a printing company, was able to enroll him in one of the only two child-care centers in the state that offered nighttime care. Because Renee was a single parent and making only $10 per hour, she qualified for a state subsidy for child care, which meant she had to pay only $200 per month for care. But that good fortune didn't last long. After the woman who directed the infant-care program at the center quit (turnover at centers is a major problem), the center decided to scrap its infant-care services.

Because most child-care centers don't offer night care, Renee's only option was to find a family day-care provider—someone who watches several children in her home. The first provider she found was located in a very bad neighborhood—so bad, that a few months after watching Ben, the provider closed her business because she felt the neighborhood was too dangerous for kids. The second family provider didn't work out because several times when Renee went to pick Ben up, neither Ben nor the provider was there. After selecting provider number 3, Renee finally thought she had found someone perfect: she was reliable and good-natured and was located in a good neighborhood near Renee's home and work-place. The downside was her fee, $100 more a month than the previous providers, which Renee thought reflected better quality of care. Instead of finally getting sterling care, what Renee got for the extra expense was an even more chilling glimpse into the world of unregulated family day care. Several times when Renee arrived to fetch Ben she heard yelling and screaming coming from the basement. When the woman noticed Renee's presence she immediately started hugging the children and cooing to them. The final straw was when Renee showed up to pick up Ben and she heard the woman punish a child who had wet his pants by refusing to feed him dinner. Renee quickly withdrew Ben from her care.

Renee decided to change jobs so that she could work during the day, allowing her to enroll Ben in a formal child-care setting. She got a new job as a paralegal assistant and enrolled Ben in a day-care center near her home. The cost was about the same as the family providers, just under $200 a month with her subsidy. The new center was a beacon of light for the family. It had a great curriculum, was well-staffed, and offered Webcams so that Renee could check in on Ben anytime. Ben loved going to the center and his mood changed dramatically; he no longer cried every time he was dropped off.

Renee was doing well at her job and got a $1,000 raise after a year. For most people this would be terrific news. But for Renee "it was the worst thing that could have happened." The slight bump in pay resulted in her losing much of her subsidy for child care. Her co-payment rose from $192 to $385 per month. This increase meant that Renee could no longer afford both the rent and day care, so she and Ben moved in with her parents. A few months later, as her home state of Minnesota grappled with a gaping budget deficit, Renee lost her subsidy entirely. Between 2001 and 2004, Minnesota "raised" the eligibility bar for child-care assistance from those who earn less than $42,300 a year to families earning less than $26,700.[17] The cut in eligibility left thousands of parents in the lurch, Renee included.

After spending two years living with her family, Renee got lucky when a family friend offered to rent her basement out to

Renee and Ben for $200 a month. The house was closer to Renee's job and she was able to enroll Ben in a branch of the child-care center near the house. However, even with a 25 percent discount arranged by her employer, the monthly payment was still close to $600 a month. It was a major financial struggle to make the rent and the day-care payment, so Renee kept looking for another provider. After several visits to different providers, Renee settled on a woman who had two children of her own. Ben seemed to bond with her immediately and the price was right—$400 per month.

Ben is now in kindergarten and still goes to the same provider for after-school care. Now that Ben is enrolled in school, it costs only $200 a month for half-day care. But Renee still feels that she can't afford the ideal care for her child. She'd like to enroll Ben in an after-school program at the Y, but she can't afford it. She feels lucky to have found the woman she uses now, but admits that she wishes Ben could have been in a child-care center all along. For Renee, child-care centers offer more peace of mind because there are more adults around, lessening the chances of her child's being treated poorly.

Renee is one of millions of parents who aren't able to afford the type of care they'd like to have for their child. Most child-care advocates agree that the main problems with America's child-care system are affordability and quality. And in many respects, the two go hand-in-hand. Because child care is largely paid for by parents and providing good child care is expensive, there simply is not enough demand for high-quality care.[18] If providers actually offered high-quality care, most parents wouldn't be able to afford to pay the real costs of providing that care, which would include higher wages to draw well-qualified teachers. The average wage for child-care providers is an unattractive $7.86 per hour, resulting in high turnover and a dearth of well-qualified providers.[19] Unlike other education services, parents pick up the tab for the largest portion of child-care costs: parents pay 60 percent; federal, state, and local governments pay 39 percent; and businesses and foundations cover 1 percent.[20] Contrast this to the current system of college tuition, where parents tend to pay only about 23 percent of the real costs of educating a student and the government and private sector pick up the rest.[21]

Is anything being done to help parents afford quality child care that is both safe and developmentally sound? The short answer is, not very much.

For the average middle-class family, the only benefit that eases the burden of child care is the child and dependent-care tax credit. The federal tax credit allows families to claim as a deduction up to 35 percent of their child-care costs; the maximum credit for families with *two or more* children is $2,100. However, most families get a credit of less than $1,000, which is better than nothing but in no way substantially reduces the cost burden they face.[22]

By far the biggest source of investment in child care is the federally funded Child Care and Development Fund (CCDF), whose sole purpose is to subsidize the costs of child care for low-income parents, mostly single parents transitioning off welfare. This is the type of subsidy that Renee received in Minnesota. The CCDF awards block grants to states, which issue vouchers to parents to purchase child care in the market or reimburses the child-care providers directly for enrolling eligible children. Parents make a co-payment on the basis of their income and the subsidy covers the difference. In 2003, the federal government allocated $10 billion to CCDF. Ten billion dollars may seem like a lot of money, but it's only enough to cover one out of seven children in families eligible for the child-care subsidy.[23] The rest may be on waiting lists or in informal care arrangements with a parent or other family member.

Many families who need help paying for child care earn too much to qualify for any assistance. Sixteen states cut off eligibility at 150 percent of the poverty level—which is $23,500 for a family of three. The state fiscal crisis that began in 2001 has made matters only worse. Most states cut their child-care spending by raising co-payments, by reducing eligibility by lowering the income cut-off level, and by lowering their reimbursement rates to providers.

More than one third of the states have waiting lists for child-care assistance, and young families who qualify for assistance are likely to find themselves on a rather long one.[24] In 2004, there were over 46,000 children on the waiting list in Florida, 26,500 in Texas, nearly 25,000 in North Carolina, about 23,000 in Tennessee, over 16,000 in Massachusetts, and almost 36,000 families in Georgia.[25] As a result of not having access to child-care subsidies, parents often make decisions that aren't in their economic interests or in their child's best long-term interest. Numerous studies show that parents on waiting lists often quit their jobs or change their working hours to care for their children, place their children in unreliable care, or go into debt to pay for care.[26]

Meanwhile, average-income young families, who don't qualify for any child-care subsidy, face difficult choices in the trade-off between buying child care and sending both parents into the workforce. When the cost of child care is prohibitively high, it may make sense on paper for one parent—usually it's the mother—to stay home, particularly when there are two children under the age of 5. For example, let's say a husband and wife each earn $22,000, or $44,000 together. Paying for child care for two children under the age of 5 could easily wipe out nearly all of one parent's earnings. In this situation, the best option is probably to reduce one of the parent's hours to part-time, but they may still need child care, so that too would cancel out that earner's income. Most families can't sustain a substantial drop-off in income, particularly during a time when their grocery bills and health-care costs are increasing as the family grows. What most families in this situation end up doing is looking for the cheapest available care for their child so both parents can continue to work.

The economics of child care has resulted in a wide disparity in the types of environments in which families can place their children. Lower-income families are much more likely than higher-income families to rely on family day care and informal child-care arrangements. Higher-income families tend to send their children to formal child-care centers, where the quality of care is much higher.

Glorified Baby-Sitters versus Baby Colleges

While Renee's son Ben was being shunted from one bad day-care situation to another in Minneapolis, Robin and Jack in Connecticut were sending their new baby, David, to a Montessori child-care center that had been around for decades. The couple earn over $160,000 a year, so they can afford to purchase the best care for their son and the peace of mind that all parents deserve. David's child-care center is the same one that Robin went to as an infant. Many of the staff have been there for over twenty years, and they have two teachers for every four infants. Top-quality child-care centers like this often have very long waiting lists that require parents to sign up well before a child is even born. Robin and Jack put their names on the waiting list when Robin was three months pregnant and it wasn't until David was seven months old that a slot opened up. It helped that Robin's employer, a Fortune 500 company, has preferred waiting lists at all the best centers in town. Robin and Jack pay $1,300 a month for their infant care at the center—and that is with a company discount.

The stark contrasts between little Ben's and little David's child-care quality isn't an aberration. By and large, working mothers with higher incomes use formal child-care centers more than lower-income working women, who are more reliant on relatives for care or on family day care, both of which are consistently less reliable and of poorer quality.[27]

What starts as a financially constrained choice for care during the earliest years often continues into the preschool years. In the last two decades, there's been a new consensus that preschool is essential to the development of children's full intellectual and so-cial capacities. At the same time, however, most states have failed to provide universal-access to preschool. The nation's Head Start program, a preschool program for the United States' poorest chil-dren, reaches only about three out of five eligible children because of low funding.[28] As a result, some children get a major leg up on structured learning while others are getting the equivalent of a baby-sitter. Not surprisingly, enrollments in preschool programs are strongly correlated with income. The Census Bureau reports that in 2000, 52 percent of those 3 to 5 years old were enrolled in nursery school, defined as a group or class offering educational ex-periences for children before kindergarten. Household income was a predictor of whether children were enrolled, and whether they were enrolled in public or private programs. The average rate of enrollment for families with incomes below $50,000 was 44 per-cent, compared to 65 percent of children in families with incomes above $50,000.[29] In my final chapter, I'll outline a comprehensive plan to ensure that all children get the quality care and education critical to their development in their earliest years, regardless of their parents' financial position.

The Free Market Won't Build the Village

Carolyn and Ryan, a teacher and a police officer, represent the all-American middle-class family. They, too, have had their share of child-care panic. When Carolyn was 30 and Ryan was 33, they had their first child, Max. A year later, they had another son, Ian. As a police officer, Ryan keeps very odd hours. His workweek is from Saturday to Tuesday, in ten-hour shifts from 6 P.M. to 4 A.M. Luckily, Carolyn's hours are predictable (7 A.M. to 4 P.M.) and eventually will parallel the children's schedules once they enter kindergarten.

As public-sector employees, Carolyn and Ryan have pretty good family benefits. Carolyn took twelve weeks of maternity leave, six of which were paid. Ryan got two weeks' paid leave from the force. They had arranged for Ryan's sister, a stay-at-home mom, to watch Max when Carolyn went back to work, and needed child care only for Monday, Tuesday, and Wednesday because Ryan could watch them on the other two weekdays he was off from work. About four weeks before Carolyn was to return to work, Ryan's sister told them she couldn't watch Max because her family needed money, so she was going back to paid work. Here comes the panic. Because they had counted on her sister, they hadn't researched any of the local centers or gotten on any waiting lists.

Luckily, they were able to find a woman who runs a family day care from her home and accepted infants. Carolyn and Ryan really liked her, and felt that Max would be safe and would be given a lot of attention. The major bonus was that the woman charged only $3 per hour to watch Max, a very budget-friendly arrangement, especially for infant day care. She had about ten kids in her care, though generally there are only six at her house at any one time. Max was with her Monday through Wednesday and on other days as needed. When Carolyn and Ryan had Ian, the plan was to have the same woman watch him as well. But life threw them a curve ball. Carolyn got a new job that was in the opposite direction of the family day care, resulting in an extra hour of driving time every day. Although she and Ryan were satisfied with their child-care arrangement, they decided to explore their options and went to visit several other child-care centers that would be closer to work and home.

Unlike most parents, Carolyn is an expert in early child development. Armed with a master's degree and teaching experience in the field, she can tell the difference between a spotless center that looks attractive but doesn't offer good care and a mediocre-looking center that provides top-notch care. She also knows what reams of social science data confirm: high-quality child care is beneficial to children. She knows to ask about staff-to-child ratios, staff turnover, and group size. Most parents aren't as able to judge whether a center offers quality care or not, and most don't know what to look for to distinguish between good and bad.

The first thing Carolyn did was get a list of certified family day-care providers that took infants. She called every single one and they were all booked up. So Carolyn and Ryan started checking out child-care centers. Because Max was 18 months old and Ian a newborn, they needed to find a place that could meet the needs of both an infant and a toddler. The first problem was that most of the centers didn't accept infants. The second problem was that the centers that did offer such care were abysmal—and very expensive. Several times they walked into the center and walked right out. Carolyn recalls visiting centers with long waiting lists that were run-down, had few toys, and were overcrowded. One center had twenty-eight cribs simply lined up in a room. Their average cost was between $900 and $1,200 a month for each child. The other problem they ran into was that many required that the child be enrolled year-round, which they didn't need, since Carolyn is a teacher.

After visiting places that were good on paper and awful in reality, Carolyn and Ryan realized they should stay with the provider Max had been with all along. For now, Max and Ian are getting high-quality care at a very affordable price. At age 2, Max already knows the alphabet and Ian is progressing rapidly as well. The kids often ask if they can go to their child-care provider's house, even on the weekends. The kids think of her as family, and Carolyn does, too.

But unfortunately the perfect arrangement would end when Max turned 3. Carolyn wanted to enroll him in preschool so he would get a developmentally formal education. They started looking into options and encountered obstacle after obstacle. Most preschools don't offer full-day hours, so someone would need to pick up Max and take him to another child-care provider. That wasn't going to work. Another challenge was finding a center that offered both a preschool curriculum for Max and toddler care for Ian. And of course, they were looking for good quality. The couple visited a few different centers and saw the gamut from one extreme of quality to the other. Some places were so sterile they felt like hospitals and lacked the creative environment Carolyn knows is critical for this age group. Finally, Carolyn's friend recommended that she check out the center she used. It offered full-day preschool and provided care for toddlers. As soon as they walked in, Carolyn and Ryan knew they had found the perfect place.

But the "perfect place" came at an enormous financial cost. To enroll Ian cost $780 a month and Max's preschool cost $500 a month. Carolyn explained that they lived paycheck to paycheck because they were saving almost every extra dollar of income toward retirement and college for the kids. Every month, they put away $200 in a college fund, 10 percent of their salaries into retirement accounts, and another $200 every month into an emergency fund. They also put $50 away each month for vacation and paid an extra $200 to pay down their mortgage. But in order to afford $15,000 in annual child care, Carolyn and Ryan decided to cut back on their retirement savings. For the next four years, all that extra money would go to paying for high-quality child care and preschool for Max and Ian.

Both Renee's experience with poor-quality child care and Carolyn and Ryan's difficult quest to find high-quality care illustrate that the U.S. child-care system is riddled with problems. For the average young family, finding high-quality care that's affordable is like finding the proverbial needle in a haystack. According to several studies, most child care in this country is of poor to mediocre quality.[30] And yet, most parents believe their kids are getting good or excellent care.[31] Unable to distinguish between good- and bad-quality care, they do not create a significant demand for high-quality care in the market. And even if demand were higher, it's very unlikely that the private-sector supply would expand because the majority of parents can't afford to pay for good care. As Anne Mitchell, president of Early Childhood Policy Research in Albany, New York, states the problem: "The child-care market doesn't work because the product quality can only be produced at a cost greater than what most consumers can afford to pay."[32] The signs abound that the private sector won't provide high-quality care unless parents can afford to pay for it, which most can't.

The fact that poor-quality child care is rampant in the country isn't too shocking, given that there is very little regulation or oversight of child-care providers. Formal child-care settings are subject to more standards, but they vary from state to state. Each state has different licensing regulations concerning staff-to-child ratios, teacher qualifications, and health and safety measures. Most small family day-care providers are exempt from state regulations, particularly those where a person is watching only one or two unrelated children—the majority of such situations.[33] It means that just about anyone can set up a family day-care center. The lack of regulation of family day care is a major reason why child-care centers offer better consistent quality. And it's a major reason why most parents can afford family day care but not center-based care.

Wanting It Better Versus Wanting It All

The enormous challenge of raising a family today is a bitter pill for young adults to swallow, particularly given their attitudes towards parenthood, which are profoundly different from those of their predecessors. Unlike their Baby Boomer parents, who are often described as overly self-centered, today's young adults are more aptly described as family-centered. Consider that in 1977, when most Boomers were in their twenties, only 45 percent of them agreed that "having a child is an experience everyone should have." In 1999, when Gen Xers were asked this same question, a whopping 68 percent answered in the affirmative.[34] In poll after poll, this children-of-divorce generation expresses their commitment to putting family first.

Social critics may decry Generation X for "wanting it all," but a closer look reveals something else entirely. They don't want it all. Instead, they want it better.

Today more than half of all children under the age of 18 are being raised by Gen X parents, and today's young adults are bringing a fresh perspective to the parenting job. Numerous polls confirm that Gen Xers have turned on to family in a big way, particularly Gen X men. Today's young married men are spending more time with their kids than did male Baby Boomers of the same age. A study by Reach Advisors found that nearly half of Gen X fathers spend three to six hours a week on child rearing, compared to just under 40 percent of Baby Boomer dads.[35]

When it comes to prioritizing work and family, Gen X parents are more likely than Baby Boomers to put family before work. According to a study from the Families and Work Institute, Baby Boomer parents are more likely to put work before family.[36] Today's young parents in their twenties and thirties put a premium on jobs that allow them to spend more time with their families, saying they'd trade less money for more family time.[37]

In survey after survey, Gen X parents are distinguishing themselves as parents. Dads are spending more time with their kids and doing household chores. Moms with professional careers are entering the workforce feeling less pressure to prove themselves, and have begun taking more time off after childbirth. The labor participation rate of women with children less than 1 year old declined between 1998 and 2000, dropping from 59 to 55 percent, the first significant decline since 1976.[38] Of course, the labor participation rate for mothers with infants is still much higher than it was in 1976, when just 31 percent of women with infants were in the workforce. Another sign that Gen X moms are feeling more comfortable taking some time off is illustrated by the growth of professional women working part-time, by choice. Between 1994 and 2000, the percentage of mothers working part-time grew 17 percent, to 2.9 million women.[39] This generation of dads is also charting new courses in the work-family continuum: the number of stay-at-home dads grew 18 percent since 1994. Though their numbers remain small, at 189,000 it's enough of a movement to have sparked several blogs and websites dedicated to stay-at-home fathers.[40]

Of course, expressing a desire to put family first isn't the same as achieving that goal. In the quest for a less frantic, more balanced family and work life, today's young parents have hit a few brick walls.

The first obstacle is family leave, which we've already covered. As new parents settle into a routine, they'll quickly find little support available at work. Although much has been made of "flex-time" and other benefits designed to help parents fulfill their responsibilities to both work and family, most people don't enjoy the basic right to a paid sick day, not to mention flex-time. According to the Bureau of Labor Statistics, 49 percent of workers, or 59 million people, don't get paid sick days either for themselves or to care for a sick family member.[41]

Being able to stay home with a sick child or take the child to the doctor is particularly important for new parents. Children under 5 have higher rates of illness and need more doctor's visits than school-age children.[42] Because women are still typically the primary caregiver in the family, paid sick leave is particularly important for working mothers, yet, ironically, women are less likely than men to have either paid sick leave or paid vacation time.[43] Single mothers are even less likely to have a sick-day benefit, adding even more stress and vulnerability to their situations. The bottom line is that most workers can't use sick time to care for a child. Just one third of all workers in the United States are afforded this very basic type of support, which would go a long way toward helping families better balance their work and family demands.

Our society isn't doing a very good job of helping new parents to be good parents. Whether it's a corporate culture that frowns upon absenteeism or low-paying service-sector jobs that provide no paid time off whatsoever, workers all across the spectrum find little support from their employers or from our government to properly discharge their family responsibilities.

The "family values" debate has been one of the defining features of American culture in the last two decades. You'd be hard-pressed to find a member of Generation X who doesn't remember the

Murphy Brown single-mother controversy. Thankfully, the tone and nature of the conversation have changed quite dramatically since the eighties. There's less waxing nostalgic these days about the era when moms were home, kids were disciplined, and nobody got divorced. Today the struggles facing single parents and the need to help all parents better meet the demands of work and family have gotten the attention of politicians on both the left and right. Unfortunately, the new debate, while healthier, is still just debate, while millions of young families are desperate for immediate action.

In order to make real progress in addressing the overwhelming stress that parents, particularly Gen X parents, are feeling today, we need to acknowledge that a return to exclusive domesticity for women is now no longer economically viable, socially preferable, or required for healthy child development. The frustrations that women face as they try to juggle both work and family have spawned countless books and magazine articles predicting a mass exodus from the rat race by professional women. But many of the well-educated women who drop out of the labor market often do so as a second or last choice—when they're faced with zero opportunities to work part-time or find jobs offering flex-time. For lower-income married couples, it is often the high cost of child care that determines whether or not a mother will return to work. But dropping completely out of the labor force after having children is a risky enterprise, for both the mother and her child. First there are the financial and career implications of leaving the workforce, which are rarely good. In addition, women who are in the paid labor force lose bargaining power in the family and are financially more vulnerable in the case of divorce or the early death of a spouse. What young parents are desperate for are real choices, not the lesser-of-two-evils decisions about how many hours to work when children are young, the type of child care the family desires, or the ability to take a paid day off to attend school functions or take a child to the doctor.

It's a Young-Adult Issue

Most parents with children under the age of 6 are in their late twenties or early thirties, so issues of family leave, child care, and work flexibility are of core concern to those under the age of 34. Young families across the income spectrum are financially and emotionally stressed by the demands of work and family, yet our nation has failed to address these issues in any systematic or holistic fashion. Caring for young children is still viewed primarily as a family responsibility, despite the fact that our economy and society have dramatically changed over the last three decades. Today the typical family with young children is one in which the mother goes to work and the children go to day care. While the debate continues about whether this is ideal, millions of children are languishing in poor-quality care that often contains little to no educational value and their parents are working longer hours just to keep their heads above water. There is little point to feeling guilty or engaging in hand-wringing when it comes to whether or not Mom should go back to work when she has young children. In the vast majority of cases, she simply has to and even wants to. If the United States offered families real choices about how to care for their newborn and young children, much of the debate about working mothers would go away.

Most women want to spend more than the first three months at home with their child, and increasingly, so do fathers. Study after study shows that high-quality infant care offers positive benefits to children, especially those from poorer families. The guilt that so many parents feel is in large part due to the realization that child care is hit or miss, especially for those parents who know they can't afford the best care. The guilt continues to grow as parents feel torn between their jobs and their families, because the boss always expects "the job" to come first.

There is no more time for guilt. Young adults can inject some much-needed common sense into the public debate about work and family responsibilities. We can demand a better way for society to reconcile the emotional and economic burdens caused by our country's unique "each family for itself" approach to raising the next generation of citizens. We've been quiet for too long.

CHAPTER SIX

Without a Fight: Explaining Young Adults' Political Retreat

In page after page of this book, I've detailed the declining economic prospects facing a new generation of young adults. I've also pointed out how changes in public policy and woeful inaction by politicians have contributed greatly to our economic insecurity. In case the connection isn't clear, public policy isn't debated or enacted in a vacuum—it's determined through a rather lengthy political process that includes public debate in the media, legislative debate, and elections. While young adults have been consistently tuning out and checking out of the political process in the last two decades, the politicians have all but stolen our future. While we weren't keeping tabs on the government, Congress decimated college financial aid, let the minimum wage fall to historic lows, and reengineered the tax code to tax income more than we tax wealth. Our health-care system continues to be riddled with inequity, and it is young adults who are the most likely to lack health insurance. We are the first generation of Americans to start our lives with five-figure debt and the first generation to start our careers in the unforgivably Darwinian new economy. The economic unraveling that has occurred and is hitting our generation leads to the question: Why are young adults still on the political sidelines? Why have we been so complicit in our economic plight?

Political scientists have been scratching their heads for decades to string together a coherent theory about America's declining political participation. A good deal of this work has focused on the generational backslide in voting, newspaper readership, and civic participation that began with the Baby Boomers and accelerated with Generation X. Volumes of research and essays have been published in the attempt to pinpoint why this generation is turned off and tuned out, presenting explanations ranging from a declining trust in government to the effect of television. Three prominent themes emerge from the dizzying array of political analysis.

The first explanation for young adults' political disengagement is our antigovernment views and embrace of free-market ideology. Even if young adults acknowledge that they've been dealt a bad hand economically, the last place they'd turn for help is the government. After all, this generation grew up during the 1980s under the leadership of President Reagan, who was an opponent of (so-called) big government and a firm believer in laissez-faire capitalism. Recognizing the importance of this social context and the power of the conservative drumbeat over the last two decades, we'll call this explanation the Reaganization effect.

The second theme behind young adults' lack of political engagement is that they are simply too checked out, uninformed, and apathetic to get involved in the process. How can young adults even begin to challenge the status quo if most of them aren't aware of how public policy impacts their lives? By not keeping up with current and political affairs, this generation deprives itself of both a current and historical perspective with which to assess their own experiences. Newspapers are still the best source for this type of information, but most young adults admit they don't read the daily paper, either in print or online. Without knowing any better, young adults resign themselves to their economic fate. We'll call this the Publicly Unaware factor.

The third explanation for young adults' reticence to challenge their economic destiny is that they lack political power, in terms of both their numbers and their ability to think about their problems collectively. The Baby Boomers had a rallying cry when they were in their twenties and thirties: a major movement to help them forge a generational identity. We don't view our experiences as shared ones, and so we lack the basic wiring to build a social movement. Given that older Americans have become a formidable voting bloc, we'll refer to this political power problem facing a new generation as Voter's Block.

The Reaganization of a Generation

Today's late-twenty- and early-thirty-somethings were born in the 1970s, graduated from high school in the late '80s and early '90s, and entered and graduated college during the early to mid-1990s. They came of age under Ronald Reagan and George Bush Sr., and when they hit the job market, Bill Clinton had taken the reins. By the time they entered their teens, in the 1980s, the country was on track to witness the greatest growth in income and wealth inequality since the Gilded Age. The rhetoric of the Reagan years, a rhetoric that characterized government as the enemy of virtue and an obstacle to market-driven prosperity, pervaded the country's psyche. At the behest of Wall Street and to fend off hostile take-overs, companies embarked on a new journey of becoming leaner and meaner, slashing payrolls, and gutting the middle-management positions that had been a stronghold of middle-class security. You could grow up during the 1980s never hearing one positive word about government, while being deluged with messages about the virtues of free enterprise and wealth—even greed.

More than previous postwar generations, today's young adults were taught from an early age to look to themselves for their own security and success. We grew up in the political era of "personal responsibility," and at home we learned to be self-sufficient as latchkey kids as our Baby Boomer mothers entered the workforce. And now, as we struggle to buy homes and start families, we tend to question our ability to be completely self-reliant rather than ask if our nation's priorities are in the right place. The last place we'd look for help is the government. And that's exactly what Reagan conservatives and their successors hoped to achieve.

When Reagan took office, the country was reeling from high inflation, high interest rates, and a deficit that seemed to grow without end. The Vietnam War and the Watergate scandal had rocked the nation just years earlier, shaking Americans' trust in their government and its leaders. The Iran Hostage Crisis, which had bedeviled the last year of the Democrat Jimmy Carter's presidency, was still fresh in people's minds and the economy was tanking. Reagan's message to the American people was a simple one: "In this present crisis, government is not the solution to our problem. Government is the problem."[1]

Those two sentences hit a raw nerve among Americans. After we watched the United States withdraw from an unwinnable war, after we waited in gas lines for hours during the 1973 oil crisis, and after we learned that a president can also be a crook, Reagan's message created an easy target for people to channel their anger, frustration, and vulnerability: the government. Reagan went on to flesh out the ideology that he'd offer the country, brilliantly articulating a trifecta of conservative philosophy: government is the problem; tax cuts and free markets are the engines of growth; and individual responsibility is the cornerstone of democracy. A genius at "staying on message," the aptly named Great Communicator would touch on these three tenets continuously throughout his presidency. A well-funded network of radio talk-show hosts, newspaper columnists, and TV pundits created an echo chamber for the conservative movement. If rhetoric indeed commands the power it so often is credited with, then young adults' socialization during the Reagan years is important to understanding their political attitudes and actions today.

What happens when a whole age cohort comes of age under a steady diet of conservative rhetoric? The result is a generation whose members view government and related institutions with distrust and blame their economic struggles on their own decisions or missteps. A whole generation that is inclined to see the free market as the best tool to deliver opportunity, even though the market has failed to deliver adequate child care or health care. The Reaganization theory may help explain why so many young adults view student loan debt as simply the price of going to college, or why they believe that finding quality child care is something parents should deal with on their own. Young adults certainly can relate to a debate over health insurance coverage, since they have the highest uninsured rate of any age group, but they're too skeptical to think that any elected leader or government could effectively solve this problem. In their Reaganization mind-set, it never occurs to young adults that the government could or should do anything to make their lives better.

Do the responses of young adults to survey questions lend credibility to the Reaganization theory? Yes and no. Let's start by looking at whether or not Gen Xers are more likely to be Republican, as politicos often emphasize. Some polls show Gen Xers leaning Republican, and others have found they're more likely to lean

Democratic. For example, according to the American National Election Study, in 2000, members of the 18-to-34-year-old age group were more likely to identify themselves as Democratic (45 percent) than Republican (36 percent), whereas the early Baby Boomers were more solidly Democratic (53 percent). Yet a poll conducted by the Gallup organization in 2003 found that Gen Xers were more likely to identify as Republican than Democratic, 33 to 26 percent.[2] But when the Gallup poll included the political leanings of independents, Gen X was split more evenly down party lines.

A book that came out a decade ago, *After the Boom: The Politics of Generation X*, edited by Stephen C. Craig and Stephen Earl Bennett, provides a comprehensive overview of Generation X's early political attitudes. In "The Partisanship Puzzle," Jack Dennis and Diana Owen discuss how this generation's party identification is uniformly weak—they don't have strong attachments to either political party. This generation's alienation from the two political parties is not a new trend. Over the past several decades since the war, each successive age group has become less partisan than the generation before it.[3] The trend began with the postwar Baby Boomers in the 1960s and became more evident throughout the 1980s and 1990s as Generation X came of voting age. What this means is that with every election, more votes are up for grabs—particularly those of young people. In political science lingo, this is called "electoral volatility." A look back at how Gen X voted in the last four presidential elections underscores their unpredictability at the polls.

In 1988, the first presidential election in which Gen Xers were eligible to vote, George H. W. Bush, the Republican nominee, won the majority of the under-30 vote. Four years later, Gen Xers resoundingly cast their votes for Bill Clinton, the Democratic nominee, and set a new high for young voter turnout in the process. But the win for Clinton among Gen Xers was only a plurality, not a majority, because more than a fifth of Gen X votes went to the third-party candidate, Ross Perot.[4] Four years later, however, Gen Xers reelected Bill Clinton, this time by a majority. Ross Perot garnered just 10 percent of the Gen X vote, and Clinton's gain of those independent voters gave him 53 percent of the votes, to Senator Bob Dole's 34 percent.[5] In the razor-thin nail-biting 2000 election, 4.7 percent of adults under 30 voted for Ralph Nader, the third-party candidate. The rest of the youth vote was pretty evenly split among the Republican and Democratic nominees, with Al Gore barely edging out George Bush, 47.6 to 46.2 percent. In the 2004 election 54 percent of the under-30 vote went to the Democratic candidate John Kerry; Ralph Nader received only 1 percent of the youth vote.

So the partisan scorecard since 1988 for Gen X and then later for the Millennials is two solid Democratic wins, one solid Republican win, one split evenly between both parties, and one election in which the independent candidate received a surprisingly large percentage of the under-30 vote.

Perhaps the most important statistic concerning the under-30 vote is that in three out of the last five presidential elections, a majority of young people *didn't go to the polls.* Consequently it is unknown whether the youth vote in these elections represents a true generational preference.

The next assertion important to the Reaganization theory holds that young adults are more conservative than liberal in their political beliefs, particularly when it comes to the role of government. If this generation is more distrustful of government, then it would make sense that they wouldn't view government as a way to solve their problems. As it turns out, Gen Xers are slightly *less* likely to identify themselves as conservative compared to Baby Boomers, though their ideological convictions are weak (see Table 3). In fact, Gen Xers are as likely to describe themselves as moderate as they are to say they're conservative. A poll conducted by the Kaiser Family Foundation found similar results.

Table 3. Political Ideology of Gen Xers and Baby Boomers, 2000

	2000 Baby Boomers Today Aged 45–54 (Percentage)	2000 Gen Xers Today Aged 18–34 (Percentage)
Total liberal	30	36
Extremely liberal	3	3
Liberal	9	17
Slightly liberal	18	16
Total moderate	29	32
Slightly conservative	21	17
Conservative	17	15
Extremely conservative	3	0
Total conservative	41	32

Source: Author's calculations, American National Election Study, 2000.

Like most Americans, Gen Xers' views on issues don't easily fit into the liberal/conservative paradigm. On some issues their beliefs skew liberal. On others their beliefs skew conservative.[6] Underlying their political positions on various issues is a strong libertarian streak—something that could be related to the Reaganization phenomenon. They tend to eschew most aspects of the social welfare liberalism that characterized American politics from the Great Depression through the late 1960s—a position that would be characterized as conservative. On the other hand, they oppose limits on personal freedom and expression in respect to abortion, sexual orientation, and artistic freedom—positions that are typically characterized as liberal. It's important to note that very few Americans of any age hold ideologically consistent views across the whole range of issues, so this ideological inconsistency among young adults is not exceptional.

How young adults view the role of government is a key element in understanding their political mind-set. Whatever conservative rhetoric maintains, the reality is that government plays an active role in our society by reflecting the priorities we have set and spending tax dollars accordingly. So whether or not Gen Xers have embraced or rejected the antigovernment sentiment espoused during their formative years is an important question. A national telephone survey conducted by the Center for Information and Research on Civic Learning and Engagement (CIRCLE) in 2002 offers some insight, on both Gen Xers and their juniors, the Millennials. Respondents were given two competing beliefs about government in three areas and asked to choose the statements that most represented their own opinions (see figure 2, p. 186):

- Government should do more to solve problems, *or* government does too many things better left to businesses and individuals.

- Government regulation of business is necessary to protect the public interest, *or* government regulation of business usually does more harm than good.

- Government is almost always wasteful and inefficient, *or* government often does a better job than people give it credit for.

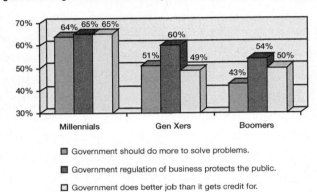

Figure 2. Pro-government Views by Different Generations, in 2002

Government should do more to solve problems.

Government regulation of business protects the public.

Government does better job than it gets credit for.

Source: Scott Keeter, Cliff Zukin, Molly Andolina, and Krista Jenkins, "The Civic and Political Health of the Nation: A Generational Portrait," report (College Park, Md.: CIRCLE 2002).

As the graph shows clearly, the Millennials are more supportive of government than are Gen Xers. More than 6 out of 10 Millennial adults took a pro-government position across all three questions. It's too early to know whether these pro-government attitudes will stick among the Millennials and inform their voting behavior, but their more supportive disposition raises a question as to what the cause might be. Perhaps it's because they grew up under President Clinton, who offered a more balanced and optimistic view of government. Unlike Reagan, Clinton emphasized that government, the private sector, and the nonprofit sector all had important roles to play in carrying out the nation's work.

Gen Xers, on the other hand, held fairly consistent, albeit ambivalent, beliefs about the role of government. In the 2002 poll, 60 percent of Gen Xers supported the pro-government sentiment on the question of regulation, while about half of them believed that government does too much already and that it tends to be wasteful and inefficient. Earlier analyses of this generation in the mid-1990s also found similarly divided opinions, noting that "ambivalent attitudes concerning the role of government are particularly widespread among citizens who have entered the electorate since 1965—and among Xers more than boomers."[7] Ambivalence—not clear-cut cynicism or distrust—best defines young adults' views of the role of government.

This ambivalence is especially obvious when we examine young adults' attitudes on certain policy issues. As the last chapter detailed, the problem of finding affordable child care is something many young adults experience firsthand. And yet, when asked whether the federal government was doing too much, too little, or the right amount to help working parents pay for child care, 42 percent of 25-to-34-year-olds thought the government was doing about the right amount and 44 percent thought the government did too little.[8] A poll conducted of parents with children under age 5 found that only 27 percent supported the idea of the government creating a universal child-care system similar to that of European countries, instead favoring (47 percent) tighter regulation of the existing child-care industry.[9] In general, the majority of parents with young children believe the primary responsibility for making sure working parents have child care rests with them (60 percent), not with the government (22 percent) or employers (15 percent).[10] This type of ambivalence is a common characteristic of young peoples' policy preferences. In their analysis of 1992 National Election Study data, Stephen C. Craig and Angela C. Halfacre found that respondents "frequently complained about 'big government' and high taxes—and then in the next breath stated their desire for government to do 'more things' and to provide additional services even at the cost of raising taxes."[11]

I encountered this ambivalence quite often in my interviews

for this book. Robin, whom we met in the last chapter, talked passionately about the lack of paid parental leave in the United States, calling it an "absolute crime." She acknowledged that there are benefits to government's lack of involvement in social issues in that we don't have socialized medicine, which she dislikes, and that we are a true capitalistic society, which she favors. At the same time, she said that "families really hurt because government isn't as involved in these policies." Toward the end of our conversation, I asked her about her politics specifically. She's a Republican who would have voted for Bush in 2000, but had just moved and hadn't reregistered. Given her passion about paid family leave, it's interesting that she would vote for the son of the president who twice vetoed the Family and Medical Leave Act. When I asked her specifically what government could do for her, she told me lower taxes. Then she told me that she thought it should be illegal for credit card companies to issue credit cards to college students. Robin's views on specific issues such as maternity leave and the regulation of credit would be considered liberal positions. Her vote for George W. Bush then would be inconsistent with her policy preferences. But her views about government—that overall it's good for them to stay out of such affairs—are typical of conservative ideology. She wants lower taxes, but also wants paid maternity leave. Robin is both inconsistent and ambivalent. And she is far from alone.

Anna is the young adult who found herself short of the money needed to go to college and is now finally working her way to a bachelor's degree in her late twenties, which is going to leave her about $70,000 in debt. She said, "There's always something I like about the Democratic party and there's always something I like about the Republican party." She told me she went from being a Democrat to a Republican and is now going back to being a Democrat. In 2000, Anna voted for George Bush; in 2004, she voted for John Kerry. Her Catholic faith and position on abortion were two reasons she voted for Bush in 2000. She also liked what he said about education and the environment. Four years later, though, she said that after seeing the effects of the Bush administration, it didn't make sense for someone in her income bracket to vote Republican. She admitted that she may not always like the particular positions of the Democratic party, but economically it made sense for her to vote Democratic in 2004.

There's a major problem, however, in using polling data to assess whether the Reaganization theory holds water. Compared to older generations, young adults today are vastly uninformed about public affairs, which means their answers to survey questions are based on sketchy and superficial knowledge of the issues at hand. This gets us to the second major reason underlying young adults' acceptance of the status quo: they may not know any better.

Publicly Unaware: What We Don't Know Is Hurting Us

When Shaney, 24 years old in 2005, was a senior in high school she participated in Girls State, a political simulation camp for high school students sponsored by the American Legion. Students were assigned to floors, which represent a county, and each county had two cities. Elections were held for both city- and countywide offices, and then people were selected to run for state office. Shaney and the other students also spent a lot of time hanging around the state capital, getting a close-up view of how the political machinery functions. Programs like Girls State are designed to get young people excited about the political process and deepen their understanding of how our democracy works. According to the American Legion's website, one of the main outcomes of Girls State is "participation in the citizen's communities when [a participant] returns home and begins a life-long commitment to be active in all levels of our government."

Unfortunately, Shaney walked away from the experience with anything but an appreciation of the political process. Girls State "left a bad taste in my mouth," she told me. Instead of inspiring activism in government affairs, Shaney instead learned "that nothing seems to work." As a result of her hands-on citizenship training, Shaney stopped paying attention to current affairs, and changed her college major from political science to French and art education. She no longer reads the newspaper or watches the news because she "just doesn't see the point."

There are millions of Shaneys out there who have reached the same conclusion, even without direct exposure to the political process. Indeed, if there is one definitive characteristic of young adults regarding politics, it is their lack of interest in public affairs.

In the spirit of full disclosure, I must come clean by admitting that until my mid-twenties, I was the epitome of an uninterested, ill-informed Gen Xer. I didn't read the newspaper regularly. I didn't know who represented me in Congress. I could name only one or two members of the president's cabinet. I didn't follow politics at all. I didn't know what legislation was pending in Congress, or have any inkling about the history of our modern welfare state. I was completely in the dark. But that didn't stop me from entering the voting booth my junior year of college in 1988 to exercise my franchise for the first time. My decision was little more than a guess about who could best run the country. It wasn't until several years later, after diving into politics and learning more about the issues, that I realized I had committed "reckless voting."

What is reckless voting? It's voting for a candidate on the basis of a gut feeling, your parents' beliefs, or instinct rather than a real understanding of the candidates' positions on issues. Reckless voting can take many forms. It may be voting on the basis of personality or looks, information gleaned from campaign commercials or late-night talk shows, or advice from parents or friends. Reckless voting certainly isn't a crime. If it were, it's likely that most voters would at some point be doing time. Some people of all ages commit reckless voting, but our generation is much more at risk of doing so. Of course, our generation is also more likely not to show up at all—a trend I'll discuss later in this chapter.

The conventional wisdom about young adults is that we are uninformed. Unlike a lot of the insults and condescension heaped on us, this is one charge that is fully merited. We are derelict in keeping up with current events, government, and politics—we are a grossly uninformed sliver of the electorate. We are the "derelectorate." It is an irony that our generation can especially appreciate: as the first adults to come of age in the information society, we are remarkably tuned out of the world around us.

On any number of indicators—newspaper readership, knowledge about news and politics, or talking about current events with friends—Generation Xers and the Millennials are less informed and engaged than the older generations. In a 2002 poll conducted by the Center for Information and Research on Civic Learning and Engagement (CIRCLE), half of all Baby Boomers said they followed politics and government "most of the time," compared to just 37 percent of Gen Xers and only a quarter of Millennials.[12] Only a third of Xers and Millennials read the newspaper regularly (defined as five of the last seven days), compared to just under half of Boomers. While 63 percent of Boomers regularly watch the TV news, only 47 percent of Gen Xers and 38 percent of Millennials do so. Radio programs fare somewhat better among Gen Xers, with 52 percent getting their news from the radio on a regular basis, but just over one third of Millennials turn the radio dial for news. And contrary to expectations, we're not making up for our smudge-free fingers by surfing the Web for news. Only 22 percent of Gen Xers and 17 percent of Millennials regularly use the Internet as a news source. Even lowering the bar to "occasional" use of the Internet for news, the Millennials are the least likely to seek out news on the Net, compared to over one-third of Xers and Boomers.

Why don't young people pay attention to politics? In the CIRCLE survey, respondents were asked, "Do you not follow it more often because you dislike politics and government, because it's not very important to you, or some other reason?" Nearly one third of Gen Xers volunteered a different reason: they were too busy and didn't have the time—a higher percentage than any other generation to give this response. This was also the most frequent reason cited by this age group, followed by lack of interest (23 percent) and a dislike of politics (22 percent).[13] The time pressures of keeping up with current events are very real, and it's not at all surprising that Gen Xers experience this time crunch more than other groups. As I've detailed in the rest of this book, young adults in their early to mid-thirties are under enormous economic and time pressures, working longer hours for less money than their parents did at the same age.

In his best-selling book *Bowling Alone,* published in 2000, Robert Putnam reports that young people's tendency to be less informed is not simply something we'll grow out of but is indeed a new generational development. According to Putnam, polling data taken between 1940 and 1960 indicate that in those decades younger people were at least as well informed as their elders. Beginning with the Baby Boomers in the 1970s, the information gap between generations began widening and then turned into a chasm-like gap as Gen Xers came of age in the 1980s and 1990s.[14] We are both less informed than older Americans and less informed than they were at our age.

Polls confirm that most young people both lack interest in and have a distaste for politics. Another important component in explaining their aversion to public affairs is that Gen Xers and the Millennials are more distrustful of people and institutions in general. We simply do not trust the intentions of the people around us. Six out of ten Gen Xers and seven out of ten Millennials believe that "most of the time people are just looking out for themselves" versus "most of the time people try to be helpful."[15] They also believe that people are more likely to take advantage of each other if given the chance than they are inclined to be fair. The lack of interpersonal trust gnaws away at our ability to think about people other than ourselves. As a result, we are more inwardly focused than other generations and less connected to each other and to the world overall.

The other main reason we haven't become interested in public affairs is related to the larger social and political context in which we came of age. Unlike previous generations, there are no great political movements to feed our passion. We weren't around to march for civil rights or women's rights. We were not born yet or possibly were toddlers when our parents were out protesting the Vietnam War. By the time we hit voting age, the Cold War was over and the country was on its way to a period of sustained prosperity. While many Baby Boomers have since rejected politics and become just as tuned out as their children, they at least had a reason to get into the game. Only history will tell if the events of September 11 and the ensuing war on terrorism will turn out to be a collective generational experience for the Millennials. Already, polls show that the Millennials have a greater sense of themselves as a generation than Gen Xers, 70 percent saying their age group is distinct, compared to just 40 percent of Gen Xers.[16]

It may well be that the adults coming of age amidst the new conflicts of the twenty-first century will indeed coalesce around favoring or protesting our nation's foreign policies. Young people's vote for Kerry in the 2004 elections does seem to indicate that they are less supportive of the current approach to the war on terrorism than older generations. But as I explained earlier in the chapter, Gen Xers came of age during a time when our nation's leaders were extolling the virtues of the free market and denigrating the role of government in society, so it's entirely possible that the Reaganization effect underlies their lack of interest in political affairs.

Finally, we should see the navel gazing of younger adults in the context of widening economic inequality in the United States. Growing inequality carries a host of cultural and social implications. As our society has grown less egalitarian, Americans have lost their sense of community, particularly young adults, who have never experienced the broad-based middle-class society in which the Baby Boomers were raised. Rising inequality has resulted in deeper class segregation in our workplaces, schools, and neighborhoods. Research shows that this inequality has resulted in lower levels of trust and social cohesion, traits that are particularly pronounced among the two youngest generations in society.[17] History shows that progressive changes have come about when Americans band together to protect their common interests. It was no accident that the broad safety net cast by the New Deal emerged from the collective trauma of the Great Depression. The current inequality has broken that collective spirit apart, leaving today's young adults with a more pronounced individualistic outlook than that of their parents and grandparents.

So far, we've examined the effects of young adults' political upbringing as a way to explain why young adults are reticent to demand or expect government to change their economic situation. The argument holds broad explanatory potential, but is probably most pertinent to understanding why young adults aren't interested in and therefore don't follow public affairs. This brings us to the last reason why young adults have failed to challenge their bleak economic circumstances: their absence from the polls.

Voter's Block

Young adults' sense that politics is neither interesting nor relevant to their lives could certainly help explain their depressingly low voting records. After all, it doesn't make sense to participate in something you don't care about. But this is far from the only reason for not voting. Many young adults also suspect what is true: the political system is dominated by wealthy candidates and even wealthier donors. Natalie, aged 26, who works as an office manager and has moved back and forth from her mom's house, doesn't think politics can make a difference in her personal financial situation. "Politicians are all more or less wealthy and they have an agenda—they're looking out for their own. There are some politicians who say they are looking out for you, but they are constantly contradicting themselves. I wouldn't trust a politician to help me save money. Unless they're going to give out free education and health care, I don't see politics benefiting me." Despite her skepticism about the worthiness of the endeavor, Natalie still votes, at least in presidential election years.

Nancy, on the other hand, was unabashed about her reasons for not voting. The 24-year-old medical assistant, who lives in suburban Cleveland, doesn't care who gets elected, because she believes both Democrats and Republicans have done nothing to help "the people—not the rich, nor the poor, the people in the middle." As a result, she doesn't think it's worth her time to vote.

Matt, who is 35, sees lots of problems in the political system. He believes the system needs revamping so that there are more candidates that are reflective of our society—and this is why he supports campaign-finance reform. He votes in all national elections but is frustrated with the choices put before him; something he takes full responsibility for. "I haven't done enough to voice my concerns. I'm the worst kind of American voter—I voice my displeasure but I don't do anything about it." Matt is a registered Democrat, though he says he judges candidates on their own merits.

Matt, Natalie, and Nancy are far from alone: a full 61 percent of Gen Xers believe the statement "Politicians and political leaders have failed my generation."[18]

And they're right. But at some point, this becomes a self-perpetuating cycle: young adults don't vote because their issues aren't addressed and policymakers don't address young adults' issues because they don't vote.

The 2004 presidential election seemed to indicate a much-needed crack in our armor of alienation. Millions of new voters under 30 swarmed the polling places, often standing in line for much longer than their supposed pea-sized attention spans would predict. The record-shattering youth turnout of the 2004 elections showed that when young adults feel there's a real stake in the outcome, they'll tune in and turn out. But here's the bad news: the rest of America's sleeping electorate will also turn out in high-stakes elections—at even higher numbers. Our generation's small size relative to the Baby Boomers and other older voters makes it that much more difficult for us to impact the outcome of an election.

In the 2004 election, exit polls show that 52 percent of 18-to-29-year-olds voted. Even in a banner election year, about half of the under-30 crowd stayed home, which is one reason why the "youth" vote didn't swing the election. Not only are we less likely to vote than older Americans, but our small numbers make it harder for our votes to pack a punch. Back in 1972, Baby Boomers, aged 18 to 29, made up a third of the entire voting-age population. By 2000, the eligible young-voter population represented only a fifth of all eligible voters.[19] The demographic bulge—the pig in the python phenomenon—of the Baby Boomers means that Generation X and the Millennials have to vote in much higher percentages to exert any influence in the electorate as generations. Turnout of just over 50 percent won't be enough to match the demographic juggernaut of aging Boomers, who already vote in higher percentages than the younger generations.

How did young adults vote in 2004? Unlike in the previous three presidential elections, this time around the under-30 voters didn't go for a third-party spoiler candidate. In fact, the under-30s were the only age group that voted for John Kerry over President Bush, by 54 to 44 percent.[20] According to some pundits, what drove their Democratic-heavy vote were fears about an impending draft and their experiences in the economy under Bush. Whether or not the 2004 election indicates a politically rejuvenated and more progressively minded slice of the electorate is far from certain. Just four years earlier, the under-30 vote was practically split between Al Gore and George Bush. Ralph Nader siphoned off just under 5 percent of the young adult vote, in all likelihood from Gore.[21] Unfortunately, because exit poll data isn't provided in easily identifiable generational age groups, it's not as easy to discern differences between the Millennials and Generation X. But given the big swing toward the Democratic party in 2004 by 18-to-29-

year-olds compared to that age group in 2000, it's likely that the Democratic tilt in the 2004 presidential race owed much to the new presence of Millennial voters. The high stakes in this country's first post–September 11 presidential election, combined with the war in Iraq and a slumping economy, made the outcome of this election more directly relevant to young adults than the 2000 election. As a result, they paid attention to the campaigns and showed up on Election Day.

Under-30 voters turned out despite the fact that neither candidate showed much interest in winning their votes in 2004. Remember how heavily Clinton courted young adults in 1992? This time around, neither Kerry nor Bush made any real attempt to speak directly to the particular experiences or interests of young adults. I'm not convinced that the high under-30 turnout will improve the candidates' courting behavior in 2008 either. Why? Because at the end of the day, young adults may vote, but they're far from a unified voting bloc. Until young adults can rally behind a unified agenda and have an energetic and committed leader or two actively promoting such an agenda, they'll continue to lack political power. Hans Reimer, Washington director for Rock the Vote, sees a real need for a youth-based political agenda. Once just a get-out-the-vote enterprise, Rock the Vote is now trying to become the "AARP for young people," says Hans. If they're successful, young adults may have a fighting chance at gaining political power and pushing for change.

There are no easy answers as to why young people vote in much lower numbers than their predecessors. Members of older age groups have always voted more frequently, but over the last four decades the voting gap between old and young has grown wider.[22] For example, since 1972, voter turnout in presidential elections has declined by about 4 percentage points, but among 18-to-25-

year-olds it has declined by 15 percentage points.[23] Even among the under-30 population, there was a 12 percent decline in voter turnout between 1972 and 2000.[24] Figure 3 shows voter turnout among the under-30s compared to the over-30s. It should be noted that since 1972, the voter turnout rate for the under-30s in presidential elections has dropped much more steeply than it has for midterm elections, in part because fewer people vote in these elections to begin with and those who do tend to be more attached to the political system in general. Between 1972 and 2000, the under-30 vote in midterm elections has hovered between 25 and 30 percent.[25] The turnout numbers for the 2004 election are not included in this analysis because the only data currently available are from exit polls, whereas data for all other years come from the Census Bureau's Current Population Survey.

Figure 3. Voter Turnout Among 18-to-29-Year-Olds, 1972–2000

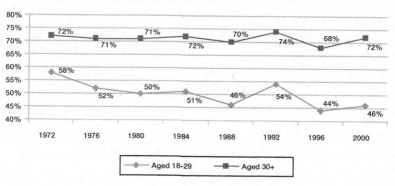

Source: CIRCLE, "Youth and Adult Voter Turnout from 1972–2000," reporting data in November supplements of the Current Population Survey.

But not all young adult populations vote in equal strength, and there are wide disparities by level of education and, to a lesser extent, by race. Young adults with college degrees are much more likely to vote than those without, a trend not isolated to this age group. In the 2000 election, just over one third of 18-to-24-year-olds with high school diplomas voted, while 70 percent of those with a college degree showed up at the polls.[26]

Other Civic Dilemmas

The trends are undeniable: young people aren't voting and they aren't keeping up with news and current events. Thankfully, voting is only one way of getting involved in our democracy, although I would argue it's both the easiest and most important responsibility of citizenship. People can sign petitions, participate in protests, write their representative in Congress, volunteer for political campaigns, attend public meetings, or simply give money to candidates. It could be that young adults are exerting their influence on our democracy in other ways besides voting.

When it comes to letter writing, signing petitions, and protesting, young adults are holding their own against other age groups, though all age groups engage in these activities in relatively small numbers. When it comes to getting involved in political campaigns—volunteering for a campaign, donating money, or displaying buttons or stickers—politics truly is a spectator sport. Survey after survey has shown that only a small percentage of any age group is actively involved with electoral politics. As parties have gone from being run by largely local outfits to being managed by national-level operatives with highly professionalized polling technology, call centers, and cadres of consultants both on the ground and in DC, politics has become less accessible to citizens.[27]

Today, most people get contacted by generic prerecorded phone calls or through mass e-mails, but it wasn't always this way. In the 1950s and 1960s, political outreach was done by committed people who volunteered for the party and hosted meetings and visited neighbors to spread the word about the party's candidates. Both of the major parties operated offices in towns and communities across the country. Social events from barbecues to dances were held on behalf of the party, offering the average citizen a chance to learn more about the party's platform and candidates. Today, during a presidential election the major parties may have one office in each state, and sometimes not even that. Any local organizing is done by committed individuals on their own initiative and rarely with any assistance from the party. The big exception to this pattern is the many dinners, salons, and other high-end functions that are major fund-raisers for the political parties and their candidates. The rich are still assiduously courted by and closely associated with the political parties, while most other Americans receive only prerecorded telephone messages and are bombarded with paid political ads on TV.

With little chance of getting into the political game, it appears Americans of all ages are finding other ways to take a political or social stand: the consumer boycott. According to one survey, over a third of the public reported that they had "not bought something because of the conditions under which the product is made, or because you dislike the conduct of the company that produces it."[28] About 40 percent of Millennials, Gen Xers, and Boomers have reported using the power of their wallets to send messages to corporate America. They also engage in positive wallet-based actions, buying certain products because they liked the social and political values of the company. While it's good news that individuals are starting to view their purchasing decisions through broader social or political lenses, it's a bit ironic that people think that their vote doesn't matter but that by switching brands or buying a different toothpaste they can influence the behavior of major corporations. However, it's quite likely that these consumer activists are also more politically engaged; people who keep up with the news are more likely to know where they want to put their purchasing dollars.

At this point, it's worth asking whether there is any good news about the younger generation's civic engagement? The answer is a shaky yes. During the 2004 elections and in the 1992 election, young people ramped up their involvement in presidential politics. This past election sparked the emergence of numerous coalitions, organizations, and Internet initiatives. Young people breathed energy and life into the campaign of Howard Dean before its very public implosion. Through the efforts of Rock the Vote, Smackdown Your Vote, and the Hip Hop movement, young people registered to vote in record numbers—and also showed up on voting day. In both the 1992 and 2004 elections, young people sensed that the outcome really mattered this time around. Of course, the outcome always "really matters." But in some election years, there is a greater sense of urgency and deep-seated conviction of the need for change. Indeed, the pulse that younger generations felt was also felt by the rest of the usually slumbering electorate, and all groups voted in higher numbers than in other election years. Since we are a smaller proportion of the population than other generations, flexing our generational muscle would require turning out in much higher percentages than our supersized generational predecessors.

Since the first of the Millennials turned 18, in 2000, much has been written and speculated about the political potential of this generation. According to two experts on the sociopolitical aspects of generations, William Strauss and Neil Howe, the Millennials are perfectly situated to become the next "great generation." They write in their book, *Millennials Rising,* "Today's kids are on track to become a powerhouse generation, full of technology planners, community shapers, institution builders, and world leaders, perhaps destined to dominate the twenty-first century like today's fading and ennobled G.I. Generation dominated the twentieth."[29] Already this generation has caught the eye of the commentariat for what appears to be an exceptionally high commitment to volunteer work.

The Rise of the Do-Gooders

The only positive trend in an otherwise steady decline in civic and political engagement is being driven by the teenagers and early twenty-somethings of the Millennial generation. Some studies show that 70 percent of Millennials volunteer in their communities, thus outperforming any other generation.[30] Other studies find that Millennials volunteer more often than their elders, with about 40 percent of this age group volunteering their time in the last year.[31] But we shouldn't award them the "Most Altruistic" trophy just yet. Although high school and college kids appear to be volunteering in much higher numbers than older generations, their civic activism tends to evaporate when examined more closely. A significant portion of "volunteering" is due to the influence of organized activities coordinated by high schools and colleges, and the cynical reality that volunteering looks good on a résumé. About a third of high schools require students to do community service for them to graduate, double the fraction a decade ago, when Gen Xers were attending school.[32] Volunteer rates drop off significantly between high school and college, and drop off once again when young people are no longer in high school or college. Adding further reason for skepticism regarding the notion of a generation of do-gooders is the fact that most of the volunteering is a one-shot deal. The percentage of Millennials who volunteer on a regular basis is essentially the same as that of Gen Xers and Baby Boomers.[33]

Young people's volunteerism, although short-lived, is worth praising, but so far lacks any real staying power or connection to political engagement. Like most people, young adults don't view their volunteering as a way to address a "social or political problem." Even those who volunteer for political or environmental groups are resistant to the idea that their work is a social or political statement. Less than half of political volunteers and only a fifth of volunteers for environmental organizations identified their work in this way.

Unfortunately, there is very little evidence to support the over-optimistic heralding of a new generation of volunteers. Even if young adults were more inclined to help their neighbors, their altruism does not reflect a desire to address social problems but rather to provide direct help to those in need—a very worthy and commendable goal, but not one that will help these young adults win the political battle for their and others' economic security.

Snap Out of It: Awakening from Our Political Slumber

Earlier in this chapter, I admitted to once being checked out of politics. As a former checked-out Gen Xer, then, I hope my generational peers will accept the following challenge with more credibility than if it were issued by a parent, professor, or other well-intentioned adult. My challenge to all Gen Xers and Millennials is this: *read a major newspaper regularly for one month*—either on the Web or in print. We can't fight what we don't acknowledge or know is happening. Failing to understand that many of the economic struggles we face are related to decisions being made every day in Congress and across the country in state capitals, we are instead blaming ourselves. Meanwhile, the politicians are running away with the country, leaving us more indebted and less economically secure. In the process, our nation's leaders have also stuck us with an enormous national debt that we will be required to pay down through higher tax rates and even shoddier schools, roads, parks, and air than what we experience today. Already, the Bush administration and many Republicans in Congress are actively seeking to destroy our retirement security by hobbling Social Security. Their plan would allow individuals to put some of their payroll taxes into private accounts—a policy that would stick our generation with a $2 trillion dollar tab in transition costs and greatly decrease our security, and our parents' security, in retirement.[34]

We don't all need to become hypervigilant political activists, but we should at least know enough to identify and stick up for our economic interests. And we should at least know enough to get involved. I'm willing to bet that after one month of reading a major newspaper, every reader will find one policy debate or legislative vote that provokes their ire. The level of involvement that follows this provocation of political awareness will vary by individual, but I'm optimistic it can and will happen. In a gesture of this optimism, I'm including an appendix that lists organizations and websites that can help you put that newfound passion into action.

Our generation has proved to be more ambitious, practical, and family-loving than the critics ever dreamed was possible. The only noxious stereotype that's been lobbed at us that is still rooted in reality is our lack of political participation and knowledge of current events. We don't keep tabs on politics and we don't vote. As a result, we're invisible to our nation's leaders. As every chapter in this book demonstrates, most of the economic obstacles we encounter on the path to adulthood are the result of policy changes or willful inaction by our nation's leaders. To counteract the declining opportunity and increasing risk that now define life in America, we need a political agenda rooted in common sense and fairness. The rug has been pulled out from under us for too long.

CHAPTER SEVEN

Changing Course: An Agenda for Reform

It is often said (and is said too often) that today's younger generation suffers from a sense of entitlement. The thinking goes that because this age group came of age during an era of prosperity, they believe their lives should be easy, that they should be able to achieve a comfortable lifestyle without putting in too much effort. Of course there are some spoiled young people who think the world should be their oyster—I even know some of them. The truth, however, is that the overwhelming majority of young adults suffers from something quite the opposite from a sense of entitlement. Their biggest character flaw is that they expect too little from our society—and everything of themselves. Socialized during the era of "personal responsibility" and capitalism on steroids, the young adults in this book didn't whine to me about their troubles, they simply told me their story with very little colorful commentary. Running through these conversations was the thread of complacency or perhaps fatalism: an acceptance of one's lot as just being the way things work. Having grown up in the new go-it-alone America, young adults personalize their problems, blaming themselves rather than questioning the structural inequalities and public policy failures that squash their aspirations and choke their chances of upward mobility. Unlike our parents' generation, which believed the personal is political, we view the personal as personal.

They sense the reality that the American dream is close to broken, but fail to connect their problems to a wider story about our nation's priorities. Millions of high school seniors can't achieve their fullest potential because going to college is too expensive. New moms and dads are struggling to handle the new economic pressures of having a baby without any official paid leave or help with child care. As the majority of today's young adults struggle to keep their heads above water, they suffer alone. Even worse, they judge themselves against the riches of some of their peers and wonder how it is that they struggle so hard while others seem to be easily passing them by. They see new McMansions being filled by families with young children and wonder how in the world someone their age could afford the half-million-dollar price tag. They can't comprehend that some couples their age can afford to spend $12,000 every year on child care. On their way to work, they see people their age driving Mercedes and SUVs, while the repairs on their ten-year-old car put them deeper in credit card debt. They're community college students who are working full-time to get a two-year degree while others their age are living in dorms at elite colleges, going to keg parties, and taking spring break trips, all on Mom and Dad's dime. The widening gap between the young haves and the have-nots can be a bitter pill to swallow. "It just isn't fair," said one woman, and she's right. Yet the goal of "fairness" seems to have fallen completely out of fashion in America. Asserting that something isn't fair is seen as the equivalent of a child stomping their feet when they don't get what they want. Or the notion of fairness is viewed as Pollyannaish, a naive idealism that has no place in today's winner-take-all capitalism.

Today the people who are working the hardest and making the biggest sacrifices are not getting ahead. Over the last two decades, the information-based economy has left them behind. And our public policies—our government—has done little to soften the blow. In some ways, it's amplified the blow. Today's young adults who come from families where neither parent has a college degree face enormous odds in trying to get into the middle class. The problem is not that all young adults get to drive SUVs, get Ivy League degrees, and summer in the Hamptons. The problem is that the majority of young adults can't even get into the game. From the very first hurdle, college, most young adults are locked out of the four-year-degree system. The labor market for young workers with only a high school diploma is brutal. Many young people work in jobs that offer little advancement, minimal benefits, and zero job security. But even for those who get their college degrees, five-figure student loan debt puts them financially behind for a decade or longer. If you are not born well-to-do, your chances of becoming well-to-do, or even moderately secure, are diminishing with each passing year.

How can we remove some obstacles from the course? How can we restore some semblance of a level playing field, some semblance of fairness? How can we ensure that this generation can make it into the middle class, or stay in the middle class?

The first thing we as young adults can do is question the values that have become dominant in our society. Three decades of laissez-faire ideology have left us more unequal, alienated us from our communities, and created a dog-eat-dog economy that rewards only a handful of players and leaves everybody else with scraps. It's time to ask ourselves, what good is an economy that generates $11 trillion where one third of us go without health insurance? Where three quarters of us can't afford to get a four-year degree? Where more than half of us lose a day's pay if we're sick? Where half of us must go back to work less than three months after having a baby?

Corporate profits continue to rise, but our incomes are either falling or stagnating, and benefits like pensions and health insurance are growing ever more scarce. Universal child care and paid sick days and parental leave are dismissed as "socialism" in the United States, but are considered good corporate, labor, and family policy in most developed countries across the world.

As young adults, we must begin to push back against this extreme form of capitalism that is crippling our quality of life. Throughout American history, whenever corporate power became too omnipotent and capitalism too extreme, reforms were enacted to temper the harsh fallout of the economic life. These reforms weren't pushed on people, they were demanded by them.

In order to return to a society that embraces collective purpose over individual gain, we as young adults need to reassess our views about government. Government is nothing more or less than the vehicle for advancing the shared goals and purposes of the nation. There is nothing inherently "bad" about the idea of government stepping up to the plate and doing things that otherwise would go undone by the private sector. By pooling the resources of over 300 million people, we can get a lot more accomplished than if we all tried to patch together our own system of schools, roads, drinking water systems, or libraries, as a pure free-market ideology would require.

We have been socialized to believe that our government is ineffective, wasteful, and nothing but an unnecessary evil, and that is no accident. Conservatives have worked diligently over the last three decades to undermine our trust in government. Government became the bungling idiot that could do nothing right. Government was the spoiled child that took your money and blew it on baseball cards and lollipops. It's time to shed this tired old view and create the government that we want. If we want to live in a society where health care is a right, not a privilege, where college is affordable, and where parents get a helping hand, then we'll need to push our government toward setting new priorities, rather than starving it of resources and dismantling it.

Finally, young adults need to transform their steely individual resolve into collective action. We can remove the obstacles, but only if we build a shared agenda of commonsense reforms, and only if we begin holding elected officials accountable for doing what we want them to do. That means showing up at every election, not just presidential elections. If our votes were as reliably cast as older Americans', the politicians would have to pay more attention to us and our concerns. We've rolled over for too long.

We need an agenda that addresses the problems we face as we try to build our lives, one that lowers the hurdles on the obstacle course, not eliminates them altogether. An agenda for reform shouldn't try to detach success from hard work. Rather, it should ensure that success becomes the reward for hard work. This agenda needs to be rooted in the common values that have a long and rich tradition in the United States. Today's economic situation is fundamentally out of sync with key American values. New policy initiatives are needed to close a growing disconnect between effort and reward, and to ensure that moving into the middle class and the ability to stay there remain realistic and achievable goals. The agenda I outline in the following pages is based on the following core American values:

Education is the cornerstone of social mobility. The United States has historically emphasized the importance of education as the engine for social and economic advancement. Today, too many young people who aspire to become the first in their families to graduate from college are falling short of that goal because they can't afford the tuition. Major new reforms in federal financial aid are needed to ensure that no one who wishes to make an investment in their future through college or vocational training will be deterred by financial obstacles.

Work should be rewarded. Americans revere the notion of hard work. Yet today, millions of young adults work in jobs that pay wages too low to cover basic living expenses or allow them to save for the future. This trend shows no signs of abating, but rather stands to worsen, for much of the future U.S. job growth is predicted to be in the lower-level, lower-paying service sector. People who currently work in assistant capacities in education and health professions—the helping professions—should themselves be helped to achieve their fullest potential in these occupations.

Everyone should have a stake in our society. The vast inequality of wealth that exists today has resulted in declining opportunity, as our nation's policy priorities have been set and skewed toward those of wealthy individuals and powerful corporations. Too few young people are able to save for their future and instead are moving in the opposite direction, toward long-term burdens of personal debt, often at very high interest rates. New investments and strategies are needed to help bring the benefits of asset accumulation to the millions of young adults who struggle to amass a down payment for a home, build a nest egg, or save for their retirement. Reregulation of the lending industry is necessary to curb widespread abusive lending practices that strip income and wealth from young adults.

Family life should come first. Few values unite Americans more than the importance of family. To be sure, the term "family values" has been appropriated by conservatives, who have transformed it into shorthand for regressing to the father-as-breadwinner and mother-as-homemaker model. Most Americans, however, reject this thinking and instead seek a balance between family life and their other commitments. Today's young adults, particularly young men, have embraced their roles as parents and search for ways to put their families before their work. Unfortunately, too many parents rush back to work after having a child and too many are forced to leave their children in mediocre or potentially harmful care while they work. Addressing the problems of quality, availability, and affordability of child care will require leveraging the resources of the federal government, private sector, and nonprofit sector. In addition, reforms are needed to help young adults be both good parents and good workers.

This agenda offers some real benefits for others besides young adults. As the pressures facing young adults have intensified, it's trickled up to their middle-aged parents and even their grandparents. The policy solutions I propose would help ameliorate the trickle-up burden that has parents taking out second mortgages for their kids' college education. It would end the need for parents to defer their own retirement needs in order to help their kids buy a decent house. It would prevent all workers from suffering the stigma and penalty of absenteeism because of a problem with child-care arrangements. It'll make your lives and your children's lives better.

The following proposals are rooted in the simple belief that if you provide an environment for people to achieve their fullest potential, they will give every fiber of their being to achieve it. So many young adults today are toiling without reward and are scared about being able to provide for their children. They're not aiming for the Ivy Leagues and the exclusive suburbs; they're aiming for the middle class. As one young adult told me, "I just want my children to have what I didn't. I don't want them to struggle so much." Another young woman wants to give her children a window to the world: she wants them to travel beyond their hometown, something she herself has never done. Another young man told me he doesn't want to be rich, he just wants to have a family and a safe backyard for his children to play in. Young adults' dreams are surprisingly old-fashioned, modest, and rooted in the values of family, hard work, and sacrifice. They don't want penthouses or hot tubs or fancy cars. They dream of achieving what we've come to classify as a middle-class life. In one generation that dream has become elusive.

The policy reforms I suggest are not modest in scope, but they are practical and rooted in common sense. One of the major impediments to solving the current crisis in opportunity is that our elected officials have lost the spirit of innovation and boldness critical for addressing domestic problems. In addition, Congress is increasingly hamstrung by ideologues who place politics ahead of progress. Progressive advocates have largely failed to offer new ideas or put forth bold solutions to the problems outlined in this book. Instead, most of the think tanks and advocacy groups work within the margins of the status quo and often find that playing "defense" to preserve funding or stop massive cuts consumes their energy. Meanwhile, conservative think tanks and advocacy groups have spent the last thirty years developing new ideas aimed at dismantling the gains made for average Americans in the twentieth century. Many of them now pervade our national debate—ideas such as public school vouchers, privatization of Social Security, and tax cuts for the wealthy.

Through my work at Dēmos—a New York City think tank whose mission is to build a more democratic, stronger American society—my colleagues and I are seeking to help fill the vacuum in ideas that exists among progressives. Several of my policy-reform proposals are based on the research and thinking that my Dēmos colleagues and I have engaged in over several years. Some of my proposals have been inspired by existing proposals or culled from the recommendations of various congressional commissions and advisory groups. Other proposals are to "scale up" scattered local- or state-level initiatives that have proved effective. Finally, some of my recommendations are based on existing legislation that has languished in Congress, stalled by entrenched special interests or partisan politicking. In almost every area, I argue for major policy initiatives that will necessarily demand sustained advocacy for several years. Balancing the need for action in the near term, I try to lay out some smaller-scope ideas or shorter-term fixes that are already on the congressional radar. Toward the end of this chapter, I discuss the financial implications of acting on these proposals—and the financial and social cost of *not* acting. We are beyond the point where taking baby steps toward reform will solve the opportunity crisis that plagues the nation.

Making College Affordable: The Contract for College

Our debt-for-diploma system is a failure. As I detailed in Chapter 1, the student loan debt burden to get a bachelor's degree ensnares young adults with hefty payments for at least a decade. The high cost of college also scares away smart young adults from families with modest incomes. Today, about three quarters of high school graduates take some type of college-level courses after high school, but only about 29 percent of today's 25-to-34-year-olds have a bachelor's degree. The percentage of young adults that want a degree and are capable of the academic achievement is much higher. Their talents are being wasted and their contributions to society minimized instead of maximized. At the root of these problems is a financial-aid system in desperate need of reform.

The fundamental problem is rooted in the reality that our government no longer really helps people pay for college—it helps them go into debt for college. In a Dēmos report, *Millions to the Middle: Three Strategies to Grow the Middle Class,* I proposed creating a new system called the "Contract for College." The Contract for College is based on a simple premise: if you study hard and are academically ready for college, money will not be an obstacle to your fulfilling your potential. The Contract is similar to a set of proposals made by the bipartisan National Commission on Responsibilities for Financing Post-Secondary Education, a body mandated by Congress in 1991 through legislation sponsored by Senator James Jeffords of Vermont, then a Republican.[1] The Commission's recommendations, which were never implemented by Congress, were released in a final report in February 1993.

The Contract would unify the existing three strands of federal financial aid—grants, loans, and work-study—into a coherent, guaranteed financial aid package for students. The Contract would shift federal financial aid funding away from loans and toward more grant aid. For example, students from households with incomes below $25,000 would be eligible for an annual grant to cover 75 percent of tuition and room and board costs at a state college, while a student from a household with income between $75,000 and $100,000 would receive a smaller grant, covering perhaps only 40 percent of the costs. Part of the Contract for every student would include some amount of student loan aid and/or a work-study requirement. But by providing grant aid for low-to-middle-income students, it would end the five-figure student loan debt that stunts the progress of young adults.

An important component in designing the program would be to ensure that families have early knowledge of the financial resources available for their children to attend college. One of the weaknesses of the current financial aid system is that parents and students do not have adequate information about the amount of aid available to them until just months before the students register, and aid amounts tend to change from year to year. The Contract could allow all households with students in the eighth grade and above to receive an annual estimate for aid based on the average cost of attendance at public four-year institutions. For example, low-income families would be informed that they could receive a Pell Grant that covers 75 percent of the cost of college, and get subsidized loans and do work-study to finance the rest. Although legislation to increase the maximum Pell Grant amount is regularly introduced in Congress, major increases in grant amounts have failed to materialize. In his budget for FY 2005, President Bush asked for funds to enable a $500 total increase in Pell Grant money available to each student over five years, from $4,050 to $4,550 in 2010. This is truly a marginal increase, given that the average four-year state college costs $12,000 per year. Other legislation has been introduced to increase Pell Grants; Senator Hillary Clinton of New York proposed to raise the maximum Pell Grant to $11,600 by 2010.[2]

The contract would also end the Federal Family Educational

Loan Program (FFELP), the government-guaranteed loan program in which the federal government acts as an intermediary between students and banks and, in effect, provides massive subsidies to ensure a guaranteed rate of return to lenders. Back in 1992, Congress tried to create an alternative plan to this subsidy-rich deal for private lenders whereby, instead of using private lenders, the government would put up the capital for student loans and disburse the money directly to the college. The Contract for College would incorporate this program, called the Direct Loan Program, which started as a pilot program in 1992 and was made an option for all colleges in 1993. Unlike federally guaranteed student loans, which cost taxpayers 12 cents on every dollar, the Direct Loan Program costs only 1 cent per dollar lent.[3] The Congressional Budget Office estimates that by switching all federal loans to the Direct Loan Program, the federal government would save over $60 billion over ten years from the reduction in subsidies and administrative costs associated with the FFELP system.[4] President Bush seems to agree that the Direct Loan Program is a better deal, stating in his FY 2005 budget that "significantly lower Direct Loan subsidy rates call into question the cost effectiveness of the FFELP structure."[5] Several pieces of legislation with bipartisan sponsorship have been introduced to encourage schools to participate in the Direct Loan Program.[6]

On the basis of enrollment projections, including increases owing to the availability of enhanced financial aid, I estimate that the Contract for College would cost about $48 billion per year.[7] The federal government already spends about $18 billion per year on all financial aid programs; these funds would be redirected to the Contract, meaning that an additional $30 billion would be needed to fund the program. By reversing the last Bush tax cut, the entire $30 billion could be found.

In exchange for the federal government picking up more of the tab for college, states need to do their part to keep tuition prices under control. That means increasing, rather than decreasing, state appropriations for higher education. Over the last several years, states have consistently slashed their support for state and community colleges as a way to deal with their budget deficits. Back in the late 1990s, when states were flush with extra money, instead of stockpiling those revenues for a rainy day, most states enacted tax cuts. When the tech bubble burst, states were left with no reserves and the political nonstarter option of raising taxes. State governments need to be more fiscally responsible about providing stable support for higher education. State tax money is the biggest source of operating funds for state colleges.

Colleges, too, have an important role to play in keeping costs in check. The state university system in this nation is the envy of the world, but far too often state colleges compete to excel in all areas, instead of concentrating on developing special academic strengths. In any given state, public universities could save the system money by eliminating redundant programs, coordinating research expertise, and collaboratively reaching agreements for each university to home in on certain academic fields.

Creating More Good Jobs

A fundamental tension exists between the American ideal of college for everyone and the reality that the largest growth in jobs is and will continue to be in the low-wage sector of the economy. These are the jobs that don't demand bachelor's degrees and often require little more than a few days of on-the-job training. Among the expanding occupations over the next ten years will be jobs in health services such as medical assistants, personal home and

health-care aides, and higher-paying jobs in the field, such as registered nurses. The teaching field shows the same job-growth trends.
Over the next decade, robust growth is projected at both the low
end (paraprofessionals, also known as teaching assistants or aides)
and the high end of K-through-12 teaching positions.

The fact that in two major occupational categories—teaching
and the health professions—both low- and high-wage job growth
is projected over the next decade signals an opportunity to design
formal career ladders in these fields. To fully develop the training
and educational process to allow young adults to advance from the
low-wage end of these occupations to the high-wage end, I propose scaling up local and state initiatives that have proved effective
in moving people up the professional ladder in these occupations.
Such programs are often called career-ladder programs.

An apprenticeship, or career-ladder, program in the health and
teaching professions would address the reality that many young
adults can't return to school full-time. It also recognizes that attending a four-year college is not possible nor even ideal for every
high school graduate. Many young people face enormous pressures
to enter the labor market in order to help support family members. Still others may not be academically prepared for the rigors
of college-level study. Career-ladder programs are also successful in
diversifying occupations by reaching young people who are not on
a traditional four-year-college path.

Successful examples of local partnerships designed to build career ladders in the teaching field include models in Los Angeles
and New York City, two major urban areas that continually face
shortages in teachers, particularly teachers of color and bilingual
teachers. In New York City, the United Federation of Teachers
created a program that paid for teaching assistants to take up to

six college credits per semester, allowed them time off to take classes, and provided a summer stipend. Since 1970, when the program was launched, more than 7,000 New York City teaching assistants have become teachers.[8] In Los Angeles, the Paraeducator Career Ladder was established by the local Service Employees International Union and the Los Angeles School District in 1995. Funded by the school district and the state, the program provides tuition reimbursement and mentoring and has successfully helped 1,200 paraprofessionals become teachers in the Los Angeles school system.[9] Eighty-five percent of the graduates are minority and 65 percent are bilingual. Other types of programs are aimed at recruiting high school students of color and bilingual students for paraeducator positions that are on a teaching track.[10] According to the National Education Association, 182 programs throughout the country offer some type of career-ladder program for teaching assistants.[11]

Similar programs abound in the health services occupations. To address the shortage in health-care workers, the Council for Adult and Experiential Learning, in collaboration with the U.S. Department of Labor, has implemented an education and training program at five pilot sites across the country.[12] Known as a "career lattice," the apprenticeship-based program helps nursing assistants advance to registered-nurse positions. In California, a public-private partnership between the Shirley Ware Education Center (a non-profit specializing in the education of health-care workers), Kaiser Permanente (the largest nonprofit HMO in California), and local community colleges provides training for current Kaiser Permanente staff to move into better-paying occupations within the company. Funded by a federal grant, the program has an 89 percent success rate in training employees to become medical assistants, nurse assistants, or surgical technicians. Another component of the grant helps licensed practical nurses graduate into registered-nurse positions by combining part-time work with full-time studies.[13] The grant also pays for books and supplies.

The results of these partnerships have proved successful in moving lower-wage workers into higher-paid positions within the fields of teaching and nursing. But in order to address the acute shortages facing the nation in these fields, these programs need the boost of federal funding and nationalized standards. Apprenticeship programs have a long history in the craft and trade professions. Bringing the apprenticeship model to the health services and teaching professions could go a long way in helping young people move up the career ladder into better-paying positions that would place them in the middle class. I talked to many young people who wanted to become teachers or nurses, but didn't have the financial support or mentors they needed to accomplish these goals. In the decades ahead, the aging of the Baby Boomer generation will result in more demand for registered nurses, along with an explosion in the need for low-wage home and health-care aides and other health assistant occupations. Similarly, the United States' population of young people is also growing rapidly, leading to an expanding need for educators.

Rather than allowing low-wage jobs in these fields to remain dead-ends, we could take active steps to convert these dead-end jobs into apprenticeships that would lead to more skilled positions and managerial opportunities.

Unfortunately, many of the largest growing occupations over the next decade—including food preparation, retail sales, security guards, and janitorial work—are not ripe for career ladders. What can be done to improve the wages and quality of life for the millions of young people whose work makes our own lives easier?

After all, someone has to clean our hotel rooms, serve our fast-food meals, and cash us out at the grocery. The key to improving these jobs lies in tearing down the many barriers workers currently face in trying to form unions at their workplaces. Unionized workers earn higher wages and have better benefits than workers in the same occupations who don't have collective bargaining power. Legally all workers in the United States have the right to form unions, but over the last two decades, it has become nearly impossible to exercise this right. Today employers can marshal a thriving union-busting industry of lawyers and consultants to defeat organizing attempts. Today, three quarters of employers facing a union drive hire anti-union consultants.[14] The first step in forming a union involves getting workers to sign forms indicating their desire to have the union represent them. If a majority of workers sign these "union cards," the employer has the option of either recognizing the union or refusing to recognize the union and insisting on an election supervised by the National Labor Relations Board (NLRB). It is during the NLRB election process that employers tend to pull out all the stops by hiring union-busting consultants, who often engage in illegal coercion and intimidation of workers. Delays of months or even years are common during this process, depressing the chances of a successful organizing campaign. Workers seeking union representation are outgunned, outspent, and outmaneuvered. As was mentioned earlier in the book, many workers are summarily fired for trying to organize their workplace. Federal law needs to step in to ensure that the right to organize is again exercisable. Legislation was introduced in Congress in November 2003 to address the reality that the legal right to organize is under attack. The Employee Free Choice Act would mandate that employers recognize and authorize the formation of a union when a majority of employees have signed union cards. The act would also provide for mandatory arbitration of the first contract, prohibiting employers from refusing to enter into a contract once a union has been formed. The bill has 36 cosponsors in the Senate and 207 cosponsors in the House. On July 16, 2004, the Senate Subcommittee on Labor, Health and Human Services held hearings on the Employee Free Choice Act, and there were few surprises in who testified in support of and in opposition to the bill. The U.S. Chamber of Commerce objected to the bill and the AFL-CIO gave it wholehearted support.

Spread-the-Wealth Incentives

Home ownership and savings are key to middle-class security. Families that sacrifice to build wealth for the future are more likely to prosper over the long term, and amid the difficult economic times of recent years, many American households have been reminded that the ability to tap into savings or home equity is crucial to weathering the loss of a job or other financial misfortune. Unfortunately, millions of young adults have neither savings nor significant home equity. Home-ownership rates, which are at historic highs, have largely been driven by older home buyers. Young adults have found themselves priced out of the market, particularly in the Northeast and on the West Coast. In addition, the ownership rates for minorities are still much lower than those of whites. The finances of many young families that do own homes are stretched thinner than they should be. The advent of new low-down-payment, or 80-10-10, plans (80 percent loan-to-value first mortgage, a 10 percent equity loan, and a 10 percent down payment) might get a young family into a new home, but it does little to ensure they can protect and maintain their asset.

The federal government helps Americans build personal wealth in a variety of ways, most notably with tax breaks related to home ownership and retirement savings. However, most of this assistance goes to people who are already doing fairly or very well. In 2003, the home mortgage interest deduction cost the federal government $69.9 billion in missed taxes, the bulk of which advantaged better-off families.[15] Nearly 90 percent of the mortgage interest deduction benefit accrues to tax filers with adjusted gross income over $50,000. Homeowners are even able to deduct mortgage interest on a second residence. Another $22 billion in forgone revenue stems from the property tax deduction. The federal government also forgoes about $101 billion yearly in tax breaks and incentives for retirement savings in IRAs, Roth IRAs, and 401(k) plans. Finally, another $53 billion in revenue was lost with the reduction of the tax rate on capital gains enacted into law in 2003.

All told, the federal government spends or forgoes $335 billion each year to promote individual asset building. The lion's share of these gains goes to wealthy investors who would already be inclined to invest and save even without the tax incentive. An analysis by the Corporation for Enterprise Development shows that the biggest beneficiaries of the three largest tax expenditures—the home mortgage deduction, the home property tax deduction, and the reduced capital gains tax rate—are America's richest households. Roughly one third of these tax savings are enjoyed by the top 1 percent of taxpayers, those with average annual incomes above $1 million. Meanwhile the bottom 60 percent of taxpayers, those with average incomes below $48,000, share about 5 percent of the savings.[16]

New steps are urgently needed to extend asset-building efforts down the economic and generational ladder. Expanding home ownership should be a major priority. The most significant impediment toward purchasing a first home is the difficulty of saving enough money for a down payment, particularly as housing prices have rapidly increased. The low percentage value of down payments is why many young families find themselves overextended in a mortgage. Combine these challenges with existing low levels of asset accumulation and it becomes clear that several types of new policies are needed to help young Americans become stakeholders in our society.

My next suggestion would require immense political courage, but given our nation's soaring deficit and debt, trimming excess fat from the budget inevitably means making tough decisions. The mortgage deduction has become a major runaway freebie. It should be limited so that it provides incentives for home ownership without making the deduction yet another tax boon for the wealthy. Currently, families whose earnings are low enough to be exempt from federal income taxes, those with incomes below $50,000, can't claim the deduction—even though they pay property taxes and payroll taxes just like other home owners. The mortgage interest deduction should be made refundable for families earning less than $50,000 and the benefit level for all families should be capped at $10,000. Capping the deduction at $10,000 would lead to $8.5 billion in extra revenue, which could be used to spread the wealth incentives to younger households. A note of definition is in order: a refundable tax credit is one that enables the tax filer to receive a "refund" (literally a check in the mail from the U.S. Treasury) even if they did not have to pay taxes (or when the credit is more than the amount owed in taxes). A non-refundable tax credit allows a household to reduce only its tax burden, but any leftover credit amount is of no value.

In place of the bloated deduction, the federal government should develop a matched savings program that would help young Americans and other lower-income families save toward a down payment on a home. First-time homebuyers earning less than $50,000 should receive a $1 for $1 tax credit for money they save toward a down payment. There could be limits on the total amount of the match, say, $7,500, which would help a first-time buyer accumulate $15,000 toward a home purchase—much more than the average young adult puts toward a down payment today.

Finally, young adults who struggle to pay down student loan bills are also having a tough time saving for retirement. Once they start having families, the need to begin saving for a child's college tuition may also lead to a decline in retirement savings. As the polls show, most young adults don't believe that Social Security will be around for them, and the young adults I spoke with are no exception. But the Bush administration's plans to allow young workers to divert some of their payroll taxes into private accounts is the wrong approach. In fact, it does nothing to strengthen the Social Security system—which most young people want to see preserved.

Social Security was always intended to be one leg of a three-legged stool for retirement security. The two other legs are supposed to be pensions and personal savings. As young people can attest, saving for retirement has become a struggle and often a pipe dream. Many young parents make the choice to save for their children's college education rather than their retirement, or they simply don't have much left over after the mortgage and bills are paid. We must both preserve Social Security for today's young workers and enhance their capacity to save on their own.

Let's start with the first leg of the stool. Contrary to the hyperbole being spread by the Republicans, Social Security is not in crisis. According to the Social Security trustees report, the program can pay all benefits through the year 2042, with no changes whatsoever. The nonpartisan Congressional Budget Office has an even more optimistic view of the system's health: it projects that

Social Security can pay all benefits through the year 2052 with no changes whatsoever.[17] By either measure, Social Security is financially sound today. To ensure that it will still be sound for us when we and our children retire, there are better solutions than private accounts. One solution would be to raise the taxable-income ceiling for payroll taxes. Currently, no Social Security taxes are paid on earnings over $87,900. What that means is that most Americans pay Social Security tax on all their income, while richer Americans pay Social Security tax on very little of their income. The regressive nature of the tax is kept well hidden from the American people. Recent polls show that once it is explained to them, most people are surprised and support lifting the ceiling.

Now for the second leg of the stool needed to enhance young workers' retirement planning: personal savings. What young people—and all workers, for that matter—need is a retirement savings account that isn't tied to their employer. Over half of all workers do not have a pension, and 85 percent of those without a pension are young, low-wage, or individuals who work for small firms or are self-employed.[18] The availability of IRAs has not solved the problem because only 3.9 percent of adults made an IRA contribution in 1996. What is needed is an easily accessible, portable, and equitable savings vehicle. During the 1990s, the Clinton administration proposed something called Universal Retirement Savings Accounts, and since then, there have been numerous similar proposals.[19] The common thread among varying proposals is the need for the accounts to be universal, meaning that they are offered to everyone and that they offer progressive incentives to save. In a matching system, the federal government matches the savings of those families who have the hardest time saving to begin with—those with lower incomes. The match could be provided through a refundable tax credit that is directly deposited in the workers' accounts. The match could be $2 for every $1 saved by the lowest-wage earners and then progressively phasing out to a 50 percent match for middle-income earners. Unlike 401(k)s, these accounts would be invested in diversified, low-risk funds, preventing the massive loss of wealth that happened to so many during the wave of corporate scandals in the early years of the twenty-first century. One viable and administratively efficient approach would be to offer universal accountholders the same investment options as the Thrift Savings Plan available to federal employees.

Although there is bipartisan agreement on the need to increase savings among Americans of all ages, the debate on this policy is currently caught up in the debate about privatizing Social Security. For young adults, it is critical that Social Security be strengthened and preserved—it remains the linchpin of retirement security and of our commitment as a society to collectively ensure the well-being of our oldest citizens. At the same time, there are common-sense reforms such as universal savings accounts that would help young people save, much as the tax code currently helps high-income households save.

Unlock the Debtor Prison

A rising tide of credit card debt is threatening young adults' shot at the American dream. More and more young people are financing their early years on credit, as they deal with slow growth in wages, prolonged unemployment, and higher prices for housing, gasoline, and other essentials. This credit has become brutally more expensive, thanks to deregulation of the credit card industry. Rising credit card debt takes a heavy toll on the family budget: every year the average indebted household pays over $2,175 in interest charges. Young adults probably pay more in interest because often they're still using cards they got during college.

My colleagues at Dēmos and I have proposed the Borrower's Security Act to address the most egregious and abusive lending practices of the credit card industry. Young adults who are routinely paying interest rates in the high teens and mid-twenties have little chance of digging themselves out of debt. Meanwhile, the credit card industry rakes in $2.5 billion in profits each month.[20] Credit card companies now routinely triple or quadruple the interest rate for a tardy payment or for any payments made late to other creditors. Congress needs to stop the gravy-train profits that come from bilking customers as opposed to responsible lending. If card companies want to raise the interest rate, the new rate should apply only to future purchases on the card instead of being retroactively applied to the existing balance. Imagine if you bought a new computer tomorrow with cash and then the company sent you a bill for $150 because they've raised the price of the computer since you purchased it. That's essentially what credit card companies are doing every day to thousands of borrowers—changing the terms and applying them retroactively. Representatives Bernie Sanders (I–VT) and Barney Frank (D–MA) have introduced legislation that would stop these abusive practices. A similar bill was introduced in the Senate by Senator Christopher Dodd (D–CT) in 2004.

The Borrower's Security Act would also get the credit card companies off our college campuses. While some states have passed legislation restricting credit card marketing at state universities, far too many of our institutions of higher learning are getting kickbacks for every student who signs up for a card. More states should enact legislation curtailing free giveaways on public campuses.

Finally, legislation is needed to end predatory lending practices that strip home owners of their equity during refinancing. These lenders aggressively market mortgages in lower-income and minority communities that leave home owners worse off thanks to bloated fees, points, and prepayment penalties.

The entire lending industry—from mortgage companies to payday lenders to credit card companies—long ago completely shed any adherence to ethical business practices. Contrary to what the deregulatory denizens promised, the lending industry has become increasingly concentrated among a handful of global and national banks that leave young adults and others with little choices to find a better deal. Deregulation has also left borrowers with higher prices—in a underregulated race to the bottom. Young adults are starting their lives in debt, and without any action from Congress, they will likely be paying off those debts well into middle age.

Building a Family Trust

Today, young families face a one-two punch as soon as their first little one comes along. The first punch is the lack of paid family leave, leading most parents to scramble back to work before their baby is even 12 weeks old. The second punch lands shortly after the first, when the parents begin their search for child-care arrangements.

For the last three decades our nation has pondered the need for a coordinated, national system of child care, from infant care to prekindergarten programs, and then has repeatedly rejected the notion. Yet the creation of such a care system is not just the right thing to do for working parents, but the smart thing to do for the future of the nation. Child development experts have confirmed that the first three years of a child's life are a critical stage in cognitive and emotional development. Our nation currently leaves the outcome of this critical stage largely to chance.

The nation has made more impressive progress in moving toward prekindergarten programs, with 46 percent of three-year-olds and 69 percent of four-year-olds enrolled in some kind of center-based preschool program.[21] Unfortunately, the majority of these programs aren't geared toward working parents, and offer only part-day care. Prekindergarten classes help make sure kids are school-ready, which saves the public school system dollars all the way up to grade 12. Big business has been urging the nation's leaders to establish universal preschool for our nation's three- and four-year-olds. Both the Committee for Economic Development, a public policy organization made up of business leaders, and the Business Roundtable, a forum for top executives in large companies, have come out in support of universal preschool.

The United States government needs to join the international community by supporting new families rather than turning its back on them. After two decades of trying to get the job done on the cheap, it's time to solve this crisis once and for all.

More easily said than done, of course. Experts put the cost of providing universal prekindergarten and improved infant and toddler care at $50 billion to $75 billion per year.[22] The federal government currently spends about $15 billion on child care and the states spend about $4 billion, so a major source of new revenue must be found or raised.[23] Where should the money to support a system of paid leave and 0-to-5 child care come from?

One idea would be for business and government to combine their resources by establishing an American Family Trust to fund the creation and maintenance of paid parental leave and universal child care and education. While business leaders have come out in support of a publicly subsidized system of prekindergarten, they haven't offered to pony up any money for the cause. Business leaders rightly understand that the key to a good future workforce is good early-childhood education. Employers also have a stake in a national policy that allows paid leave after the birth of a child. Evidence from other countries shows that paid leaves increase the likelihood of a mother returning to her employer. Given how much American businesses stand to gain, a small tax on corporations seems justified to support the American Family Trust. Federal and state governments will need to find new sources of revenue to support the system, but again, by pooling resources the burden is more widely shared. A handful of states already have financing mechanisms for paid leave or prekindergarten. For example, New York, New Jersey, Hawaii, and Rhode Island all use a mandatory payroll tax of .5 percent to defray the cost of short-term paid parental leave after the birth of a child.[24] In Georgia, revenues from the state lottery are used to pay for prekindergarten programs, which now enroll more than half of all 4-year-olds in the state.

After finding ways to raise the revenue, the next question becomes, what does this system look like? While child care experts have outlined a number of different approaches, there is widespread agreement that the system must address three current problems: cost, availability, and quality. Some advocates propose direct subsidies to providers while others promote integrating early childhood care and education into the existing public school system.[25] Another model exists in the child-care program for members of the military; it provides care to children aged 4 weeks to 18 years old. The child-care centers are subsidized by the federal government, with parents paying fees on a sliding scale according to income.

Paid parental leave is also critical to ensure young parents have the financial flexibility to stay home with a newborn child. A commonsense length of time would be six months, with up to 50 percent of the parent's wage replaced up to some specified maximum. Following the lead of other countries, the United States should mandate that one month of the leave must be taken by fathers or be forgone. But even with paid leave, parents will still need to find high-quality infant care, although at a later age than is currently the case. While many child advocates and policymakers have joined the pre-K bandwagon, there has been very little acknowledgment of the need for infant and toddler care, which is often the hardest care to find and afford.

The specifics of creating a universal system of paid leave and child care still need to be carefully hammered out, but the need for such a bold advance is crystal clear. Business leaders have provided support for a universal system, while many advocacy organizations are on the case for expanded child care and paid leave. The Family Initiative, run by Legal Momentum, is working to mobilize families to press for better access to child care and paid leave.[26] There are plenty of ideas out there about how to "build the village"; what's missing is political leadership and public will.

The Price Is Too High Not to Act

The United States must rearrange national priorities to afford major new efforts to ensure that young adults today and in the future can make it into the middle class and stay there. The agenda I propose comes at a time when the United States faces major budget deficits and rising burdens for its entitlement programs for seniors. However, additional expenditures will be unavoidable. It's important to keep the cost of the major new initiatives I propose in some historical perspective.

First, the agenda I propose is not inordinately expensive compared to investments this country made during the early post–World War II period. That era saw very high levels of investment through the GI Bill, widely used home mortgage deduction, massive infusions of federal and state money into both the public and private university system, and the large-scale public investments in the infrastructure needed to convert open space into suburban communities. These investments more than paid for themselves by helping to fuel decades of dynamic economic growth. The investments I propose will not only help fuel growth but will be recouped many times over by saving the taxpayers dollars down the line.

Second, the revenue to fund many of these initiatives can be found within existing spending. There are major inequities in how public subsidies are currently distributed across age and income groups. This is particularly notable in the area of tax breaks, leading the scholar Christopher Howard to posit the existence of a "hidden welfare state." As discussed earlier, these tax expenditures subsidize home ownership, retirement savings, and asset-building to a total of several hundred billion dollars a year. Most of these tax expenditures benefit middle-aged and wealthier Americans.

Third, the cost of the initiatives I propose is actually small compared to the tax cuts enacted by the Bush administration, which will total over $2 trillion by 2010. Rolling back portions of those tax cuts would generate significant new revenues. More generally, if federal spending returned to levels that prevailed during the Reagan administration—roughly 22 percent of gross domestic product, as opposed to 20 percent today—significant new resources would be available to pay for the agenda.[27]

Fourth, by providing the right incentives, government can creatively leverage resources from business and nonprofits and make taxpayer dollars stretch further. My proposal for the American Family Trust explicitly makes this connection; other initiatives will help generate partnerships between all sectors of society. The public sector should not be expected to solve all systemic social problems alone, nor can it. Through matching grants and other mechanisms, government can catalyze major new initiatives by the private and nonprofit sector to help all Americans realize their potential for advancement and economic success.

Finally, there is no real alternative to dramatic action if the United States wishes to retain some of its signature strengths as a nation, including widespread economic opportunity and mobility. Already, the inequities and challenges facing today's young adults have robbed too many of the hope and aspirations that make this country exceptional. Unless the United States takes bold action today, these inequities will only worsen. While the aging of the Baby Boomers has grabbed much attention in terms of the burden it will place on our national resources, there are looming demographic challenges throughout the age spectrum. For example, the current crisis in access to higher education will be further strained as the largest generation since the Baby Boomers begins to age out of high school.

Further threats to our social cohesion could arise as the largely white Baby Boomers retire and an increasingly non-white labor force is left paying the bill for entitlement programs. In their book, *The Coming Generational Storm,* Lawrence Kotlikoff, a Boston University economics professor, and Scott Burns, a personal finance columnist, estimate the fallout if our nation's leaders fail to act now. Absent major action in the near term, the combined obligations of paying down the national debt and paying out Medicare and Social Security payments will result in a tax burden on today's young adults double that of our parents.

The clock is ticking. In 2011, 76 million Baby Boomers will

start retiring. The agenda needed to bolster economic security among young Americans today and tomorrow must be addressed before this financial collision occurs. It won't happen unless young adults band together and flex our political muscle. While our parents fought for civil and women's rights, we must battle against the economic inequity and lack of opportunity that now defines this country. The stakes are high. In thirty years, we could be known either as the generation that saved the American dream or the one that suffered silently through its demise.

"A lot of kids don't know what work is. They think 'work' is a four-letter word. We've got to send a different message to our young people. America didn't happen by accident. A lot of people worked really hard. They've got to do their part, too."

If you're under 35, chances are you've heard some variant of this argument, either from a conservative pundit or even more likely, your parents. What may be surprising is that this scolding was courtesy of Hillary Clinton, senator for New York and (at the time of writing) the Democratic party's presidential front-runner.

We've got our work cut out for us. And Senator Clinton, or any other potential nominee, has their work cut out for them, too. After all, whoever hopes to win the nomination, let alone the presidency in 2008, is going to need the young-adult vote. Which means it's time for some reeducation on this issue. In Clinton's case, her accomplished twenty-something daughter Chelsea promptly phoned it in; for the rest of the country, it's time to start thinking differently.

Putting the clumsy remarks of the senator aside, I'm optimistic that more and more people are "getting it." Since *Strapped* was released in January 2006, there's been a flurry of reporting on the economic challenges facing today's young adults. Articles taking the position that this generation is just a bunch of spoiled, self-entitled whiners are harder and harder to come by. Instead, there's been a wave of news reports on college costs and the impact of student loan debt; on how soaring property values are delaying home ownership; how today's young workers are making less and facing higher costs.

And most importantly, I'm optimistic because the response of the under-35 crowd to the book has been incredible.

Over the last year I've traveled the country, speaking to audiences packed with young people thirsty for an empowering message about the economic challenges they confront. In Minneapolis, 250 people—not a gray hair in sight—packed the Varsity Theater for an event about the book. In Boston, over 175 crammed into a conference room at Jurys Hotel. From Denver to Durham, throngs of young adults showed up to get a different view about why it's gotten harder to get ahead—something other than the finger-wagging, condescending lectures and admonishments they've become accustomed to hearing. They've called into radio stations to share their stories and reinforce the argument that this isn't a personal problem. I've also been gratified by the number of parents who have e-mailed their thanks for providing a better understanding of what's happening to their adult children, and who have also called in to air their grievances about the enormous obstacles they think this generation faces.

I'm convinced that, if given the opportunity, young people will channel their personal frustrations into political action. Up until now, the only explanation given to young people about why they couldn't get ahead was because they were throwing their money away on $4-a-day latte habits, flat-screen televisions, expensive cars, and too many dinners out. For the majority of young people who don't imbibe overpriced coffee, own new cars, much less flat-screen

TVs, this advice is not only irrelevant to their lives, it's politically paralyzing. And so, when I talk to young people about how as a generation we've been raised to believe that our economic struggles are personal, not political, I see sparks light in their eyes and their heads nod.

Changing the discourse is a big first step. Now, it's time to kick the issue into the political arena. Because even though problems facing young people are gaining traction in the media, the political battle in Washington, D.C., is far from won. While it is now almost universally recognized that rising college tuition and student loan debt are serious problems, it still didn't stop the Republican-controlled Congress from cutting $12.7 billion in student loan aid—the largest single cut in the program's history. The changes, which raise the interest rate on Stafford loans and Parent Loans for Undergraduate Students (PLUS), took effect on July 1, 2006 and will cost the typical undergrad borrower thousands of extra dollars. It was a political decision largely assailed by the media and opposed ferociously by student advocacy groups. The bill passed the House in a 221–199 vote, with 207 Republicans and 14 Democrats voting for the bill. In response to the cuts, Representative George Miller (D-CA) and Senator Dick Durbin (D-IL) have introduced legislation that would cut the interest rates on subsidized college loans in half. As of press time, the bill was languishing in committee.

At the same time they're cutting student aid, congressional Republicans continue to push for more tax cuts—extending the breaks on capital gains and dividends that, along with spending on the war, have helped fuel the nation's soaring deficits. As I argue throughout the book, the diminished opportunities that young people face are the result of changing political priorities. The federal minimum wage hasn't been raised since 1997. The number of uninsured Americans—of which those under 30 are the largest group—continues to grow.

And the problems facing new parents in finding affordable child care is nowhere close to being on the political agenda.

And yet, as I said earlier, I remain optimistic. Why? Because I believe the tide is turning against the ultra-individualistic, greedy, and market-driven politics that have dominated the country for the last three decades. Americans—including young people—are growing wary of the tired mantra of personal responsibility, tax cuts, and small government. It's a paradigm that has fostered too much inequality, too little opportunity, and cultivated a culture of greed and selfishness most Americans find repulsive. As the country heads into the next presidential election, the declining opportunity and stalled life chances of today's young adults should be front and center in the national debate.

I'm doing whatever I can to kick these issues up the political food chain by meeting with policymakers and their staff to educate them about the issues raised in *Strapped*. I'll continue to write and speak out about the declining opportunities and diminished economic chances facing young people today. In the months leading up to the 2008 elections, I hope we'll see a renewed energy to organize young voters, and not just those on traditional college campuses. There's a latent, enormous voting bloc that's yet to be given attention—the 11 million students at community colleges all across the country. If we can energize this group, along with the traditional college students and young professionals, we can deliver a political message that can't be ignored.

If you're enraged or excited—or both—about taking the *Strapped* cause to the voting box, be sure to check out the expanded resource section in the back of the book. There's a step-by-step guide on how to get engaged, get organized, and get heard. You can also access this information on the book's website, **www.strappedthebook.com**.

The 2008 presidential election is our chance to demand a better future. So let's make good on a simple promise: "We're strapped and we vote."

Acknowledgments

There are many people I need to thank for their help with this book. First, I must thank all the young adults whose stories make this book come alive. I deeply appreciate their willingness to share their time and their experiences.

As a first-time book author, I was very fortunate to be in the hands of a superb editor, Gerry Howard. I thank him for his endless enthusiasm and brilliant editing. I must also thank my agent, Andrew Stuart, who championed this book from the start and sharpened the project along the way. I had two research assistants, both of whom worked tirelessly to help recruit and interview the young adults in this book—thank you, Heather Rogers and Sara Glassman. I also had the help of a wonderful researcher, John Summers, who tracked down endless statistics and studies, never giving up when the research seemed elusive. Finally, I owe thanks to three people who crunched reams of new data for the book: Danielle Gao, Gabriela Fighetti, and Javier Silva.

I am very fortunate to work at an organization with terrific people, and I thank them all for their support. I especially want to thank Miles Rapoport, president of Dēmos, who embraced this book and gave me the flexibility and time off needed to write it.

Thank you so much, Miles, for your enthusiasm and fostering of my talent. I also want to thank Heather McGhee and Javier Silva at Dēmos, who kept our program running smoothly and picked up the slack while I was busy writing. Another thanks to my colleague at Dēmos David Smith, who provided razor-sharp insight and feedback on several chapters. I owe enormous gratitude to my mentor, friend, and colleague at Dēmos, David Callahan. Thank you for convincing me I could write a book in the first place and for your patient guidance and support throughout the entire process.

I also need to thank my family and friends, whose support and enthusiasm kept me going while writing this book. A special thank-you to my parents for their endless support and for instilling in me the values of hard work and fairness that are central to this book. A big thanks to my lifelong best friend, Laura Parker. Your friendship has made the journey all the better and I can't imagine doing this without you. I'd also like to thank my father-in-law, Steven Fink, for his thoughtful comments on earlier drafts of the manuscript.

Finally, thanks to my husband, Stuart Fink, for his love, respect, support, and laughter—and the many creative touches, skillful edits, and hours he spent helping me with this book.

Introduction

[1] This analysis is based on data from the 1960 and 2000 censuses. Men are defined as "financially independent" if they are in the labor force; women are defined as "financially independent" if they have completed all transitions except employment in the labor force.

[2] Frank F. Furstenberg, Jr., Sheela Kennedy, Vonnie C. McCloyd, Ruben G. Rumbaut, and Richard A. Settersten, Jr., "Between Adolescence and Adulthood: Expectations About the Timing of Adulthood," Network on Transitions to Adulthood and Public Policy, Research Network Working Paper no. 1, July 29, 2003, available at http://www.transad.pop.upenn.edu/news/between.pdf.

[3] Sandy Baum and Marie O'Malley, "College on Credit: How Borrowers Perceive Their Education Debt: Results of the 2002 National Student Loan Survey," Nellie Mae Corporation, February 6, 2003, available at http://www.nelliemae.com/library/research_10.html.

[4] College Board, "Trends in College Pricing 2004," available at http://www.collegeboard.com/prod_downloads/press/cost04/041264TrendsPricing2004_FINAL.pdf.

[5] College Board, "Trends in Student Aid 2004," available at http://www

.collegeboard.com/prod_downloads/press/cost04/TrendsinStudent Aid2004.pdf.

[6] Lawrence E. Gladieux, "Low-Income Students and the Affordability of Higher Education," in Richard D. Kahlenberg, ed., *America's Untapped Resource: Low-Income Students in Higher Education* (New York: Century Foundation Press, 2004), p. 29.

[7] College Board, "Trends in College Pricing 2004."

[8] U.S. Department of Education, National Center for Education Statistics, *The Condition of Education 2004 and 2006.* 2006 edition available at http://nces.ed.gov/program/coe/2006/section2/table.asp?tableID=473.

[9] John M. Quigley and Steven Raphael, "Is Housing Unaffordable? Why Isn't It More Affordable?" *Journal of Economic Perspectives* 18, no. 1 (Winter 2004): 191–214.

[10] Amy Feldman, "Will It Last?" *Money,* June 2003, p. 82.

[11] Ann Crittenden, *The Price of Motherhood* (New York: Metropolitan Books, 2001), p. 94.

[12] Edith Rassell, Jared Bernstein, and Heather Boushey, "Step Up, Not Out: The Case for Raising the Federal Minimum Wage for Workers in Every State," Economic Policy Institute, 2001, available at http://www.epinet.org/content.cfm/issuebriefs_ib149.

[13] Robert Reich, *The Future of Success: Working and Living in the New Economy* (New York: Vintage Books, 2000), p. 78.

[14] "American Attitudes Toward Unions," based on a poll conducted by Peter D. Hart Research, Inc., for AFL–CIO, 1999, available at http://www.aflcio.org.

[15] U.S. Department of Commerce, Bureau of the Census. 1975 and 2003. *Current Population Survey.* Public Use Microdata File. Washington, D.C.: U.S. Government Printing Office (March).

[16] Jeffrey Jensen Arnett, "Learning to Stand Alone: The Contemporary American Transition to Adulthood in Cultural and Historical Context," *Human Development* 41 (1998):295–13.

[17] Furstenberg et al., "Between Adolescence and Adulthood," p. 9.

Chapter 1: Higher and Higher Education

[1] Advisory Committee on Student Financial Assistance, *Empty Promises: The Myth of College Access in America* (Washington, D.C.: Advisory Committee on Student Financial Assistance, June 2002).

[2] Robert Zemsky, "Labor, Markets, and Educational Restructuring," *Annals of the American Academy of Political and Social Science,* no. 559 (September 1998):77–90.

[3] Lawrence E. Gladieux, "Low-Income Students and the Affordability of Higher Education," in Richard D. Kahlenberg, ed., *America's Untapped Resource: Low-Income Students in Higher Education* (New York: Century Foundation Press, 2004), p. 22.

[4] Nicole Stoops, *Educational Attainment of the United States: 2003,* Current Population Reports P20-550 (Washington, D.C.: U.S. Census Bureau, June 2004).

[5] Tracey King and Ellyne Bannon, "The Burden of Borrowing: A Report on the Rising Rates of Student Loan Debt," State PIRGS' Higher Education Project, March 2002, available at http://www.studentpirgs .org/BurdenofBorrowing.pdf.

[6] Gladieux, "Low-Income Students," p. 29.

[7] U.S. Department of Education, Office of Postsecondary Education, "2002–2003 Title IV/Federal Pell Grant Program End-of-Year Report," table 3A, available online at http://www.ed.gov/finaid/prof/ resources/data/pell0203.pdf.

[8] College Board, "Trends in Student Aid 2003," available at http://www .collegeboard.com/prod_downloads/press/cost03/cb_trends_aid_ 2003.pdf.

[9] Robert Lowe, "The GI Bill Doesn't Vouch for Vouchers," *Rethinking Schools Online* 9, no. 4 (Summer 1995), available at http://www .rethinkingschools.org/special_reports/voucher_report/vgibill.shtml.

[10] College Board, "Trends in Student Aid 2003."

[11] The GI Bill cost $5.5 billion dollars per year over seven years; adjusting

for inflation brings the annual amount to $13 billion. See Paul Simon, "A GI Bill for Today," *Chronicle of Higher Education,* October 31, 2003, available at http://chronicle.com/free/v50/i10/10b01601.htm.

[12] Arthur Levein and Jana Nidiffer, *Beating the Odds: How the Poor Get to College* (San Francisco: Jossey-Bass, 1996), p. 35.

[13] College Board, "Trends in College Pricing 2003," available at http://www.collegeboard.com/prod_downloads/press/cost03/cb_trends_pricing 2003.pdf.

[14] College Board, "Trends in Student Aid 2003."

[15] Ibid.

[16] Thomas R. Wolanin, ed., *Reauthorizing the Higher Education Act: Issues and Options* (Washington, D.C.: Institute for Higher Education Policy, 2003).

[17] Advisory Committee on Student Financial Aid Assistance, *Access Denied: Restoring the Nation's Commitment to Equal Educational Opportunity* (Washington, D.C.: Advisory Committee on Student Financial Aid Assistance, 2001).

[18] Daniel J. Phelan, "Enrollment Policies and Student Access at Community Colleges," paper, Education Commission of the States Community College Policy Center (Denver, Colo.), 2000, available at http://www.communitycollegepolicy.org/pdf/3306_Phelan_policy.pdf.

[19] Sandy Baum and Marie O'Malley, "College on Credit: How Borrowers Perceive Their Education Debt: Results of the 2002 National Student Loan Survey," Nellie Mae Corporation, February 6, 2003, available at http://www.nelliemae.com/library/research_10.html.

[20] Jean Johnson and Ann Duffett, "Life After High School: Young People Talk about Their Hopes and Prospects," report (New York: Public Agenda 2005), available at http://www.publicagenda.org/research/pdfs/life_after_high_school_pdf.

[21] Baum and O'Malley, "College on Credit."

[22] Gary Hoachlander, Anna C. Sikora, and Laura Horn, "Community

College Students: Goals, Academic Preparation, and Outcomes," report (Washington, D.C.: U.S. Department of Education, National Center for Education Statistics, 2003).

[23] Richard J. Coley, "The American Community College Turns 100: A Look at Its Students, Programs and Prospects," Policy Information Report (Princeton, N.J.: Educational Testing Service, March 2000).

[24] Ibid., p. 20.

[25] U.S. Department of Education, National Center for Education Statistics, "Trends in Undergraduate Persistence and Completion," in *The Condition of Education 2004* (Washington, D.C.: U.S. Department of Education, 2004) and Richard J. Coley, "The American Community College Turns 100: A Look at Its Students, Programs and Prospects," Policy Information Report (Princeton, N.J.: Educational Testing Service, March 2000).

[26] Richard D. Kahlenberg, *America's Untapped Resource: Low-Income Students in Higher Education* (New York: Century Foundation Press, 2004), p. 2.

[27] See, for example, James T. Patterson, *America's Struggle Against Poverty in the Twentieth Century* (Cambridge, Mass.: Harvard University Press, 2000).

[28] Paul Simon, "A GI Bill for Today," *The Chronicle of Higher Education*, October 31, 2003, available at http://chronicle.com/free/v50/110/10b01601.htm (accessed March 15, 2005).

[29] Laurent Belsie, "A Stronger Link Between Degrees and Dollars," *Christian Science Monitor*, July 18, 2002.

[30] King and Bannon, "Burden of Borrowing."

[31] Nancy Hoffman, "College Credit in High School: Increasing College Attainment Rates for Underrepresented Students," *Change*, July–August 2003.

[32] Kahlenberg, *America's Untapped Resource*, p. 22.

[33] U.S. Department of Education, National Center for Education Statistics, "Trends in Undergraduate Persistence and Completion," in

The Condition of Education 2004 (Washington, D.C.: U.S. Department of Education, 2004). Available at http://nces.ed.gov//programs/coe/2004/pdf/19_2004.pdf.

[34] Kahlenberg, *America's Untapped Resource,* p. 22.

[35] U.S. Department of Education, National Center for Education Statistics, "Trends in Undergraduate Persistence and Completion," paper, 2004, available at http://nces.ed.gov/programs/coe/2004/pdf/19_2004.pdf.

[36] Anthony Carnevale and Stephen Rose, "Socio-Economic Status, Race/Ethnicity and Selective College Admissions," report (Washington, D.C.: Century Foundation, March 2003).

[37] Marianne Costantinou, "The Great Admissions Race," *San Francisco Chronicle Magazine,* August 10, 2003, p. 9.

[38] Prices quoted for the 2004 East Coast Tour on www.collegecampustours.com.

[39] Fredreka Schouten, "Getting In, with Some Help," *USA Today,* April 30, 2003, p. 8D.

[40] Ibid., citing the National Association for College Admission Counseling.

[41] Stacy Berg Dale and Alan B. Krueger, "Estimating the Payoff to Attending a More Selective College: An Application of Selection on Observables and Unobservables," National Bureau of Economic Research Working Paper Series no. 7322, August 1999.

[42] Carnevale and Rose, "Socio-Economic Status, Race/Ethnicity and Selective College Admissions."

[43] Dale and Krueger, "Estimating the Payoff."

[44] Donald Heller and Patricia Marin, eds., "Whom Should We Help? The Negative Social Consequences of Merit Aid Scholarships," August 23, 2002, report developed from research commissioned for the conference State Merit Aid Programs: College Access and Equity, December 8, 2001 (Cambridge, Mass.), available at http://www.civilrightsproject.harvard.edu/research/meritaid/fullreport.php.

[45] Susan Dynarski, "Hope for Whom? Financial Aid for the Middle Class and Its Impact on College Attendance," National Bureau of Economic Research Working Paper Series no. 7756 (Washington, D.C.: National Bureau of Economic Research, June 2000).

[46] Patrick T. Terenzini, Alberto F. Cabrera, and Elena M. Bernal, "Swimming Against the Tide: The Poor in American Higher Education," College Board Research Report no. 2001–1 (New York: College Board, 2001).

[47] Judith Glazer, "The Master's Degree: Tradition, Diversity, Innovation," ASHE-Eric Higher Education Research Report no. 6 (Washington, D.C.: Association for the Study of Higher Education, 1986).

[48] Clifton Conrad, Jennifer Grant Haworth, and Susan Bylard Millar, *A Silent Success: Master's Education in the United States* (Baltimore: Johns Hopkins University Press, 1993).

[49] U.S. Department of Education, National Center for Education Statistics, *Digest of Education Statistics 2003* (Washington, D.C.: Department of Education), table 249, available at http://nces.ed.gov//programs/digest/d03/tables/dt249.asp.

[50] Baum and O'Malley, "College on Credit."

[51] The statistics in this paragraph are taken from U.S. Department of Education, National Center for Education Statistics, *The Condition of Education 2003,* "Trends in Graduate/First—Professional Enrollments, Indicator 7" (Washington, D.C.: U.S. Department of Education, June 2003), available at http://nces.ed.gov/programs/coe/2003/pdf/07_2003.pdf.

[52] Catherine Millett, "How Undergraduate Loan Debt Affects Application and Enrollment in Graduate Degree or First Professional Schools," *Journal of Higher Education* 74, no. 4 (July–August 2003), pp. 386–427.

[53] Advisory Committee on Student Financial Assistance, *Empty Promises: The Myth of College Access in America* (Washington, D.C.: Advisory Committee on Student Financial Assistance, June 2002).

[54] Ibid.

[55] Population growth estimates from U.S. Census Bureau, "U.S. Interim

Projections by Age, Sex, Race and Hispanic Origin," http://www
.census.gov/ipc.www/usinterimproj/.

56 Advisory Committee on Student Financial Assistance, *Empty Promises,* 2002, available at www.ed.gov/about/bdscomm/list/acsfa/empty
promises.pdf.

Chapter 2: Paycheck Paralysis

1 Robert Reich, *The Future of Success: Working and Living in the New
Economy* (New York: Vintage Books, 2000), p. 78.

2 Jennifer Cheeseman Day and Eric C. Newburger, "The Big Payoff:
Educational Attainment and Synthetic Estimates of Work-Life Earnings" (Washington, D.C.: U.S. Census Bureau, July 2002).

3 U.S. Census Bureau, "Income, Poverty, and Health Insurance Coverage in the United States: 2003," table C2, "Health Insurance Coverage
by Age: 1987 to 2003." In 2003 there were over 8 million uninsured
adults aged 18 to 24 and over 10 million uninsured adults aged 25
to 34.

4 Kaiser Family Foundation, "Uninsured Workers in America," fact
sheet, July 2004, available at http://www.http://www.kff.org/unin
sured/upload/44470_1.pdf.

5 Kevin Quinn, Cathy Schoen, and Louisa Buatti, "On Their Own:
Young Adults Living without Health Insurance" (New York: Commonwealth Fund, May 2000), available at http://www.cmwf.org/
usr_doc/quinn_ya_391.pdf.

6 U.S. Census Bureau, "Income, Poverty, and Health Insurance Coverage
in the United States."

7 Sara R. Collins, Cathy Schoen, et al., "Rite of Passage? Why Young
Adults Become Uninsured and How New Policies Can Help" (New
York: Commonwealth Fund, May 2004), available at http://www
.cmwf.org/usr_doc/collins_ritepassage.pdf.

8 Employment Benefit Research Institute, "The Decline of Private

Sector Defined Benefit Promises and Annuity Payments: What Will It Mean?" *EBRI Notes* 25, no. 7 (July 2004).

[9] Economic Policy Institute, "Retirement Security: Facts at a Glance," February 2003, available at http://www.epinet.org/content.cfm/issueguides_retirement_facts (accessed August 27, 2004).

[10] United States General Accounting Office, "Contingent Workers Incomes and Benefits Tend to Lag Behind Those of the Rest of the Workforce," table 1, available at http://www.gao.gov/archive/2000/he00076.pdf.

[11] Stephen P. Bercham, "ASA's Annual Economic Analysis of the Staffing Industry," American Staffing Association, 2002, available at http://www.staffingtoday.net/staffstats/annualanalysis03.htm.

[12] Bureau of Labor Statistics, "Contingent and Alternative Employment Arrangements, February 2001," news release, May 24, 2001, available at http://www.bls.gov/news.release/conemp.nr0.htm.

[13] Arne L. Kallenberg, Barbara F. Reskin, and Ken Hudson, "Bad Jobs in America: Standard and Nonstandard Employment Relations and Job Quality in the United States," *American Sociological Review* 65 no. 2 (April 2000):256–78.

[14] Steven Hipple, "Contingent Work: Results from the Second Survey," *Monthly Labor Review,* November 1998, pp. 22–35.

[15] Bureau of Labor Statistics, "Contingent and Alternative Employment," table 2, 2001.

[16] Bureau of Labor Statistics, "Contingent and Alternative Employment Arrangements," table 10.

[17] Hipple, "Contingent Work."

[18] Ibid.

[19] Bureau of Labor Statistics, "Contingent and Alternative Employment Arrangements," table 6.

[20] Ibid., table 11.

[21] New York Department of Insurance, "Premium Rates for Standard

Individual Health Plans, May 2005," available at http://www.ins.state .ny.us/acrobat/newyork.pdf.

[22] Sara Horowitz and Stephanie Buchanan, "Educated, Employed and Uninsured: How Independent Workers Fall out of the Social Safety Net" (New York: Working Today, July 2004).

[23] Michelle Conlin, "For Gen X, It's Paradise Lost," *Business Week Online,* June 30, 2003.

[24] This statistic is widely acknowledged by labor economists and is cited in numerous articles on wage mobility of workers. See Robert Topel and Michael Ward, "Job Mobility and the Careers of Young Men," *Quarterly Journal of Economics* 107 (1992):439–79.

[25] See, for example, Kurt Schrammel, "Comparing the Labor Market Success of Young Adults from Two Generations," *Monthly Labor Review* 3–9 (February 1998); Annette Bernhardt, Martina Morris, Mark Handcock, and Marc Scott, "Trends in Job Instability and Wages for Young Adult Men," *Journal of Labor Economics* 17, no. 4 (October 1999):S65–S90; and Greg J. Duncan, Johanne Boisjoly, and Timothy Smeeding, "Economic Mobility of Young Workers in the 1970s and 1980s," *Demography* 33, no. 4 (November 1996):497–509.

[26] Bernhardt et al., "Trends in Job Instability and Wages for Young Adult Men."

[27] Heather Boushey and John Schmitt, "Hard Times in the New Millennium," report (Washington, D.C.: Center for Economic and Policy Research, November 2003), available at http://www.cepr.net/publications/state ofnationsyouth.pdf.

[28] Geoffrey Paulin and Brian Riordan, "Making It on Their Own: The Baby Boom Meets Generation X," *Monthly Labor Review,* February 1998, pp. 10–21.

[29] U.S. Department of Commerce, Bureau of the Census, 1975 and 2003. *Current Population Survey.* Public Use Microdata File. Washington, D.C. U.S. Government Printing Office (March).

[30] Schrammel, "Comparing Labor Market Success," p. 6.

[31] Ibid.

[32] Bureau of Labor Statistics, "Occupational Employment and Wages, May 2003," news release, April 30, 2004, available at http://www.bls .gov/news.release/archives/ocwage_04302004.pdf.

[33] Ibid., table 1, p. 12.

[34] Daniel E. Hecker, "Occupational Employment Projections to 2010," *Monthly Labor Review,* November 2001, pp. 57–84, available at http:// www.bls.gov/opub/mlr/2001/11/art4full.pdf.

[35] John F. Stinson, "Multiple Jobholding," *Monthly Labor Review,* March 1997, pp. 3–8.

[36] Families and Work Institute, "Generation and Gender in the Workplace," issue brief (New York: Families and Work Institute, October 2004), available at http://familiesandwork.org/eproducts/genand gender/pdf.

Chapter 3: Generation Debt

[1] Tamara Draut and Javier Silva, "Generation Broke: The Growth of Debt Among Young Americans," report (New York: D⁻ emos, 2004), available at http://www.demos-usa.org/pubs/Generation_Broke.pdf.

[2] Margaret Webb Pressler, "Swimming in a Sea of Debt," *Washington Post,* December 14, 2003.

[3] Thomas A. Durkin, "Credit Cards: Use and Consumer Attitudes: 1970–2000," *Federal Reserve Bulletin,* September 2000.

[4] Suze Orman, *The Money Book for the Young, Fabulous and Broke* (New York: Penguin, 2005), pp. 83–84.

[5] U.S. Department of Education, National Center for Education Statistics, "Debt Burden: A Comparison of 1992–93 and 1999–2000 Bachelor's Degree Recipients a Year After Graduating," report, p. 27, available at http://nces.ed.gov/pubsearch/pubsinfo .asp?pubid=2005170.

[6] College Board, *Trends in Student Aid 2003,* available at http://www.collegeboard.com/prod_downloads/press/cost03/cb_trends_aid_2003.pdf.

[7] U.S. Department of Education, National Center for Education Statistics, "Debt Burden: A Comparison of 1992–93 and 1999–2000 Bachelor's Degree Recipients a Year After Graduating," March 2005, p. 32, available at http://nces.ed.gov/pubs2005/2005170.pdf.

[8] Sandy Baum and Marie O'Malley, "College on Credit: How Borrowers Perceive Their Education Debt. Results of the 2002 National Student Loan Survey," Nellie Mae Corporation, February 6, 2003.

[9] Ibid.

[10] Ibid.

[11] Robert B. Avery, Gregory E. Elliehausen, and Glenn B. Canner, "Survey of Consumer Finances, 1983: A Second Report," *Federal Reserve Bulletin,* December 1984, available at http://www.federalreserve.gov/pubs/oss/oss2/83/bull1284.pdf.

[12] Ana M. Aizcorbe, Arthur B. Kennickell, and Kevin B. Moore, "Recent Changes in U.S. Family Finances: Evidence for the 1998 and 2001 Survey of Consumer Finances," *Federal Reserve Bulletin,* January 2003, available at http://www.federalreserve.gov/pubs/oss/oss2/2001/bull0103.pdf.

[13] For a good review of free-market ideology and its promise to enhance democracy, see Thomas Frank, *One Market Under God: Extreme Capitalism, Market Populism, and the End of Economic Democracy* (New York: Knopf, 2001).

[14] Vincent D. Rougeau, "Rediscovering Usury: An Argument for Legal Controls on Credit Card Interest Rates," *University of Colorado Law Review,* Winter 1996.

[15] Ibid.

[16] Lucy Lazarony, "States with Credit Card Caps," Bankrate.com,

March 20, 2002, http://www.bankrate.com/brm/news/cc/2002 0320b.asp.

[17] "Card Fees 2003," Cardweb.com, http://www.cardweb.com/cardtrak/news/2003/july/18a.html.

[18] Robert D. Manning, *Credit Card Nation: The Consequences of America's Addiction to Credit* (New York: Basic Books, 2000), pp. 12–13. Figures adjusted to 1999 dollars.

[19] In 2005, the House voted 302–126 to pass the bankruptcy "reform" legislation and the Senate passed it 74–25. The bill was signed into law by President Bush in April 2005.

[20] Manning, *Credit Card Nation,* and *Frontline:* "The Secret History of the Credit Card," *Frontline,* broadcast on PBS, March 17, 2005; see also the graph at http://www.pbs.org/wghb/pages/frontline/shows/credit/more/marketshare.html.

[21] See Federal Deposit Insurance Corporation (FDIC), "Bank Trends— The Effect of Consumer Interest Rate Deregulation on Credit Card Volumes, Charge-Offs, and the Personal Bankruptcy Rate," May 1998, available at http://www.fdic.gov/bank/analytical/bank/bt_9805.html; see also David A. Moss and Johnson A. Gibbs, "The Rise of Consumer Bankruptcy: Evolution, Revolution or Both?" *National Conference of Bankruptcy Judges,* 1999, p. 13.

[22] See Rougeau, "Rediscovering Usury."

[23] Federal Reserve, "Federal Funds Rate, Historical Data," released April 28, 2003, available at http://www.federalreserve.gov/releases/h15/data.htm.

[24] U.S. Census Bureau, *Statistical Abstract of the United States: 2002* (Washington, D.C.: U.S. Census Bureau, 2003), p. 728.

[25] Patrick McGeehan, "Soaring Interest Compounds Credit Card Pain for Millions," *New York Times,* November 21, 2004.

[26] Nellie Mae Corporation, "Undergraduate Students and Credit Cards:

An Analysis of Usage Rates and Trends," April 2002, available at http://www.nelliemae.com/library/ccstudy_2001.pdf.

27 "Virginia Colleges Make Policies Against Credit-Card Vendors," *Credit Cards Magazine,* December 30, 2003.

28 U.S. General Accounting Office, "Consumer Finance: College Students and Credit Cards" (GAO–01–773), report to congressional requesters, June 2001, p. 53, available at http://www.gao.gov/new .items/d01773.pdf.

29 Cheryl Hystad and Brad Heavner, *Graduating into Debt: Credit Card Marketing on Maryland College Campuses* (Rockville, Md.: Maryland Public Interest Research Group, 2004).

30 The absolute figures (for example, the average household reported $5,219 in credit card debt) are based on data that consumers reported about themselves in the *Survey of Consumer Finances.* Aggregate data on outstanding revolving credit reported by the Federal Reserve estimates the average credit card debt per indebted household at about $12,000—nearly three times more than the self-reported amount. See also Robert Manning, *Credit Card Nation,* p. 319.

31 Teresa A. Sullivan, Deborah Thorne, and Elizabeth Warren, "Young, Old, and in Between: Who Files for Bankruptcy?" *Norton Bankruptcy Law Advisor,* no. 9A, September 2001, pp. 1–12.

32 Milt Marquis, "What's Behind the Low US Personal Saving Rate?" Federal Reserve Bank of San Francisco, *Economic Letter,* Number 2002–09, March 29, 2002, and U.S. Department of Commerce, Bureau of Economic Analysis, http://www.bea.gov/briefrm/saving.htm.

33 Federal Reserve Board, *Survey of Consumer Finances,* 1989 to 2004. Expanded tables based on public data provided online at http://www. federalreserve.gov/pubs/oss/oss2/2004/scf2004home.html.

34 Ibid.

Chapter 4: The High Cost of Putting a Roof over Your Head

[1] U.S. Census Bureau, "Table AD–1, Young Adults Living at Home, 1960 to Present," September 15, 2004, available at http://www.census.gov/population/socdemo/hh-fam/tabAD-1.pdf.

[2] Dara Duguay, "For New Graduates: How to Avoid Returning to the Nest," *Consumers Research Magazine,* March 1, 2003, p. 19.

[3] Ibid.

[4] John M. Quigley and Steven Raphael, "Is Housing Unaffordable? Why Isn't It More Affordable?" *Journal of Economic Perspectives* 18, no. 1 (Winter 2004):191–214.

[5] Rachel S. Franklin, "Migration of the Young, Single and College Educated: 1995 to 2000," Census 2000 Special Report no. CENSR–12 (Washington, D.C.: U.S. Census Bureau, November 2003).

[6] William H. Frey, "Generational Pull," *American Demographics,* May 2004, pp. 18–19.

[7] Ibid.

[8] Ibid.

[9] Christopher J. Mayer and Gary V. Englehardt, "Gifts, Down Payments, and Housing Affordability," *Journal of Housing Research* 7, no. 1 (1996):59–77.

[10] Author's calculations, using U.S. Census Data, 1970–2000, provided by Integrated Public Use Microdata Series (http://www.ipums.org). Steven Ruggles, Matthew Sobek, Trent Alexander, Catherine A. Fitch, Ronald Goeken, Patricia Kelly Hall, Miriam King, and Chad Ronnander, *Integrated Public Use Microdata Series: Version 3.0* [Machine-readable database]. Minneapolis: Minnesota Population Center [producer and distributor], 2004.

[11] Author's calculations, based on U.S. Census Data, 1970–2000, Integrated Public Use Microdata Series (http://www.ipums.org). Ruggles et al., *Integrated Public Use Microdata Series: Version 3.0.*

[12] Quigley and Raphael, "Is Housing Unaffordable?"

[13] Chicago Title Insurance Company, "Who's Buying Homes in America?" (Chicago: Chicago Title Insurance Co., 1999), available at https://www.ctic.com/homesurvey/home.pdf.

[14] Walter Molony, public affairs associate at the National Association of Realtors, personal communication, August 17, 2004.

[15] James T. Patterson, "Grand Expectations: The United States, 1945–1974" (New York: Oxford University Press, 1996), p. 72.

[16] Ibid., p. 72.

[17] Ibid., p. 38.

[18] Ibid., p. 75.

[19] Josh Barbanel, "Behind the Region's Run-up in Prices," *New York Times,* July 13, 2003.

[20] Online search for all listings in Levittown, New York, conducted on www.realtor.com on April 9, 2005.

[21] Patterson, "Grand Expectations," p. 73.

[22] According to the Census Bureau, the median family income for households aged 25 to 34 in 2001 dollars was $20,151 in 1949 and $46,272 in 2001. See U.S. Census Bureau, "Historical Income Tables—Families," table F–7, "Type of Family (All Races) by Median and Mean Income: 1947 to 2001," available at http://www.census.gov/hhes/income/histinc/f 07.html.

[23] U.S. Census Bureau, *Housing Vacancies and Homeownership* (CPS/HVS), Table 12. "Household Estimates for the United States, by Age of Householder: 1982 to Present." Available at http://www.census.gov/hhes/www/housing/hvs/historic/histt12.html.

[24] Ibid.

[25] Lewis M. Segal and Daniel G. Sullivan, "Trends in Homeownership: Race, Demographics, and Income," *Economic Perspectives* 22, no. 2 (1998):53.

[26] Barbanel, "Behind the Region's Run-Up in Prices."

[27] Amy Feldman, "Will It Last? We Like to Think Our Homes Are Safe Havens, but That Doesn't Mean the Boom Will Go On Forever," *Money,* June 2003.

[28] Ibid.

[29] Patrick Healy, "Young Adults Call Long Island a Fine Place to Grow Up, and Leave," *New York Times,* February 21, 2004.

[30] Rauch Foundation, "Room for Growth: Long Island's Changing Economy," report, October 23, 2003, p. 2, available at http://www.long islandindex.org/fileadmin/reports/Economic_Development_Poll_ Report.pdf.

[31] Diane E. Lewis, "Fearing Brain Drain Reports Say Boston Area Needs to Retain More Grads," *Boston Globe,* October 22, 2003.

[32] Jason P. Schacter, "Geographical Mobility: 2002 to 2003," Current Population Reports (Washington: U.S. Census Bureau, March 2004), available at http://www.census.gov/prod/2004pubs/p20-549.pdf.

[33] Erica Noonan, "Through the Roof," *Boston Globe,* May 9, 2002.

[34] Julissa McKinnon, "Soaring House Prices Lock Families Out of Bay Area," *Oakland Tribune,* February 4, 2002.

[35] David Myron, "Home Equity Debt Soars," *American Demographics,* November 1, 2004, p. 9.

[36] Author's calculations from U.S. Census Data, 1970–2000, provided by Integrated Public Use Microdata Series (http://www.ipums.org). Ruggles et al., *Integrated Public Use Microdata Series: Version 3.0.*

[37] Peter Francese, "America's Gray Area Dilemma," *American Demographics,* July–August 2004, pp. 40–41.

[38] Michael Jonas, "Anti-Family Values," *CommonWealth,* Spring 2002.

[39] Charisse Jones, "Housing Doors Close on Parents," *USA Today,* May 6, 2004.

[40] The account of the town planning board in Plymouth, Massachusetts, is based on Michael Jonas, "Anti-Family Values," *CommonWealth,* Spring 2002.

Chapter 5: And Baby Makes Broke

[1] Catalina Amuedo-Dorantes and Jean Kimmel, "The Motherhood Wage Gap for Women in the United States: The Importance of College and Fertility Delay," *Review of Economics of the Household* 3, no. 1 (2005):17–48.

[2] The Financial Guide (website), "Becoming a Parent: The Financial Considerations," http://www.gofso.com/Premium/LE/02_le_bp/fg/fg-parent.html.

[3] Estimates are for a middle-income husband-wife couple with before-tax income between $40,700 and $68,400, or averaging $54,100. See Mark Lino, *Expenditures on Children by Families, 2003,* publication no. 1528–2003 (Washington, D.C.: U.S. Department of Agriculture, Center for Nutrition Policy and Promotion, 2003), available at http://www.usda.gov/cnpp/Crc/Crc2000.pdf.

[4] Elizabeth Warren and Amelia Warren Tyagi, *The Two-Income Trap: Why Middle-Class Mothers and Fathers Are Going Broke* (New York: Basic Books, 2004), pp. 6–7.

[5] Lino, *Expenditures on Children by Families, 2000.*

[6] Columbia University, The Clearinghouse on International Developments in Child, Youth and Family Policies, "Mother's Day: More Than Candy and Flowers, Working Parents Need Paid Time Off," Issue Brief, Spring 2002, available at http://www.childpolicy.org/issuebrief/issuebrief5.htm.

[7] Kenneth R. Sheets, "A Bevy of Bills Would Sock Firms for Parental Leave, Even Damages," *U.S. News and World Report,* May 21, 1990.

[8] *The MacNeil/Lehrer NewsHour,* November 11, 1991, transcript no. 4201, available from LexisNexis.

[9] Sheila B. Kamerman, "Parental Leave Policies: An Essential Ingredient in Early Childhood Education and Care Policies," *Social Policy Report* 14, no. 2 (2000), pp. 3–15.

[10] Ibid.

[11] Isaac Shapiro and Joel Friedman, "Tax Returns: A Comprehensive Assessment of the Bush Administration's Record on Cutting Taxes" (Washington, D.C.: Center on Budget and Policy Priorities, April 23, 2004), available at http://www.cbpp.org/4–14–04taxsum.htm.

[12] Kamerman, "Parental Leave Policies."

[13] According to the Census Bureau, in 2002 there were 4,302,000 families with children up to age 5, and of these 2,830,000, or 66 percent, were households headed by someone aged 34 or under. See U.S. Census Bureau, "Table F–1: Family Households, by Type, Age of Own Children, Age of Family Members, and Age, Race and Hispanic Origin of Householder: 2003," at http://www.census.gov/population/socdem/hh-fam/cps2003/tabF1–all–1.pdf.

[14] Heather Boushey, "Who Cares? The Child Care Choices of Working Mothers" (Washington, D.C.: Center for Economic and Policy Research), May 6, 2003.

[15] Linda Giannarelli and James Barsimantov, "Child Care Expenses of America's Families," Occasional Paper no. 40 (Washington, D.C.: Urban Institute, December 2000).

[16] U.S. Census Bureau, "Who's Minding the Kids? Child Care Arrangements: Spring 1997," Current Population Reports (Washington, D.C.: U.S. Census Bureau, July 2002), available at http://www.census.gov/prod/2002pubs/p70–86.pdf.

[17] Karen Shulman and Heather Blank, "Child Care Assistance Policies 2001–2004: Families Struggling to Move Forward, States Moving Backward" (Washington, D.C.: National Women's Law Center, September 2004), available at http://www.nwlc.org/pdf/childcaresubsidy finalreport.pdf.

[18] Suzanne W. Helburn and Barbara R. Bergmann, *America's Child Care Problem* (New York: Palgrave, 2002), and Jessica Brauner, Bonnie Gordic, and Edward Zigler, "Putting the Child Back into Child Care:

Combining Care and Education for Children Ages 3–5," *Social Policy Report* 18, no. 3 (2004).

19 Center for the Child Care Workforce, "Current Data on Child Care Salaries and Benefits in the United States, 2002 Edition" (Washington, D.C.: Center for the Child Care Workforce, 2004).

20 Ewing Marion Kauffman Foundation, "Families Pay More for Early Education Than for College," *Financing Child Care,* Winter 2002, p. 4.

21 Children's Defense Fund, "Good Child Care Assistance Policies Help Low-income Working Families Afford Quality Care and Help Children Succeed," Key Facts (Washington, D.C.: Children's Defense Fund, 2003).

22 Helburn and Bergmann, *America's Child Care Problem,* p. 22.

23 Children's Defense Fund, "Good Child Care Assistance Policies."

24 Helen Blank, "Taking Care of Children," *NCJW Journal* 25, no. 2 (Summer 2002):16.

25 Shulman and Blank, "Child Care Assistance Policies 2001–2004."

26 Ibid. Also, see Table 2 on page 104.

27 Boushey, "Who Cares?"

28 Children's Defense Fund, "Head Start Basics 2005" (Washington, D.C.: Children's Defense Fund), 2005, available at http://www.childrens defense.org/earlychildhood/headstart/headstartbasics2005.pdf.

29 Committee for Economic Development, "Preschool for All: Investing in a Productive and Just Society" (a statement by the Research and Policy Committee), 2002, http://www.ced.org/docs/report/report_preschool.pdf.

30 Jessica Brauner et al., "Putting the Child Back into Child Care, pp. 3–15.

31 Helburn and Bergmann, *America's Child Care Problem,* p. 163.

32 Marc Ferris, "Someone to Watch over Baby," *New York Times,* March 16, 2003.

[33] For a complete discussion on child care regulations, see Helburn and Bergmann, *America's Child Care Problem,* pp. 123–58.

[34] Pamela Paul, *The Starter Marriage and the Future of Matrimony* (New York: Villard), 2002, p. xiv.

[35] Laura DeMarco, "Generation X Parents Outshine Baby Boomers," *Cleveland Plain Dealer,* September 6, 2004.

[36] Families and Work Institute, "Generation and Gender in the Workplace," Issue Brief (New York: Families and Work Institute, October 2004), available at http://familiesandwork.org/eproducts/genandgender.pdf.

[37] Radcliffe Public Policy Center and Harris Interactive, Inc., "Life's Work: Generational Attitudes Toward Work and Life Integration" (Cambridge: Radcliffe Institute for Advanced Study, 2000), available at http://www.radcliffe.edu/research/pubpol/lifeswork.pdf.

[38] U.S. Census Bureau, "Fertility of American Women: June 2002," Current Population Reports (Washington, D.C.: U.S. Census Bureau, October 2003), available at http://www.census.gov/prod/2003pubs/p20-548.pdf.

[39] DeMarco, "Generation X Parents Outshine Baby Boomers."

[40] U.S. Census Bureau, "Children's Living Arrangements and Characteristics: March 2002," Current Population Reports (Washington, D.C.: U.S. Census Bureau, June 2003), available at http://www.census.gov/prod/2003pubs/p20-547.pdf.

[41] Vicky Lovell, "No Time to Be Sick: Why Everyone Suffers When Workers Don't Have Paid Sick Leave" (Washington, D.C.: Institute for Women's Policy Research, 2004), available at http://www.iwpr.org/pdf/B242.pdf.

[42] Virginia M. Freid, Dianne M. Makuc, and Ronica N. Rooks, "Ambulatory Heath Care Visits by Children: Principal Diagnosis and Place of Visit," DHHS Publication no. 98–1798 (Hyattsville, Md.: U.S. Department of Health and Human Services, 1998).

[43] Lovell, "No Time to Be Sick."

Chapter 6: *Without a Fight: Explaining Young Adults' Political Retreat*

[1] Ronald Reagan, First Inaugural Address, January 20, 1981, available at http://www.reaganfoundation.org/speeches/speech.asp?spid=6.

[2] Darren K. Carlson, "Ideological Crossroads: Gen X Marks the Spot (Xers Turning More Conservative as They Age; Gen Y Too)," Gallup Tuesday Briefing, September 2, 2003.

[3] Jack Dennis and Diana Owen, "The Partisanship Puzzle: Identification and Attitudes of Generation X," in Stephen C. Craig and Stephen Earl Bennett, eds., *After the Boom: The Politics of Generation X* (Lanham, Md.: Rowman & Littlefield, 1997), p. 48.

[4] Center for Information and Research and Civic Learning and Engagement (CIRCLE), "Youth Turnout up Sharply in 2004," press release, November 3, 2004.

[5] Ibid.

[6] Stephen C. Craig and Angela C. Halfacre, "Political Issues and Political Choice: Belief Systems, Generations, and the Potential for Realignment in American Politics," in Craig and Bennett, *After the Boom,* p. 74.

[7] Diana Owen, "Mixed Signals: Generation X's Attitudes Toward the Political System," in Craig and Bennett, *After the Boom,* p. 81.

[8] *Washington Post,* Kaiser Family Foundation, Harvard University, "A Generational Look at the Public: Politics and Policy," October 2003, telephone survey of a nationally representative sample of 2,886 randomly selected individuals, available at http://www.kff.org/Kaiserpdls/32B index.cfm.

[9] Public Agenda, "Childcare: Bills and Proposals," poll of 815 individuals with children under the age of 5, 2000, http://www.publicagenda.com/issues/major_proposals_detail2.cfm?issue_type=childcare&proposal_graphic=majprochilduniversal.jpg.

[10] Ibid.

[11] Craig and Halfacre, "Political Issues and Political Choice," p. 80.

[12] Scott Keeter, Cliff Zukin, Molly Andolina, Krista Jenkins, "The Civic and Political Health of the Nation: A Generational Portrait," report of a national telephone survey of 3,246 respondents undertaken for the Center for Information and Research and Civic Learning and Engagement (CIRCLE) (September 19, 2002), pp. 15–16, available at http://www.civicyouth.org/research/products/youth_index.htm.

[13] Ibid., "Questionnaires and Complete Tabulations," available at http://www.civicyouth.org/research/products/toplines.pdf.

[14] Robert D. Putnam, *Bowling Alone: The Collapse and Revival of American Community* (New York: Simon & Schuster, 2000), p. 36.

[15] Keeter et al., "Civic and Political Health of the Nation," p. 39 (http://www.civicyouth.org/research/products/Civic_Political_ Health.pdf).

[16] National League of Cities, "The American Dream in 2004: A Survey of the American People" (Washington, D.C.: National League of Cities, September 2004), available at http://www.nlc.org/content/Files/RMPamdream04srvyofampeoplesrvy. pdf.

[17] Eric M. Uslaner, "Divided Citizens: How Inequality Undermines Trust in America," working paper (New York: Dēmos, May 2004), available at http://www.demos-usa.org/pubs/Divided%20Citizens,%206.3.04.pdf.

[18] Ted Halstead, "A Politics for Generation X," *The Atlantic Monthly*, August 31, 1999.

[19] Center for Information and Research on Civic Learning and Engagement (CIRCLE), "The 2004 Presidential Election and Young Voters," October 28, 2004.

[20] Center for Information and Research and Civic Learning and Engagement (CIRCLE), "Youth Voting in the 2004 Election," report, November 8, 2004, p. 2.

[21] Center for Information and Research and Civic Learning and Engagement (CIRCLE), "Youth Turnout up Sharply in 2004."

[22] Robert Putnam, *Bowling Alone*, p. 256.

[23] Peter Levine and Mark Hugo Lopez, "Youth Turnout Has Declined by Any Measure," Center for Information and Research on Civic Learning and Engagement (CIRCLE), September 2002.

[24] Mark Hugo Lopez and Carrie Donavan, "Youth and Adult Voter Turnout from 1972–2002," Center for Information and Research on Civic Learning and Engagement (CIRCLE), undated fact sheet.

[25] Levine and Lopez, "Youth Turnout."

[26] Ibid.

[27] Putnam, *Bowling Alone,* pp. 38–40.

[28] Keeter et al., "Civic and Political Health of the Nation," p. 20.

[29] For more information about this theory, see Neil Howe and William Strauss, *Millennials Rising: The Next Great Generation* (New York: Vintage Books, 2000), and William Strauss and Neil Howe, *The Fourth Turning: What the Cycles of History Tell Us About America's Next Rendezvous with Destiny* (New York: Broadway Books, 1997).

[30] Michael DeCourcy Hinds, "Youth Vote 2000: They'd Rather Volunteer," *Carnegie Reporter* 1, no. 2 (Spring 2001), available at http://www.carnegie.org/reporter/02/vote2000/index.html.

[31] Keeter et al., "Civic and Political Health of the Nation," p. 19.

[32] Hinds, "Youth Vote 2000."

[33] Keeter et al., "Civic and Political Health of the Nation," p. 18.

[34] Jason Furman, William G. Gale, and Peter R. Orszag, "Would Borrowing $2 Trillion for Individual Accounts Eliminate $10 Trillion in Social Security Liabilities?" (Washington, D.C.: Center on Budget and Policy Priorities, December 13, 2004), available at http://www.cbpp.org/12-13-04socsec.htm.

Chapter 7: Changing Course: An Agenda for Reform

[1] The commission's final report, "Making College Affordable Again," was released in February 1993. The report identified specific policy

concerns, which led to the formulation of policy recommendations, including the Student's Total Education Package (STEP). The commission's full report is available online at http://www.ihep.org/ Pubs/PDF/makingcollegeaffordable.pdf.

[2] See Amanda Sharkey, "Paying for Postsecondary Education: An Issue Brief on College Costs and Financial Aid" (Washington, D.C.: Center for American Progress, March 2005). According to Sharkey, Senate bill 2360, the Nontraditional Student Success Act, introduced by Sen. Hillary Clinton (D-New York) on April 29, 2004, would increase the maximum authorized Pell Grant to $11,600 by 2010, and makes other recommendations focused on nontraditional students. It was read twice and referred to the Committee on Finance.

[3] Institute for College Access and Success, "Student Loan Costs Rise Despite New Law," briefing paper, March 15, 2005, available at http:// ticas.org/ticas_d/2005_03_15_TICAS_Brief.pdf.

[4] Committee on Education and the Workforce, Democratic committee staff, "Bipartisan Student Loan Bill Would Boost Funding for College Scholarships by $12 Billion Without Costing Taxpayers a Dime, Says CBO," news release, January 12, 2005, available at http://edworkforce .house.gov/democrats/releases/rel11205b.html.

[5] *Department of Education PART Assessments,* 2004. Available at http:// www.whitehouse.gov/omb/budget/fy2005/pma/education.pdf.

[6] See Sharkey, "Paying for Postsecondary Education." According to Sharkey, Rep. Thomas Petri (R-Wisconsin) and Rep. George Miller (D-California) have introduced the Direct Loan Reward Act, which would establish incentives for colleges to switch to the Direct Loan Program by offering to let them keep half of the savings for their use in financial aid programs. The bipartisan Student Aid Reward Act, introduced by Rep. Petri, Rep. Miller, Sen. Edward Kennedy (D-Massachusetts), and Sen. Gordon Smith (R-Oregon), asks the Secretary of Education to determine which student loan program is less

expensive, and then provides additional scholarship money to schools that adopt the cheaper loan program.

[7] David Callahan, Tamara Draut, and Javier Silva, *Millions to the Middle: Three Strategies to Grow the Middle Class* (New York: Demos, 2004). Available at http://www.demos-usa.org/pubs/millions_web.pdf.

[8] Daniel Gursky, "From Para to Teacher," *American Teacher,* May–June 2000.

[9] Service Employees International Union, "Better Schools, Stronger Communities: The Paraeducator Career Ladder," available at www .seiu.org/public/education/ladder.cfm.

[10] Two examples are the Teacher Track Project (TTP) at California State University-Fullerton and the Milwaukee Pathways to Teaching Careers Program at Alverno College and the University of Wisconsin-Milwaukee. See Recruiting New Teachers, Inc. (the National Teacher Recruitment Clearinghouse), "Paraeducator Program Profiles," http:// www.rnt.org/channels/clearinghouse/audience/paraeducators/1d4_ para_paraprofprogs.htm.

[11] Kerri Rossi, "Addressing Career Change Barriers for Rhode Island Teacher Assistants," *Sherlock Center Research Brief* 3, no. 1 (Winter 2005).

[12] For more information on the career lattice, see Council for Adult and Experimental Learning, "CAEL/DOL Healthcare Lattice Program," http://www.cael.org/healthcare.htm.

[13] See Service Employees International Union and the Shirley Ware Education Center, "The Career Ladder Mapping Project," December 2002, http://www.seiu399.org/documents/swec/CareerLadder MappingProject. pdf.

[14] John Logan, "Consultants, Lawyers, and the 'Union Free' Movement in the USA Since the 1970s," *Industrial Relations Journal* 33, no. 3 (2002), pp. 197–214.

[15] Corporation for Enterprise Development, "Hidden in Plain Sight:

A Look at the $335 Billion Federal Asset-Building Budget," report (Washington, D.C.: Corporation for Enterprise Development, 2004), available at http://www.cfed.org/publications/Hidden%20in%20Plain %20Sight%20Summary.pdf.

[16] Ibid., pp. 24–25.

[17] Dean Baker and David Rosnick, "Basic Facts on Social Security and Bush's Privatization Plan" (Washington, D.C.: Center for Economic and Policy Research, March 2005), available at http://www.cepr.net/ publications/facts_social_security.htm.

[18] Michael Calabrese, "Retirement Security: The Need for Universal Savings Accounts," presentation to ERISA (Employment Retirement Income Security Act) Advisory Council, U.S. Department of Labor Working Group on Pension Coverage, Participation and Benefits, Washington, D.C. (June 11, 2001), available at http://www.newamer-ica.net/Download_Docs/pdfs/Doc_File_67_1.pdf.

[19] See for example, Michael Calabrese, "Retirement Security," and Gene Sperling, "New Ways of Saving," *New York Times,* November 18, 2002, available at http://www.americanprogress.org/site/pp.asp? =biJRJ8OVF&b=14084; U.S. House Democratic Policy Committee, "Universal Retirement Savings Accounts: Giving People Control over Their Savings," February 14, 2002, available at http://www.american benefitscouncil.org/documents/universal_retirement_plan.pdf; Chris Edwards and Ernest Christian, "Turning Roth IRAs into Universal Savings Accounts," December 10, 2002, available at http://www.cato .org/dailys/12-10-02.html.

[20] Patrick McGeehan, "Soaring Interest Compounds Credit Card Pain for Millions," *New York Times,* November 21, 2004.

[21] Committee for Economic Development, Research and Policy Committee, *Preschool for All: Investing in a Productive and Just Society,* 2002, available at http://www.ced.org/docs/summary/summary_preschool .pdf.

22 See Suzanne W. Helburn and Barbara R. Bergmann, *America's Child Care Problem* (New York: Palgrave, 2002), and Committee for Economic Development, Research and Policy Committee, *Preschool for All*.

23 Helburn and Bergmann, *America's Child Care Problem*, p. 11.

24 Kevin Finneran, "Roundtable: Infant Child Care and Development," *Issues in Science and Technology* 13 (Summer 1997):72–78.

25 For example, Helburn and Bergmann, *America's Child Care Problem*, outline a comprehensive system in which families pay a co-payment based on family income. They propose a system in which the states provide direct subsidies to providers to cover the balance of the family co-payment. Professor Edward Zigler of Yale University proposes a program called "Schools for the 21st Century" whereby full-day, year-round care for 3-, 4-, and 5-year-olds would be made available through the public school system.

26 See www.familyinitiative.org for more information on the campaign.

27 Matthew Miller, *The 2% Solution: Fixing America's Problems in Ways Liberals and Conservatives Can Love* (New York: Public Affairs, 2003), p. xii.

Civics 101—The Guide to Getting Engaged, Getting Involved, and Getting Heard

To find out who represents you in Congress and to register to vote:
Visit **www.congress.org**.

In less than a minute, you can become a registered voter and learn who represents you in Congress. If you've already registered to vote and have moved since the last election, you need to update your registration. You can do that online, too. Once you know who represents you in the House and the Senate, drop them an e-mail and let them know what's on your mind. Then stay on top of them when important legislation comes up (see below).

To learn more about the issues:

Here are just a handful of websites from great organizations that make it easy to stay on top of the news and track what's happening on the issues you care passionately about. Most have e-mail alerts and news briefs that you can sign up to receive on a regular basis, all delivered straight to your inbox. This isn't the end-all, be-all list, these are just a few sites that I find helpful and easy to navigate.

Dēmos—www.demos.org

A bit of disclosure: I am the director of the economic opportunity program at Dēmos, a nonprofit, nonpartisan policy organization that works to expand economic opportunity, strengthen democracy, and revitalize the role of the public sector in helping achieve these goals. Check out the site dedicated to the issues facing young people to get the low-down on what's happening in Congress and across the country on issues affecting this generation.

18to35—www.18to35.org

A nonprofit, nonpartisan policy organization dedicated to engaging young adults in the political process. Check out their site for fact sheets, poll data, and basic information about the economic issues facing young adults.

Center for American Progress—www.americanprogress.org

A one-stop source for information on domestic and foreign policy and a political analysis of the daily news. The Center is a nonprofit, nonpartisan policy organization that promotes progressive ideas for a strong, just, and free America. Sign up for *The Progress Report*, a daily e-mail deconstructing the news and the important issues facing the nation.

Campus Progress—www.campusprogress.org

Still in college? Be sure to hook up with Campus Progress. It's an effort to strengthen progressive voices on college and university campuses nationwide; counter the growing influence of right-wing groups on campus; and empower new generations of progressive leaders.

National Partnership for Women & Families— www.nationalpartnership.org

Struggling to balance work and family? Frustrated by the lack of affordable child care? The National Partnership for Women & Families is a nonprofit, nonpartisan organization that uses public education and advocacy to promote fairness in the workplace, quality health care, and policies that help women and men meet the dual demands of work and family. Another site for information on child care and family leave policies is Legal Momentum at **www.legalmomentum.org**.

Project on Student Debt—www.projectonstudentdebt.org

The Project on Student Debt works to increase public understanding about the new reliance on borrowing to pay for college and what it means for us and our families. Visit their site to get involved in changing the student aid system. Also check out the State PIRGs' Higher Education Project at **http://pirg.org/highered/index.html**.

Rock the Vote—www.rockthevote.com

Rock the Vote is a nonprofit, nonpartisan organization that mobilizes young people to create positive social and political change in their lives and communities. Visit the site to get registered to vote, join the campaign to save social security, and sign up for e-mail alerts.

United Professionals—www.unitedprofessionals.com

UP is a nonprofit, nonpartisan membership organization for white collar workers, regardless of profession or employment status, founded by Barbara Ehrenreich in September 2006. UP reaches out to all unemployed, underemployed, and anxiously employed workers—people who bought the American dream that education and credentials could lead to a secure middle-class life, but now find their lives disrupted by forces beyond their control.

To stay on top of current affairs:

It may sound old-fashioned, but if you don't read the paper— either online or in print—you're out of the loop. Blogs are great, but they're no substitute for the primary source, which is major newspapers. *The Daily Show* is great too, but don't think for a second that means you're "caught up" on current affairs. So, why bother to read the paper? The first step in questioning or challenging the status quo is to know exactly what is going on—and that's where newspapers play a vital role. Papers pick up lots of news that the TV news doesn't cover—important stuff that just can't be molded to conform to the "deadly bacteria lurking in your kitchen" segments that now dominate the local news. Read it online, or get your fingers dirty. Either way, just read it.

To hook up with local organizations doing great work:

Over the last couple years, there's been a flurry of new groups organized by young people hoping to engage their unengaged generation, while some long-established organizations have begun anew with a focus on engaging the under-35 crowd. To find all the civic organizations in your state, visit the Center for Civic Participation (**www.centerforcivicparticipation.org**).

To get help managing your finances, including paying off debt:

Whether you need help deciding among the hundreds of personal finance books or help finding a reputable credit counseling agency, here are several resources to get you started.

Personal Finance Books

Carmen Wong Ulrich. *Generation Debt: Take Control of Your Money—A How-to Guide.* Warner Business Books. January 2006.

Suze Orman. *The Money Book for the Young, Fabulous, and Broke.* Penguin Group. March 2005.

Elizabeth Warren and Amelia Warren Tyagi. *All Your Worth: The Ultimate Lifetime Money Plan.* The Free Press. March 2005.

Websites

National Foundation for Credit Counseling—www.nfcc.org

With over one hundred member agencies and more than 900 local offices throughout the country, the NFCC can help you find an accredited credit counseling agency in your area. The site also provides a range of general budgeting and debt advice.

Bankrate, Inc.—www.bankrate.com

This site offers an array of information about financial products, from credit cards to mortgages. Bankrate also features monthly articles addressing some of the most common personal finance issues.

And don't forget, VOTE:

Yeah, I know it often feels like it doesn't matter. Or that the choice is really about voting for the lesser of two evils. But until our generation starts flexing its muscle at the ballot box, we've got no credibility. So, remind your politicians that you exist. Vote. And not just in presidential elections either. For everything you need to know about voting, check out Project Vote Smart (**www.vote-smart.org**). You won't be disappointed.

If you don't want to commit reckless voting, you can learn the difference between different candidates by visiting their websites. You can also visit your state board of elections website for campaign guides, including information about any referendums or ballot initiatives. In addition, most local papers will offer information to help you compare and contrast the positions of different candidates.